Tom Walsh in Dakota Territory

Tom Walsh in

Personal Correspondence of

Dakota Territory

Senator Thomas J. *James* Walsh and Elinor C. McClements

EDITED BY J. LEONARD BATES

With a Preface by Genevieve Walsh Gudger

UNIVERSITY OF ILLINOIS PRESS, URBANA AND LONDON, 1966

to Dotty

Preface

When my father died in March, 1933, it seemed expedient that I dispose of the Helena, Montana, home. At that time I had no thought of returning to Montana to make my official and permanent residence. As I readied the house for sale, I found, in a small trunk in the attic, hundreds of letters which my mother and father had written to each other during the years between their first meeting in 1881 and their marriage in 1889, and during the subsequent lifetime of devotion and cooperation. I was appalled by the decision, which must be mine, as to what disposition or use I would make of them. As I read and arranged them chronologically, I was impressed by the fact that, in addition to bearing witness to an unusual affection and mutual esteem, they presented a fascinating personal view of the cultural, political, and social progress of the era covered. The letters were written at a time when such correspondence, for those far separated, was the only means of transmitting one's news, one's reactions to given situations, one's hopes, and one's ideals.

For the next several years I occupied all spare moments in transcribing literally, with dates and places, such portions of the letters as seemed to me to make a continuous historical record of the years covered. The handwriting was laborious to read—thousands of pages of my father's difficult writing and my mother's precise but tiny calligraphy. I worked always at night by the light of one bulb, energy furnished by our own thirty-two-volt generator (at our home in Glacier National Park). I am not an expert typist and made no attempt at accuracy in the sense of neatness or checking for typographical errors. As for the rest, one may be very sure that the quotations are taken exactly. Where I made comments of my own, they are clearly marked. As I believed my mother and father would have wished, the originals for the years preceding their marriage are now destroyed. Needless to say, the letters written after the marriage, except for those of the very early period in Dakota when the exigencies of law practice then required my father's frequent absence from Redfield, are fragmentary. They concern largely unrelated facts about the progress of this case and that, since my mother for years acted as his law clerk. But they also recite incidents and observations which may be of interest to the historian.

With confidence in the careful work that Professor Leonard Bates of the University of Illinois will do, I have turned over to him my transcripts of the early letters as well as the letters themselves of the later era. It is my hope that the correspondence may be an inspiration to the youth of this generation, an example of what a man and a woman sincerely devoted to one another, and with a "will to do," can accomplish.

Genevieve Walsh Gudger
Lake McDonald, Montana

Editor's Foreword

Thomas J. Walsh, United States Senator from Montana (1913-33), began his public career in Dakota Territory. Indeed, the Dakota years were decisive in his political career, for the pattern of his success was established long before the voters of Montana sent him to the Senate. He worked with a will at his chosen profession of law and remained its student. He read widely and commented perceptively on his surroundings. He was an active young politician in a country he described as having "more politics to the square mile" than any place he had been, and he quickly became a Democrat of some note in Republican Dakota.

Statehood was the great issue in Dakota in the 1880's, but Walsh did not play an important part in the movement—few Democrats did. Yet Walsh would seem worthy of attention. As a rising young lawyer and Democrat, he attended county and territorial conventions. He ran for chairman of the Democratic convention of 1885 at Aberdeen, but was defeated by Bartlett Tripp, a lawyer from Yankton (who later served as chief justice of the territorial supreme court). In 1888 he was a contesting delegate to the Democratic national convention in St. Louis. His career seemed to touch upon all the issues of importance. If his success was limited and he had no great impact upon Dakota, it is clear that Dakota had a strong impact upon him. Among other things, "Tom" Walsh became a confirmed, partisan Democrat in the Dakota years.

The letters in this volume are the earliest of Walsh's letters still extant. They are a part of the collection of personal correspondence (1881-1933) lent to me by Walsh's daughter, Mrs. Genevieve Gudger. This Gudger Collection, as I think it should be designated, is quite small when compared with the Walsh

Papers in the Library of Congress, which have become fairly familiar to researchers in twentieth-century political history and occupy more than four hundred boxes in the Manuscripts Division. By contrast, the Gudger Collection has never been used. It contains virtually the only letters that exist for the first fifty years of Walsh's life (up to his first campaign for the Senate in 1910). Regrettably the originals for the 1880's are now gone, but the copies for that decade and later originals make no small contribution to an understanding of Senator Walsh. They leave no doubt, for example, of his determination to succeed, first by gaining renown as a lawyer and becoming independent economically, and second by plunging immediately into the world of politics. They reveal him as a human being, with warm personal relationships—offsetting the later interpretations of him as an austere, humorless senator. His courtship of Elinor McClements, herself ambitious and talented, produced some letters that would be difficult to match in the correspondence of other senators.

The correspondence started rather formally in July, 1881, when "Mr. Walsh" received a brief note from "Miss Ellen" McClements. Some readers may wish to begin with these early letters, which have been placed in Appendix I, "The Wisconsin Years."

Editorial procedures have been determined largely by the fact that I worked with copies and that they contained many omissions. Mrs. Gudger had indicated her omissions with ellipses (while preparing to write her father's biography and putting the letters into typewritten form). In some letters the ellipsis occurred so often—interrupting the flow of reading—that I decided to eliminate it whenever possible. The reader may assume that almost every letter contains omissions and that some are mere fragments. In some instances I am responsible for the omission of words or phrases that are unclear, garbled, or irrelevant. These are signified in the following manner: "[*editor's omission*]." A stylistic peculiarity has led to the following mechanical change. In the body of a letter where the dash was used in combination with a comma (—,) one or the other has been eliminated. Spelling has been no particular problem, for the Walshes were careful in their use of words. Occasional errors that do occur may have been typographical in origin, and therefore I have not hesitated to make minor alterations. Substantive changes or additions to the manuscript have been placed in brackets. They have also been italicized, if in the nature of an editorial comment.

In annotating the book, I decided with some misgivings not to cite general reference works. Thus the *Dictionary of American Biography*, the *Biographical Directory of the American Congress*, *Who Was Who in America*, and similar very useful volumes have not been mentioned.

Introduction

In February, 1884, taking time from his law studies at the University of Wisconsin, Thomas J. Walsh cast a look into the future. To Elinor McClements he wrote: "Now if you (or I) should ever become known to fame, with what sentiments would we regard some prowler, gloating miserly over our letters, provided we retained consciousness of things transpiring in this nether world after we take our flight hence?" And he referred to a recent example of "historical mousers" who had gone into every drawer of Thomas Carlyle and read his letters. Thomas Walsh and Elinor (Ellen) McClements thought frequently of the chance of becoming famous. There was little, in fact, that they failed to think of and to mention at one time or another in their correspondence. They did not write for publication, but they saved their letters—or most of them. Each was interested in literature, drama, art, music, law, politics, and public affairs and each had a sense of history. In his later career, Walsh acquired a keener understanding of sources for history and of the value of letters such as Carlyle's, or of his own. He appreciated the need for critical writing. To a Montana newspaperman, planning a book on Montana, he deplored what often passed for history: ". . . do avoid having the work even appear to be of the character of too many alleged histories of Montana and biographies of its prominent citizens, which consist simply of compilations of articles paid for by those whose names appear in the book or by admiring friends."

The author of these sentiments was not an ordinary lawyer and politician, who made his way eventually to the United States Senate. Nor was Ellen McClements Walsh the typical lady of a successful politician. They were people of ideas who read widely and liked to write, to entertain, and to be entertained. Walsh once said: "I'll consent always to be the butt of my friend's wit (provided it be good and racy) rather than that he, or she, should be as dull and uninteresting as myself." He may have had Ellen McClements in mind. She was seldom dull. When Walsh, for example, went into ecstasies over a camping trip and said that the two weeks had passed like two days, she replied that they would have "seemed like two months to me." She added: "Why I've never attended a picnic without a retrospective glance at my life to see what I had done to merit 'the burden laid upon me.'" Rather mischievous was her habit of addressing her envelopes to "T. J. Welch." Since he and his family pronounced the name with an *e* she believed it should be spelled that way. She was alternately gay, saucy, sad, witty, sarcastic, cool, warm, tender. However, she showed great respect for the young Walsh's ability, and urged him to use it and to have confidence in himself. She had a decided influence.

Thomas J. Walsh did become "known to fame," and his correspondence acquired a special interest. His reputation came to rest upon three achievements. First, he studied law and devoted himself to the practice of law. He loved his practice and prepared himself in scholarly ways for every case. After a period of slow progress in Dakota Territory and in Montana, he steadily moved in the late nineties toward the front of his profession. Of Walsh's success Senator James E. Murray of Montana commented (1949): "There never was a lawyer in Montana before or since so recognized for his skill." Actually Walsh gained a national prominence, and when he entered the U.S. Senate in 1913, he had a larger "courtroom." He prided himself on his knowledge of law and especially constitutional law. Of course many other senators did also, but according to a critical-minded colleague, Henry F. Ashurst of Arizona, Walsh was "generally considered as the soundest of them all," for the twenty years of his service.

Second, Walsh entered politics and became in the first decade of the twentieth century the acknowledged leader of Montana's reform Democrats. He fought the Anaconda Copper Company and its allied interests. Tireless, incorruptible, courageous, he fought a good fight—although it could not honestly be said that he greatly altered the pattern of corruption and corporate domination in Montana. Working with Walsh by 1910 was Burton K. Wheeler, a young lawyer in Butte. Each man moved ahead to a national career, Walsh entering the Senate in 1913, Wheeler in 1923.

Third, Walsh attained unusual distinction in the Senate. Almost immediately as a freshman senator he entered fully into the debates concerning Woodrow Wilson's New Freedom. His ability was widely acknowledged, and he quickly became one of the most respected leaders in the Wilson administration. As if his appetite were merely whetted, he made a run for leadership of the Senate majority—and almost prevailed. In 1916 he was selected as western manager of Wilson's presidential campaign, with headquarters in Chicago. He proved an exceedingly able manager, and the states under his direction are usually considered to have re-elected Wilson (California notably). Walsh had a superb background for many issues that came before the Senate; for example, problems of public land policy in the West. But he was interested in almost everything and gave increasing attention to foreign policy. In 1918-19 he became deeply involved in the fight for the League of Nations. He was possibly the ablest friend of the League in the U.S. Senate. In the long and bitter fight the Democrats were divided and were finally defeated on this issue. Walsh, however, went on to achieve his principal publicity and national fame in the years of Republican ascendancy. He criticized and attacked basic Republican policies in the 1920's, as the growth of monopoly and the failure to do much about it seemed deplorable to him. Most of all, he was the Senate investigator who exposed the oil leasing scandal, or Teapot Dome affair. In affairs of the Democratic party meanwhile Walsh went almost to the top. He was permanent chairman of the national conventions in 1924 and 1932, adviser to Franklin D. Roosevelt in the late twenties, and supporter of Roosevelt's candidacy for the presidency. Had he lived, Walsh would have joined Roosevelt's official family as Attorney General.

If one seeks a key to Walsh's success, it seems to be this: he had ideas and opinions which he believed in asserting. By no means was he always right, but he was a persistent force—thinking, acting, doing, giving his opposition little peace. According to one lawyer in Helena, who knew Walsh well, it would be difficult to imagine Walsh idling away his time, or with his brain full of nonsense; he would be thinking constructively and systematically at all times. Ellen McClements, who knew him better, had somewhat the same conception. She referred to "that busy brain of yours," or used similar expressions.

That Walsh had a "head full of brains," a first-class mind, there can be little doubt. He also inherited a family situation and a community environment which afforded fairly good opportunities. The impulse that carried him forward is, of course, impossible to explain adequately, although a knowledge of his early years is helpful.

Tom Walsh—as his family and close friends knew him—was born on June 12, 1859, just five weeks after his father, Felix Walsh, was elected trustee of the first ward, in the village of Two Rivers, Wisconsin. Felix later became the village clerk, and he continued for twenty years as village and city clerk. He also served as a justice of the peace, while supporting his family in part by manual labor. The people of Two Rivers enjoyed a beautiful timbered location on the western shore of Lake Michigan, north of Milwaukee. There the Walsh children (Tom was the third of ten) grew up in an almost idyllic setting. They worked and assisted their father, but also had time for fishing, baseball games, school, and books.

Quite an emphasis was placed upon education in this family, as indicated by the fact that eight of the ten children became school teachers and three became lawyers. The father and mother were Irish-born Catholics who believed in public education.

Tom Walsh attended the elementary school in Two Rivers and took advanced courses offered there, since no high school had been completed. Essentially Walsh educated himself. By 1877 he was teaching in a country school, and he continued as a teacher until the fall of 1883, when he entered the University of Wisconsin Law School. By this time he had read widely: Macaulay, Taine, Lecky, Tocqueville, Shakespeare, Bulwer-Lytton, Byron, Walter Scott, Southey, Thackeray, Schiller, Oliver Wendell Holmes, Adam Smith, Henry George, Blackstone, and Kent, among others. His high school teaching had introduced him to Jenkins' *Magnetism and Electricity* and to other scientific works. He was particularly interested in flowers and plants and in "botanizing" expeditions.

Walsh had an adventurous streak and the interest of a nineteenth-century romantic in the glorious outdoors. He was not all work and study. In the summer of 1883 he joined a party of some twenty-five who went to Strawberry Island, close to the mouth of Green Bay, for two weeks of camping and fishing. Later he reported what a great experience it had been. The group had "fished, read, and vegetated"; they spent most evenings by "a big bon-fire kindled from the driftwood on the beach or in playing poker by the light of tallow drips."

Walsh's great adventure—previous to the Dakota frontier—was his year at the University of Wisconsin. He flourished in the free and heady atmosphere. Having already read law for a year or more, he experienced no difficulty with his courses and greatly enjoyed lectures by William F. Vilas and other professors. He threw himself into campus activities. There was the excitement of moot court; of a literary society which he had determined not to join but did join; of mixing with students, professors, and town lawyers in animated conversation and debate; of being elected law editor of the student paper, *The Badger*. He made the acquaintance of, and observed with interest, a young lady in his class who had recently married a rising lawyer—Belle Case La Follette. He had time for an occasional lark, as when he and another student attempted to raid the university dairy barn for buttermilk. Walsh seems in later years to have measured all colleges and universities by his alma mater. He observed to Ellen McClements: "Don't you think it makes a vast difference what kind of air there is about a college? Whether it's laden with a large sympathy with all humanity or impregnated with a sort of we-are-the-elect idea . . .; whether a great abundance of tolerance and liberality pervades it or if one must seek the fountain of knowledge in the icy air of Puritanic or Inquisatorial holiness?"

Along the way, Walsh had been considering where to begin the practice of law. The territory of Dakota was much in the news in the 1880's. Chicago newspapers, among others, advertised the advantages of the region, and people went there in large numbers. Those from nearby states such as Minnesota and Iowa went by covered wagon or even on foot, but railroads were also available. Frequently settlers went by train to a railhead in eastern Dakota, unloaded their wagons and belongings, and continued across the plains. According to one estimate the territory had about 236,000 people in 1882 and more than 400,000 two years later.

Thomas J. Walsh was one of the multitude who migrated to

Dakota. His reasons for going west were, in some respects, unique: He was bothered by asthma near the Great Lakes, and wanted to try a drier climate. Moreover, his older brother, Henry, had preceded him; always good friends, they decided to practice law together. Tom Walsh at this time was about five feet eight inches tall, erect and quick of movement much as in later years. He sported a mustache similar to the handlebar growth of his early senatorial career. His age was twenty-five.

To leave Wisconsin and his family and friends was not entirely painless. Walsh was much interested by now in Ellen McClements, with whom he had been corresponding steadily since 1881. He had met Ellen through her sister Mary at the Glenbeulah, Wisconsin, high school where Walsh served as principal and teacher and Mary McClements was his assistant.

The McClementses lived in Sheboygan, Wisconsin, although the father, who was a Scotsman, and the mother had emigrated from the British Isles. On the mother's side there had been some wealth and luxury, and the McClements family apparently had a social status higher than the Walshes. James McClements, the father, died around 1880 and Ellen's only brother, John R., died in 1884. After Ellen obtained a job in 1882 at Chicago's Wicker Park School, her mother and three sisters eventually moved to Chicago. All was less than serene among the ladies of this household; Tom Walsh had difficulty establishing himself as a suitor worthy of Ellen's hand. Moreover, Ellen had her own career to think of, and she had strong opinions on many subjects.

Ellen McClements and Tom Walsh were products of their times. Bright and ambitious, they did not go to college—except for Walsh's one year of law study. They believed passionately in individual attainment, hard work, and self-improvement. Like so many young men after the Civil War, Walsh was affected by the drama of it and thought for a time of pursuing a military career. Upper-class views found occasional expression in Ellen's letters. She also reflected the growth of feminist ideas in a man's world. Both were romanticists. Both were Victorians. Neither, however, can be neatly classified, for they read widely and thought independently, and by the 1880's winds of change were blowing.

In the summer of 1884 T. J. Walsh, just out of law school, followed westward the "course of empire." The letters in this volume begin shortly after his arrival in Redfield, in the east central part of Dakota Territory.

Contents

1

My dear Ellen,—

After wandering around in the wilderness since you last saw me, I have reached what seems to me in the light in which I walk, to be the promised land. It is a land of promise in the sense that its advantages are prospective rather than established. It has hopes rather than existing resources. Were I not impressed with the fact that many of these will in time be realized I should not be here. Both great lines of railroad run through the town going north and south; it is connected with Chicago by one of the C. and N.W. lines, is about three years old and has a population of 800.[1] As to how it got its chromatic cognomen I am uninformed and unable to conjecture. The fields are not red at all. Corn fields are green, wheat fields are golden, and the prairie is very brown.[2] The adjacent country is said to be the finest farming land in the territory and certainly the appearance of the crops and the numerous and substantial farm houses and buildings scattered over the prairie seem to support the boast. Redfield came within one of being the capital of Dakota, and she still has hopes of becoming the seat of state government. You will remember that a commission of nine members were two years ago appointed to locate the capital and that after a long struggle Bismarck was chosen.[3] Four of the commission voted in favor of this place.[4] A scheme is now on foot, with every chance of success, as South Dakota seems to be united in its favor, to divide the territory along the line of the 46th parallel and admit the southern portion as a state during the ensuing session of Congress. Redfield, in common with the other disappointed towns of South Dakota, expects in this way to have another chance. To be sure this is only a possibility upon a possibility and rather too remote for consideration from a business point of view. But the future of the town rests upon a more substantial basis. . . .

My brother [Henry] is coming down in about two weeks and we shall then work together—in case we find any work to do. His presence during the next few months which must necessarily be dull ones, will be a great relief. We haven't seen much of each other for a number of years.[5]

The first term of court ever held in this county convenes Sept. 8. I shall have charge of two cases entrusted to me by the Huron lawyer in whose office I spent a few days.

It takes one's breath away to hear of the sums young men have laid up here within two or three years. I have met as many as a dozen who in that time on an original capital of not more than $500 have accumulated property worth from $10,000 to $50,000. No wonder either. They have been getting 15% on real estate loans and consider it as extremely modest to ask less than 3% per month on chattel security.

A good long letter from you is always welcome but it will be received with particular pleasure at any time during the dull days that are coming, by

Your devoted friend,
T. J. Walsh.

[1] The two railroads referred to were the Chicago and Northwestern and the Chicago, Milwaukee, and St. Paul.

[2] Redfield was named after James Barlow Redfield, an auditor for the Chicago and Northwestern Railway. Spink County, in which Redfield was located, was named after Solomon L. Spink, who served as secretary of Dakota Territory (1865-69) and delegate to Congress (1869-71). Dana D. Harlow, *Prairie Echoes: Spink County in the Making* (Aberdeen, South Dakota, 1961), p. 323; Doane Robinson, *Encyclopedia of South Dakota* (Pierre, South Dakota, 1925), p. 678.

[3] Dakota Territory experienced bitter sectional rivalries early in the 1880's. The leading section was the southeast, where Yankton on the Missouri River had been the territorial capital since 1861. But two sections of increasing importance were the Black Hills to the west, with

its mining, and an area of settlements in the north along the Northern Pacific Railroad, from Fargo to Bismarck. Under Governor Ordway in 1883 the capital was moved from Yankton to Bismarck. Many in southern Dakota found the situation intolerable, and they launched a movement for separate statehood. See Howard R. Lamar, *Dakota Territory, 1861-1889: A Study of Frontier Politics* (New Haven, 1956), pp. 172, 208-9, 213-14, and *passim*; Herbert S. Schell, *History of South Dakota* (Lincoln, Nebraska, 1961), pp. 211-13 and *passim*. These two books are excellent and indispensable.

[4] Redfield apparently received three rather than four of the nine votes. Schell, *History of South Dakota*, p. 211.

[5] Henry Comer Walsh was about fourteen months older than Tom. Born in 1857 in Two Rivers, Wisconsin, he attended school there, began teaching at the age of fifteen, and turned in spare moments to the reading of law. In 1882 he came to Redfield, and in 1884 he passed his bar examinations. Although senior man in the law partnership, he probably suffered some disadvantage by comparison with his college-trained brother. But he seems to have been an extremely generous and likeable person. Some significance may be attached to the fact that Senator Thomas J. Walsh, writing in 1923 of the old days, said that whenever in his dreams he got into a "desperate situation" Henry always appeared to help him out. Walsh to George Randall, February 6, 1923, Thomas James Walsh Papers, Division of Manuscripts, Library of Congress; editor's interview with Mrs. Genevieve Walsh Gudger, February 16, 21, 1950; Harlow, *Prairie Echoes*, pp. 366-67. See Tom's tribute to Henry in No. 296.

2

Sheboygan, Wis., Aug. 19, 1884.

My dear Friend,

Your letter of the 17th was received this morning—joyfully received. . . . When I saw the postmark "Redfield" I smiled; yes I may say I smiled smilingly. Shall I tell you why I smiled that smile? If anyone, during the past two months had asked my opinion as to what place in Dakota would be likely to prove a good place to locate, I should have unhesitantly said "Redfield." Shortly before leaving Chicago I had a paper containing a very long article about Redfield. It was spoken of in the very highest possible terms, its excellent location, the enterprise of its people, its prosperity, brilliant hopes for the future, etc., etc. When you decided to go to Dakota, I honestly hoped you would go to Redfield for that article impressed me deeply. But did you ever hear me say "Redfield"? Don't you think I deserve a medal for not giving any counsel unasked? For your sake I hope the brilliant prospects of Redfield may be more than fulfilled. . . .

Sincerely your friend,
E. C. McC.

3

Redfield, Dakota, August 24, 1884.

My dear Ellen,—

You certainly deserve praise for your promptness, the length of your letter, and its kindness through-out. How encouraging it is when one has taken a step involving a weighty responsibility, the event of which is still involved in doubt, to have a kind friend in whose judgment he reposes a great deal of confidence, come up and slap him on the back, tell him he has chosen well and as any sensible person would. I am inclined to be too sanguine, to trust to the future rather than to rely on the present, to magnify the advantages of a favored scheme and regard too lightly the obstacles which spring up along the line of its proposed execution. I sometimes accuse myself of coming to conclusions and forming resolutions without due reflection and then afterwards endeavoring to support them by specious arguments having only possibilities for their bases. Your letter had a wonderfully curative and reassuring effect. . . . Newspaper correspondents are likely to "exaggerate" just a little in describing western towns and it is always safest to come and see before investing largely in city property that is "boomed" in that way.[1]

I am becoming slowly acquainted with the people of the city and am happy to state that the somewhat unfavorable opinion I formed of them on my first visit to the place is undergoing a change which does them more justice. I never possessed the faculty of rapidly ingratiating myself into the favor of strangers. In fact I sometimes fear that they are inclined to shun me, as I certainly at times avoid them. I don't exactly dread an introduction but the ceremony has no attraction for me and I much prefer to "pick" an acquaintance provided the other party is willing. I must overcome this disinclination though or submit graciously to the inconvenience because the political and social gatherings, county fairs and other similar meetings, that will crowd one another during the coming two months will furnish me an admirable opportunity to extend my knowledge of the people with whom I expect to establish business relations.

Oh, so a rose by any other name would not smell as sweet to you, or rather 'twould smell sweeter had it another name. I'm sorry we can't agree on my name. You see, it wouldn't do. The name is now written over so many I.O.U.'s that confusion would arise from a change—misnomer papers are thrown out of court, put over a term, $10 costs et cet. No, you go on spelling it as you like and call it as you like and so shall I. I never investigated how my grandfather spelled the name. Perhaps he used an E and C. The change is certainly an improvement. A and S make a much better appearance in print.[2]

I shall expect your next from Chicago and shall await it longingly.

Your friend,
T. J. W.

[1] As Walsh indicated, boomers and boosters were everywhere in Dakota; frontier capitalism was rampant. See Seth K. Humphrey, *Following the Prairie Frontier* (Minneapolis, 1931). Humphrey arrived in east central Dakota about the same time as Walsh. His book, however, had more to say about the seamy side of things.

[2] Walsh and his family pronounced their name as if it were spelled "Welch." Ellen could not understand this, or she chose not to. The subject recurs frequently.

4

Chicago, Sept. 4, 1884.

My dear Friend,

Your reference to a "rose by any other name," and A or E versus E or A puzzled me for a moment, until the remarks I made in my last letter occurred to me; for which remarks I now ask pardon. They were inexcusably impertinent, though they did not appear so to me at the time because nothing of the kind was intended. It simply reoccurred to me at the time, when I directed your letter, how strange it seemed to spell the name one way and pronounce it another. Had you spelled it with an A and called it like A I should have thought it all right. I fully recognize and appreciate the patience you have always shown by your own letters, and the spirit of gentleness which always pervades them. I'll try to be better in future and therefore unlike my wilfull self.

Your remarks about dreading an introduction amused me greatly. I have a great liking for the ways of society and horrified some friends of mine once by saying I'd rather know a courteous villain than a home-spun saint. Don't lecture me. . . .

Yours,
E. C. M.

5

Redfield, Dakota, Sept. 14, 1884.

My dear Ellen,—

You must pardon my delay in answering yours of the 4th and hereafter when anything of the kind occurs you can allay your(?) anxiety and console yourself for the deprivation!!! with the reflection that it is due to that one cause which all lawyers deem a sufficient excuse for the most flagrant case of procrastination—namely, court-week. I am happy to state, and know that you will be glad to learn, that we have really been quite busy in consequence of the session. We tried and got judgment in one case and worked hard to force another to trial, but were obliged to consent to a postponement until the coming week. . . . The court house is about three miles out of town and those who are not fortunate enough to own a conveyance or wealthy enough to hire one must shift as best they can with nature's equipment. So doth your humble correspondent. A strong effort will be made to move the county seat into town but from present indications this consummation so devoutly to be wished will not be reached in the immediate future. A two-thirds vote is required for a removal and though Redfield can readily secure a majority, the dog-in-the-manger policy of two other competing towns is likely to defeat the project of removal for the present at least. The court house is a temporary shed and the surroundings are strongly suggestive of the stories we read in the lives of Clay, Lincoln and Douglas holding court on the frontier.[1] But the similarity ends here, at least it does not extend to the settlers who are much more refined and in any community would pass for intelligent.

Was not this a very nice thing for the ladies to do yesterday? They came out in force (the lawyers' wives) and spread a bountiful picnic dinner on the banks of the classic Jim,[2] to which they invited their husbands, the judge, reporter and district attorney, and us bachelors who profess to practice. To be sure the butter intercepted a good share of the adjacent stubble land that whirled in the autumn's rising blast and the frosted cake had a suspicious looking upper coat of gray, but for all that the dinner had a merit which it must have borrowed from our appreciation of the kind intentions of our fair entertainers and served as the occasion of a little gathering that had many pleasant features about it. . . .

Yours sincerely,
T. J. Walsh.

[1] Walsh was referring to the preliminary phase of what soon turned into the "Spink County War"—a county seat struggle of much notoriety. As Redfield sought the honor (and business) of the county seat, and attempted to move the courthouse from the "shed" in the wilderness, other towns sought the same honor. By the fall of 1884 violence threatened. Walsh was personally involved and described the course of events in further letters. See notes for Nos. 11 and 15.

[2] To Dakotans the James River was the "Jim."

6

Chicago, Sept. 26, 1884.

My dear Friend,

"You must pardon my delay in answering yours . . . ," etc. Now confess; isn't that a most barbarous manner in which to begin a letter?[1] . . . No. Mr. W. J. T., I was not anxious about your delay, for strange to tell, I remembered it was "court week."

My Katie has come and gone and I feel blue and generally hateful. Time, the great reliever, will come to my assistance, and in a few days Richard will be himself again, with "A smile for every fate." What does that prove, O Lawyer? That I am as changeable as—as Mary thinks me,[2] and incapable of caring for anything or anybody for any length of time, or does it, perhaps, show a desire to make the best of the inevitable, or what is, at best, bad? Since the above is addressed to you in your wig-and-gown capacity, I shall not expect a decision gratis, so send in your bill, Mr. Lawyer.

I am going to "swear off" now on the going about town business. That is I'll do so after tomorrow. I want to attend an open air concert at Lincoln Park Saturday. Then I want to see Keene as Richard III and McCullough as Brutus,[3] and I want to go to the Exposition again,[4] and—and ever so many other places. . . .

Sincerely,
Elinor C. McClements.

[1] See the first sentence of the preceding letter.

[2] Katie McClements was Ellen's youngest sister; Mary was an older sister. In all, there were four sisters and one brother whose ages (in 1884) ran as follows: Lizzie, 32; Mary, 30; John R., 28; Ellen, 26; Anna, 24; Katie, 21. The reference to Richard was apparently a literary allusion.

[3] Thomas W. Keene (1840-98) was famous for his roles as Richard III, Hamlet, and Louis XI. He went on tour annually in the 1880's. John McCullough (1832-85) was born in Ireland but trained for an acting career in the United States. From 1873 to 1884 he toured the country in various acting roles, the most notable of which occurred in *Virginius, Richelieu,* and *Damon and Pythias.*

[4] The "Exposition" building was an immense structure east of Michigan Avenue on the lake front. For much of its existence (1873-92), it was the center for trade fairs, art exhibits, musical concerts, and political conventions. Three of the national political conventions were held there in 1880 and 1884. Jacquelin Southerland in *Chicago Tribune,* December 4, 1960, pt. I, p. 16 (photo-copy courtesy of Chicago Historical Society). See also No. 105.

7

Redfield, October 5, 1884.

My dear Ellen,—

Candor compels me to acknowledge not only the indisputable logic of the proposition with which you introduced your last letter, but also the justness of the severe criticism you pass upon it as a piece of epistolary composition. . . .

I have added nine pounds to my weight since coming here. You see I bid fair at this rate of increase to become a "portly burgher" soon.

Do you not remember a remark that I once made to the effect that I should be more successful before the court than with a jury? My short experience has already exemplified the truth of the proposition.

Yes, "territory people" seem to take a great interest in the political contest. There are more politics to the square mile in the country than in any other place in which my lot has thus far been cast. . . . Do you not think it extremely likely that Wisconsin will go Democratic this fall? There is a remarkable number of "converts" from republicanism and all seem to be from the very best and purest material of that party. As the questions of division and admission are to come before the present Congress and its successor, the contest attains a special importance to the people of this territory and unusual interest is taken in the progress of the campaign though they have no voice in the contest.

Write me soon.

Yours devotedly,
T. J. W.

8

Chicago, Ill., Oct. 13, 1884.

Dear Friend,

We all went to the Exposition again last Saturday evening. I spent most of my time in the art galleries. . . .

. . . I do think it very probable that Wisconsin will go democratic. I don't think Blaine's speech making will be very effective with democrats. Wherever he goes there are great crowds present, of course, and great excitement. But the enthusiasm will die out when the light of his countenance is withdrawn.[1]

E. C. M.

[1] James G. Blaine was the Republican candidate for the presidency in 1884; Grover Cleveland opposed him.

9

My dear Ellen,—

. . . It's impossible to build a fine city on a flat [*a reference to Redfield?*]. Would not Rome have been less beautiful had she not "sat on her seven hills"? He would be a rash man who should attempt to predict what Chicago will be fifty years hence. The charm of life in such a city is so much greater than it is in such a village as this that I was almost myself induced to go there or to some other large town to begin business. I am not yet satisfied that I committed no mistake in not doing so.

Your description of the Exposition was read with great interest. When my ship comes in I am going to invest part of the proceeds of her cargo in such pictures. You couldn't tire me talking of pictures.

I attended the convention at Miller and had the distinguished honor of presiding over that august assemblage. Although the district is overwhelmingly republican the fact that they have two tickets in the field makes it probable that we shall be able to elect at least two or three of our men. Three county conventions will be held here during the coming week. Our county seat fight gives these a special importance this year. One very noticeable feature in the politics of this country is that the democrats are all young men. This was particularly apparent in the Miller convention and to my mind quite refutes the position of Storrs, Ingersoll, and their disciples that the democratic party of today is the same that it was a quarter of a century ago.[1] Hereafter, whatever the results in November, the young men will be found in the democratic ranks, the older men, those whose prejudices have become fixed by past history will stay with the republican party.[2] But the politician who in forecasting the future does not make a large allowance for the prohibition vote reckons without his host. That party will make a strong effort before the convention which will frame the constitution under which the state of South Dakota will be admitted to the union, to have incorporated a clause representing their views on the liquor question. . . .

Yours very truly,
T. J. Walsh.

[1] Robert G. Ingersoll was "the great agnostic" of this period. He

also gained fame by his speech of 1876 in which he nominated James G. Blaine for the presidency, and coined the phrase "the plumed knight." Ingersoll held public office in Illinois, lectured widely, and was an eloquent spokesman of the Republican party. Emery A. Storrs attained the reputation of a great lawyer and a strongly partisan Republican. He stumped several states for Abraham Lincoln in 1864, served as a delegate (from Illinois) to Republican conventions, and was active in support of James G. Blaine in the election of 1884. See Isaac E. Adams, *Political Oratory of Emery A. Storrs from Lincoln to Garfield* (Chicago and New York, 1888).

2 Walsh was expressing a somewhat prejudiced view. Dakota Democrats, for example, were badly in the minority and were often thought of as the saloon element. Many were working men in the towns and mining camps, or the poorer people; and not a few were Catholics. Cultural and ethnic factors, that is, had much to do with political affiliations. The farmers, including Germans and Scandinavians pouring into Dakota in the 1880's, were predominantly Protestant and Republican. One scholar observes that after 1878 it was well-nigh possible to tell a man's politics in Dakota "by his occupation or his religion." Lamar, *Dakota Territory*, pp. 174-75. See also *Chicago Tribune* (editorial), December 5, 1884.

10

Chicago, Oct. 26, 1884.

Dear Friend,

Once upon a time, I innocently remarked that I like living in Chicago and you said all manner of hateful things—called us all Philistines, and wound up by saying that a big city never should have any inhabitants. I don't think you used just those words, because the statement seems scarcely logical, and you disciples of Blackstone are always logical, are you not? You could not have meant all you said, for, in your last letter, you speak of the "charm" of living in a large city, and almost wish you had allowed that charm to ensnare you. As to whether it had been better so, I cannot say, but don't you think, mon ami, that whatever is to be, will be; and do we not usually find in the end that things happen for the best?

. . . A little cheering was indulged in as Blaine passed down the corridor, but there was no such disorder as the [Chicago] "Times" mentions. If there was, it must have occurred after we had ascended to the next floor. We had a most excellent view of the street, and the spectacle was a grand one. It made one realize that there are a great many people in the world. Blaine made a short speech looking down upon a perfect sea of upturned faces, brilliantly lighted by electric lights, gas lights, calcium lights, etc. The post-office opposite was illuminated, and every window and balcony within sight of the hotel was filled with eager spectators. I cannot form an estimate of how many people were in the streets, but, at the close of Blaine's speech, when that mighty cheer went upward to the still sky, I realized what power for good or evil lay below us in the street. I don't know why it is, but loud cheering always makes me shudder, I am positively afraid. It is ridiculous I know, but I cannot overcome it. Logan spoke after Blaine, and received his quota of cheers. Gov. Hamilton followed.[1] Mrs. Logan and Mrs. Hamilton were also on the balcony. At ten o'clock the torch bearers, some 30,000 in number, passed before the hotel. A passage had been made through the crowd and for two hours they continued to pass, five abreast at an average, in an unbroken line. There were hundreds of horsemen, the procession being led by about two hundred, each of whom, as he passed, saluted the "Plumed Knight" [Blaine] and the "Black Eagle" [Logan]. (How partial they seem to feathers.) There were torches of every kind, lanterns of various colors, costumes good, bad, and indifferent, music by voice and instrument, and transparencies witty and otherwise. State St. was well illuminated in some places. Campaign songs were sung when the bands were silent. One company kept step to a novel music. Instead of saying left, right, as they might have done, they said, "Blaine, Blaine." The perfection in time made it sound like one solemn, heavy voice.

I was slightly surprised to learn that you are a prohibitionist. I knew of course that you are, rightfully, opposed to liquor, but I did not know you make it a part of your political creed. I, too, am a prohibitionist, in witness whereof I am invited to a champagne supper tomorrow night. . . . I think you are right in what you say about the strength of the prohibition vote, but if they wish to elect a presidential candidate in 1888 let them get the elective franchise extended to women.

Yours very truly,
E. C. McC.

[1] John A. Logan of Illinois was Blaine's running mate in 1884. He had been a general in the Union army and a leader of the Radical

Republicans. John M. Hamilton, Governor of Illinois for two years, 1883-85, had served in the state senate and as lieutenant governor. Previously he was a professor of languages at Illinois Wesleyan in Bloomington.

11

Redfield, November 2, 1884.

My dear Ellen,—

Neither the sacredness of the day [Sunday] nor the unpleasantness of the weather has abated the excitement that has been running so high here during the week past. Your humble servant has just emerged from a secret conclave being held below at which schemes were being concocted and put into operation, such as mortal man never dreamed of before. . . .[1] The location of the county seat is the most important feature of our campaign. I spoke on three evenings last week of the claims and advantages of Redfield as our local seat of justice—last evening in the open air with the mercury 10 to 15 degrees below the freezing point. You see how very necessary it is under such circumstances for a speaker to "spread himself" if he desires to prevent his audience from spreading also. A special train took nearly three hundred from here to the place of meeting, about twenty miles east, last night. An equal number went north the previous evening. Business has practically been at a standstill for a week past and we shall all feel a sense of great relief when Tuesday is past.

Excuse me, please, but I must see how things are getting on below. I'll divulge the next time I write and tell you how the thing worked. Meantime, I am

Your own
T. J. Walsh.

[1] Walsh was referring, in all probability, to the county seat situation and to indignant citizens of Redfield now debating their course of action. They believed that in two previous elections they had been cheated out of the county seat. One possibility was to seize the voting records at the existing courthouse (Old Ashton) and make a determination as to whether fraud had been committed. The allusion to a conclave "being held below" is explained by the fact that Walsh and his brother lived in a hotel, and meetings often were held in the dining room.

12

My dear Friend,

Congratulations are in order I suppose, as of course every democrat feels uplifted to a height equalled only by a century's depression. Wasn't it a close run though? . . . The democrats had an immense time last night. Our lullaby was the distant booming of cannon and the shouts of the people. One hundred guns were fired at noon yesterday. I hear guns today occasionally. Mrs. Holmes states that "rum, Romanism, and rebellion" and eternal destruction will follow in Cleveland's foot-steps. Do you not tremble? [1]

E. C. M.

[1]This was the election in which the Reverend Burchard, a Baptist, denounced the Democratic party as the party of "rum, Romanism, and rebellion." James G. Blaine, who was present, failed to dissociate himself from the remark and may have lost enough Catholic votes to cost him the presidency. The state of New York went for Cleveland by 1,149 votes out of 1,000,000 cast; this vote was decisive.

13

Redfield, November 16.

My dear Ellen,—

We celebrated here last Tuesday evening but the glorious uncertainty that then still hung over the contest obliged us to "go it very mild." We have special reasons here for feeling jovial over the victory because the democrats are in such a hopeless minority that they cut no figure in local politics at all. . . . And then the party in power assumes a special importance in territorial affairs, so we are suddenly lifted from insignificance to a position that the smallness of our numbers makes all the more enviable.[1] It was a rather bold step to announce my convictions so early where everyone is taken to be a republican, but the event shows that it was not an unwise one. As I engaged actively in the work of organizing and sought nothing myself I was and am in a position to dictate in a measure on whom such honors as are to be distributed in this section are to fall. Although

Redfield secured only about 1200 out of the 2900 votes cast in the county for county seat and far from the requisite two-thirds, she comes out several hundred ahead of the two other competing towns.

Accept my thanks for your careful abstract from the Federalist. Why did you not express your opinion on the proposition I submitted? Tut, tut, don't say anything now about poor weak-minded women. I wish I might oftener have the aid of your judgment. . . . I usually see the difficulties of a subject pretty well. It's how to avoid them that usually sticks me.

Henry complains that I am too much like Erasmus, or who was it who said "When I get some money, I shall buy some Greek books and some clothes." He called my attention to the very narrow margin in [our] bank-account the other day when I sent for a work on elections.

Ever yours,
T. J. Walsh.

[1] What Walsh had in mind was the President's appointive power. If Cleveland wished, he could replace the Republican governor and other territorial officials, and in turn the new governor would have various appointments at his disposal. See Earl S. Pomeroy, *The Territories and the United States, 1861-1890* (Philadelphia, 1947) for an excellent study of the functioning of territorial government. George W. Kingsbury, *History of Dakota Territory*, Vol. II (Chicago, 1915), is in large part a compilation of primary sources; it is very useful on this period. Kingsbury was a Republican newspaperman, active in Republican conventions and in meetings aiming toward statehood. His bias is often apparent, but his collection of documents and facts has proven of great value.

14

Chicago, Nov. 23, 1884.

Dear Friend,

. . . I think Governor Cleveland will be a wise ruler. He has a level head, a strong sense of justice and right, and a powerful will. That is—I think so, and that is why I should have voted for him had I been a man. I have now another reason for being pleased since his election means so much to you and your party in Dakota.

"My sound judgment"! Thanks awfully. As Garrick said the other night, "Modesty forbids that I should contradict so complimentary a statement." [1] Your friends are perfectly right in their estimate of your powers of perception. I endorse all they say. It is proved beyond a doubt, in my estimation, by your "sound judgment" verdict.

So you, too, have a mentor. How good people will be at times. I have, no doubt, been saved from financial ruin often by a timely word. I know how to spend money splendidly. I always manage to keep within my income, however. When I take to a thing I get it, and am just about as well off in the end as more prudent people of my acquaintance.

Last Friday night, I had a real treat. I saw Lawrence Barrett as Shylock and as David Garrick.[2] You noticed what the [Chicago] Inter-Ocean said of him. Well it hardly did him justice. I like him better than any other actor I've seen. He is so perfectly nice. You can imagine how nice when he makes even a Shylock seem not far from being a man.

E. C. M.

[1] A reference to the comedy *David Garrick*, by Thomas W. Robertson.

[2] Lawrence Barrett (1838-91) became famous for his Shakespearean roles, especially Hamlet, King Lear, Richard III, and Romeo. He toured various cities of the United States. The *Chicago Tribune*, November 21, 1884, p. 6, reported that on that day, Barrett appeared in Chicago at McVicker's Theater in Shakespeare's *The Merchant of Venice* and in *David Garrick*.

15

Redfield, D.T., Nov. 30, 1884.

My dear E.—

. . . I was not surprised that your nervous system was affected by the intelligence of the scheme of the "intrepid" Redfield democrats. I hesitated on learning of it, not from any fear of possible punishment, but because it seemed to me that I could never engage in it without compromising my honesty, and I never appreciated before engaging in the active work of the profession to how many temptations the lawyer is subjected nor how

absolutely necessary it is for him to avoid any and every transaction "that has no flavor of heaven in it." I did not long consider
the matter though, when the conviction [came] which still abides
with me, that it was no more dishonest than any scheme to detect
crime and commendable in the same sense.[1]

Here's news. A correspondent of the St. Paul Pioneer Press of
yesterday parcels out a long list of Federal offices in the territory
among the resident "democratic office-seekers," and with rare
magnanimity assigns to your humble servant the post-office at
this place. No mistake about it, the thing is all fixed. Salary $1800.
But I came to Dakota to practice law, so I'll agree to assign over
to you all my claims on the position.

Your devoted friend,
T. J. Walsh.

[1] The month of December, 1884, was the high point of the "Spink
County War." Walsh's cryptic statements were followed on Friday,
December 5, by the seizure of county records at Old Ashton, with
repercussions that he describes in considerable detail. Apparently there
is no good account of the "Spink County War." Various references in
Harlow's *Prairie Echoes* are somewhat contradictory as to details, and
newspaper stories vary sharply in accordance with the source. Schell's
History of South Dakota, pp. 203-4, briefly describes the Spink County
affair as illustrative of the confusion that existed over county organization. In many cases records were taken by force; litigation and threats
of violence were the result.

16

Chicago, Ill., Dec. 7, 1884.

Dear Friend,

. . . Of course fraud deserves exposure, and my remark
was perfectly innocent of any design to criticise your action in
the matter. I know you to be so good that you could do no wrong,
and, since the other Mr. W—— is your brother, he must be somewhere near, if not quite, perfect. I admired that sentiment you
expressed, about shunning "all and every Transaction that has no
flavor of heaven in it." A man might find a better guide through
life than is held in those few words, but I doubt it. To so live that
when at last the summons came, the whole world might stand up
and say, "This was a man!"

Thanks awfully for the post-office, but I couldn't accept your generous offer under the circumstances.

Confess that I find school monotonous after a short vacation? Well, yes, somewhat, but I crush such feelings in the bud. I never yet had a school that I disliked. I am rather pleasantly situated at present, the principal is all smiles, my pupils are about the best trained I've ever had sent to me. I tell you all this to show you how ungrateful I should be if I were to consider my school-work irksome. . . .

Very sincerely,
E. C. McC.

17

Redfield, December 14, 1884.

My dear Ellen,—

The Inter-Ocean and other Chicago papers have given you daily for the past week so full and on the whole accurate accounts of the progress of the war in Dakota in which we figured so prominently that I concluded that anything I might write would, as a matter of news, be somewhat stale ere it reached you and hence have deferred. And then matters have been so unsettled here for the past week and it has been impossible to say what a day might bring forth that I could not write without exciting your apprehensions, though in my own judgment the immediate danger at anytime since Monday has been very slight. But the "cruel war is over" for good now in all probability, a telegram having been received last evening to the effect that the judge has dissolved the injunction by which the records were held here and ordered them taken back to their former resting place.

They [Redfield's leaders] now propose to begin in the legal way by mandamus as I was proceeding when some marplots stepped in and precipitated the struggle of the past week. We had a good case and there appeared no reason why it should not be brought to a speedy and successful hearing. That it has been damaged seriously by the late illegal proceeding is evident. Neither Henry nor I knew anything of the moving of the records though before the act was perpetrated and doubtless because we spared no pains to discountenance the proceeding whenever and wherever it was mentioned. Only the evening on which the act was committed I was asked by one of the business men what the outcome of such a move would be and the result has given the appearance of much wisdom to my counsel. Yet though I deprecated the lawless act that had been committed, I prepared fearlessly to resist any equally lawless attempt to remove the records from the city. The proper custodian of the books never demanded them and our injunction was obtained on Monday morning preventing anyone from removing them.

Both Henry and I belong to the militia and the whole company have "slept on their arms" since the fight began.[1] We were detailed in squads and except on one night when the citizens relieved us we have kept a constant guard about town. The exquisite pleasure of tramping about four hours every night for a week with the thermometer ranging 10 to 0 with nothing but our groundless fears to make the pastime diverting it is unnecessary to describe. But I did witness a scene on Monday which I sincerely trust I may never again look upon. A crowd of at least 500 thoroughly armed and organized men gathered together by representations that the county records were in the hand of a drunken mob who were destroying and mutilating them, were inside of the city limits and just three blocks away from the city hall in which the records were secreted. Designing men were haranguing them and inciting them to disobey the order of the court, to take the records or burn the town. Anyone who approached and who was suspected of being unfriendly to them was covered with a rifle or revolver and ordered inside the lines. The sheriff in vain tried to disperse them. Finally they sent word that we should have thirty minutes to get the women and children out of town.

Meanwhile the people in the city were not unprepared. About thirty men armed to the teeth with repeating Winchester rifles and revolvers occupied the city building. Others well armed were secreted in the buildings lining the street up which the rioters must march. A volunteer company was organized to block up the street and the military company who were without ammunition were to surround the city hall with fixed bayonets. Although we were inferior in number the advantage of our position was so great that it would be impossible for them to accomplish anything except they began firing the buildings and it was secretly understood that anyone caught in the act was to be shot down without question. Finally the mob made a proposition to disperse on condition that the Redfield men should vacate the building and leave the records there in charge of two of the county commissioners who were friendly to their cause. This was supposed by our side to be only a ruse but was at last reluctantly acceded to and the mob then broke up, most of them coming into town in small squads, a circumstance which gave much ground to our suspicions. The armistice was kept inviolate though and the malcontents had nearly all left before night, vowing vengeance and another hostile visit within a week should the court sustain the injunction.

It is fearful to think now how slight a circumstance might at any time from 11 to 4 have precipitated a scene of bloodshed such as would have been too horrible to tell. A fire, started accidentally or by design, the careless discharge of a pistol, a drunken quarrel, any one of a thousand little mishaps of daily occurrence and the result would have been the death of hundreds. The experience of the day taught me what a fearful responsibility he who arouses the passions of the mob or gives occasion to one act of lawlessness assumes. It was grim and yet laughable to see people in a civilized community parading the streets of an ordinarily quiet and orderly town (and Redfield is such) with guns on their shoulder and pistols in their belts looking about for someone to shoot at—and that as calmly and with as little fear so far as appearances went as if it were a matter of every day business, and as little compunction as though they were expecting an attack from wild beasts instead of men. Even the school-master was out with a double-barreled shotgun and he said he told his boys on dismissing them to go home and arm themselves with every weapon available in defense of their firesides. They seemed to have obeyed his injunction. Boys not yet in their teens came out with bludgeons and revolvers. The hardware stores supplied everybody with weapons without money and without price. There are two murderous looking revolvers in our desk now that are seeking for owners. I never carried one before in my life.[2]

Yours devotedly,
T. J. Walsh.

[1] The Dakota militia, by law, was composed of "all able-bodied male citizens . . . being eighteen years of age and under the age of forty-five." Certain volunteer companies were designated as the active militia. A brigadier general commanded the territorial forces. Aaron B. and L. Levissee (eds.), *Revised Codes of the Dakota Territory, 1883* (St. Paul, Minnesota, 1885), pp. 505-10.

[2] As Walsh indicated, violence was somehow prevented. Yet tension remained high for more than a week and territorial militia were sent from Fargo to keep the peace, while a judge pondered the disposition of the case. Less than two weeks after the records were taken, the judge decided that they should go back to Old Ashton in custody of the sheriff. By no means was the matter settled. In the spring of 1885, the territorial legislature passed an act temporarily moving the records from Old Ashton to Ashton. It also provided that the question on location of the county seat should be submitted to the voters at the next general election. Meanwhile, attempts were being made to identify the Redfield men who had taken the county records. Should they be caught and convicted, that town would have little chance of becoming the county seat. Walsh in his letters commented frequently on the twists and turns of this controversy. A short description, based to an extent upon newspaper accounts, is found in J. Leonard Bates, "Walsh of Montana in Dakota Territory: Political Beginnings, 1884-90," *Pacific Northwest Quarterly*, LVI (July, 1965), 115-18.

18

Redfield, December 25, 1884.

My dear Ellen,—

I was intending to answer today your letter which I confidently expected to receive last night but its non-arrival is not going to deprive me of the opportunity of wishing you, before the season has fled, a "Merry, Merry Christmas" and a "glad New Year." Hence I write this evening. I'm not in a very merry mood just now and haven't been today, owing in great part, to confess freely, to the disappointment above referred to. That photo should have been here a week ago. I am sure you spoke in jest when you accused me of not wanting it. I'm homesick too. We used to have such pleasant re-unions at home about Christmas time when we [brothers and sisters] were all teaching. The desire of leaving this place has not yet developed any strength and I should much rather meet our family here than at Two Rivers, only that if I went to Wisconsin during the holidays, as the business of our office at one time indicated would be necessary, I should have had the further pleasure of meeting a friend of mine at Sheboygan who sings very sweetly and who has contributed on several occasions to making my Christmas a merry one. . . .

The other day we summed up the cases we have already on the calendar for trial at the next term of the district court. What do you think of the list?—three appeals from the justice court, two criminal cases, one forgery and one grand larceny and four civil cases. We shall start two or three more within a week. Not very bad for strangers, is it?

Don't forget to forward that picture.

Devotedly yours,
T. J. Walsh.

19

Sheboygan, December 28.

My dear Friend,

My letter is a whole week behind time but I had not the heart to write sooner. Deep sorrow has again over-taken me. My brother, my only brother, is dead. . . .[1]

I hope you have had no more trouble in Redfield. It was too bad things were managed as they were. Before I got your letter I doubted whether removing those records was a wise step. I also felt quite sure you had nothing to do with it. I trust matters may be arranged as you wish.

Yours sincerely,
E. C. McC.

[1] John R. McClements, age thirty, died on December 21, 1884. The cause is unknown. "Registration of Deaths, County of Sheboygan," in Register of Deeds Office, Sheboygan, Wisconsin.

20

Redfield, D.T., January 4, 1885.

My dear Ellen,—

The very sad intelligence of the death of your loved brother reached me through your letter on Friday and I haste to convey what little consolation there may be in the assurance that you have my sincerest sympathy and heartfelt condolence. . . . Heaven blessed me with sisters of whose love I am proud though I do not believe I ever yet sounded its intensity. By theirs, I measure yours and can thus form an idea at least of the depth of your affliction.

The literary society of which I wrote has come to be. We held a very interesting meeting last evening at which Longfellow as a poet suffered alike from friends and foes. . . . He sings in strains of great sweetness the sorrows of the slave, but his lines have little tendency to rouse men to abolish the evil. His chief merit, as I believe, and who will say that it is not a great one, is this— that sadness always finds him a sympathetic friend. The club is composed exclusively of single men and the membership is limited to ten. It may assist to dispel any erroneous ideas you may lately have formed of Dakota if I say that after deliberation it was deemed wise to establish this rule in order to prevent the club from growing unwieldy by reason of numbers. I never lived in a town in Wisconsin where there was the slightest danger of anything of the kind. Write me soon.

Yours sorrowfully,
T. J. Walsh.

21

Chicago, Ill., Jan. 8, 1885.

My dear Friend,

Your kind letter was received yesterday morning and I thank you for it. Why should you ask pardon for having written the letter which I received at home? . . . No, mon ami, you must not feel like that. To show you how unnecessary is any regret that you wrote to me, I will truthfully say that no letter you ever wrote me gave me more comfort than that one.

Yours sincerely,
E. C. M.

P.S.—About that picture. You shall have it. I'll send two and you can take which ever you wish.

E.

22

Redfield, January 18, 1885.

My dear Ellen,—

Your last should have been answered earlier but that I was waiting to acknowledge the receipt of your picture which, by the way, has not yet appeared. Why did you not select one yourself? I am sure I should have been better pleased than by relying on my own discrimination. Are both to be mine? You didn't say I should return either.

Yours ever,
T. J. Walsh.

23

Chicago, Jan. 25, 1885.

Dear Friend,

By this time you will have received that "work of art" and been disappointed of course. Certainly return one. You already have a half dozen (or less), too many pictures of me. . . . There's a very handsome young lady here who took up my album one evening, and what do you suppose occurred? She stopped at your photo and used all manner of beautiful adjectives in speaking of it. Don't blush; that's nothing. She looks at it every chance she gets and I am so amused. Now if I could only get one of her pictures for you, it might be a mutual affair. Shall I try? She is a perfect "blond" and I know you must admire blonds.

I am sorry you were not "wholly pleased" with my rejection of [room] No. 2. However there generally is "method in my madness." Believe me, there would have been no possible advantage in my taking the room. When I reach that lofty pinnacle (the head-assistanceship) it will be by a single bound. I hate crawling.

You ask what I think of the number of cases you have for trial at the next term of court. I should judge (if you really care to have my opinion) that the people possess great wisdom and see that you are quite a nice, smart little boy. But forgery! Grand larceny! I didn't know Dakota folks were as bad as that.

Why do not you make a dramatic society of your club? You are probably all interested in the drama, and the gentleman you mentioned might prove an efficient manager. Your efforts might provide a pleasing, and I am sure necessary, entertainment for the people of your town through the winter. If you think of doing anything of the kind, and I can be of service in getting books or in any other way, just call on me.

Len.

24

Redfield, February 1, 1885.

My dear Ellen,—

I was very agreeably relieved of a somewhat anxious suspense by the receipt a few moments ago of your letter of last Sunday. It bore no marks of having gone awry or from which could be gathered the story of its wanderings for the week past. Your "fair counterfeits" have also been received for which please accept my thanks. Notice the very bad taste I display by retaining the colored one. There is exhibited in the other a paleness of countenance such as I sincerely trust does not exist in the artist's model and which in my opinion mars the picture seriously. The other is very rosy indeed, and I admire roses, you know. Frankly the work is not in my opinion at all equal to that displayed in the other picture of you which I have, which, by the way, is a very finely executed piece of work. Why if I were to relate all the pretty things that have been said of that picture my letters would every one lengthen out into next week.

No the county seat business isn't ended yet. It is proposed now to introduce a bill providing that an election shall be held in

June at which any town in the county may be voted for, the two having the highest number of votes to be declared candidates at the November election and the one having the highest number of votes then to be the county seat. The news is too good to be true, as in that event Redfield's chances become the very best.

. . . Well now that's just the thing we are going to do. Not that I am very enthusiastic over it or unqualifiedly approve of it, but we are going to resolve ourselves into a dramatic society for one occasion at least. Thanks for your kind offer to assist us in procuring books. I am already deeply indebted to you for similar favors but shall draw on your services if we purchase in Chicago. It is contemplated to conclude the entertainment with an original farce in which our honorable legislators shall play the principal parts.

Good-night. Give your next letter a better start.

Tom.

25

Chicago, February 8, 1885.

Dear Friend,

What execrable taste you show in preferring plebian color to aristocratic pallor. . . . I agree with you that those roses are pretty, though painted too deep a pink. The roses I wore were pale pink and so lovely, but art can never equal nature in making flowers. Did you notice the quantities of flowers (chiefly roses) in some of the down-town windows when you were here? When I am downtown, I see unlimited amounts of beautiful dress goods, jewels, millinery, without one wish that I might have them, but when I see the flowers I want them.

Do you know, I think you were unkind even to pretend you misunderstood what I said about being amused at what Miss —— said about your picture. It wasn't what she said that amused me. She couldn't think otherwise, in my estimation, for I—well, I think it perfect.

Let me know how your dramatic club gets along. If I were there you should certainly have my bouquet thrown to you. Did I tell you of my club, the Motette?—or the club that I belong to rather. It is a musical club of course, and meets once a week at Apollo Hall. Mr. Tomlins wrote to me about it last summer when I was at home. He said he should invite about 200 members of the Festival Chorus to join the society. There are about that many, perhaps a few more, members at present. We have just received some new music from Europe—"Saint Ursula" and "Fair Ellen." . . .[1]

Len.

[1] William L. Tomlins had a distinguished career as musical director. Born in London, England, in 1844, he was trained in choral work and as an organist. In 1870 he came to New York. In 1875 he moved to Chicago and served as musical director of the Apollo Club from 1875 to 1898. His work in organizing children's choruses and wage-workers' concerts was notable. Frequent references in Ellen McClements' letters indicate that he was busy with many singing groups including what seems to have been a chorus for the May Festival. His work in the Chicago public schools is described in Department of Public Instruction, City of Chicago, *Thirty-second Annual Report of the Board of Education for the Year Ending June 30, 1886* (Chicago, 1887), pp. 54-55.

26

Redfield, February 15, 1885.

My dear Ellen,—

I didn't know you would think me unkind for writing anything I did, or it should not have been penned and I must beg your pardon for thinking it, whatever it was. . . .

Henry and I have been doing some newspaper work and I send you a copy merely because it contains a reply to the question you ask me about the virtue of Dakota politicians. I must disclaim all responsibility for any article on the woman suffrage question, so if the views expressed do not meet with your approval you must remember that they may not accord with mine. But we shall probably have the management of the paper a few weeks more and I should like very much to read an article on either side of the question by a woman who reaches conclusions by reason and not by instinct and I should be extremely happy to "place our columns at your service" whenever you choose to do us the honor of contributing anything on the subject.

No, you never spoke of the Motette. . . . Are visitors ever allowed at the Motette? I remember your once saying, or perhaps it was in the papers I saw it, that it was in contemplation to keep a large number of the Festival singers in training to form a ready chorus for other extensive musical entertainments.

Our dramatic club is in status quo or words to that effect. But we have arranged to get together this week and outline the farce. I have advised the boys to attempt a tragedy and the thing is sure to be farcical—same principle as some prominent playwright is said to work on. . . .

Yours as ever,
T. J. Walsh.

27

Chicago, February 22, 1885.

Dear Mr. Walsh,

. . . Yes, visitors are allowed at the Motette rehearsals. Do you think of dropping in some evening? That will be nice and neighborly of you. We meet at Apollo Hall every Wednesday night from 8 to 10:30. Ours is not the opera chorus. They practice under the leadership of Mr. Pratt. I was invited to become a member last fall, but thought it best for various reasons, not to avail myself of the privilege. . . . I think I never felt more tired in my life than I felt the last night of the May Festival. I guess that was the prevailing feeling, for the singing was not as good as upon previous nights, and Mr. Tomlins considered "The Redemption" our piece de resistance. I wish you could have heard the Grand Mass on Wednesday evening instead, but I was afraid to suggest it as everyone predicted a failure because it failed in New York. Cincinnati gave it up and Chicago made it a complete success. The scene in the Exposition building that night, "after the battle was o'er," passes description. The display of enthusiasm somewhat resembled the scene in the Republican Convention when Blaine was nominated [in the same building].

Many thanks for the distinguished honor you do me in requesting me to contribute to your paper an article whose conclusions are reached "by reason." Now if only you had asked me for an immortal poem or two, I might have attempted the rhyme, but the "reason" is entirely out of my line. Have you not yet learned that fact? Honestly, My friend, without any joking, I'd be most happy to do as you desire but I cannot write at all. I read carefully the article on "Woman's Suffrage" and find no particular fault with it. However, do not put me down as one who thinks "Woman's Sphere" is a ball of darning cotton.

Heard Miss Frances Willard lecture yesterday upon the temperance question. The lecture was very fine. She is a very pleasing speaker, and, I'm sure, a deep thinker. She favors Woman's suffrage and if allowed to vote would probably do so quite as intelligently as the average hod-carrier or colored porter. . . .[1]

E. C. McC.

[1] Frances E. Willard (1839-98) was a president of the Woman's Christian Temperance Union, an educator and reformer. In 1884 she helped to organize the Prohibition party. Also a newspaperwoman, she wrote *Women and Temperance* and two other books between 1883 and 1889. When Ellen McClements heard her, she was at the height of her power. See Mary Earhart, *Frances Willard: From Prayers to Politics* (Chicago, 1944).

28

Redfield, March 1, 1885.

My dear Ellen,—

. . . No, I have not been reading the Inter-Ocean's serial. Political novels are much more of a rarity in this country than in England. Why is this? When the paragraph in the [Redfield] Dispatch was written it might be said that the wish was father to the thought [1]—that Col. Vilas would go into the cabinet but there is no longer any doubt that he is one of the elect.[2] Of course it pleases me much. If the rest of them are as able and as honest as he the administration will not suffer because of the material in the cabinet. I should much rather see some other man than Manning in the treasury department.[3] It appears to me that a further mistake has been made in taking the three leading democrats out of the senate as appears will be done. Thurman, Pendleton, McDonald, McClellan and other men in private life would have filled cabinet positions creditably [4] and the administration will soon feel the need of Bayard, Garland and Lamar in the Senate.[5] Quite a delegation from this section have gone down to Washington to witness the inaugural ceremonies and have themselves appointed to Federal offices with as little delay as may be. Two aspirants for the post-office at this place will be there to urge their "claims." It's very ridiculous. Both of them seem to think that about the first question that will engage the attention of the new president is who he will appoint as post-master of an insignificant town out in Dakota.

Now don't put yourself out about this matter but I desire to draw on your kind offer to assist us in getting material for our attempt at the drama. Our Committee haven't been successful in getting anything very desirable yet and we shall all be very thankful if you make a selection for us as early as you can conveniently. Mr. Milton, not the deceased John, but our manager, says that what is desired is a three or four act military drama but if you are unable to find any such make any selection that you think will answer our purpose well—don't forget to send the bill.

If I go to Chicago this summer, and it isn't unlikely that I shall, it will be a pleasure I shall certainly avail myself of, to drop in on the Motette.

Tom.

[1] In No. 26 Walsh mentioned his writing for a newspaper, and he has identified it here as the *Redfield Dispatch*, a Democratic organ. The paragraph referred to must have been his own. (Files of the *Redfield Dispatch* have completely disappeared, so far as this writer can discover.)

[2] William F. Vilas (1840-1908) was a man of great ability and was one of Walsh's favorites among the law professors at the University of Wisconsin. He served in the Union army, practiced law in Wisconsin, and emerged in the 1870's and 1880's as a power in the Democratic party. He was a member of the Democratic National Committee (1876-86), chairman of the national convention in 1884, and Postmaster General and later Secretary of the Interior in Cleveland's cabinet. He also served one term as senator from Wisconsin, 1891 to 1897. See Horace Samuel Merrill, *William Freeman Vilas: Doctrinaire Democrat* (Madison, Wisconsin, 1954).

[3] Daniel Manning of New York.

[4] Allen G. Thurman of Ohio, George H. Pendleton of Ohio, and Joseph E. McDonald of Indiana. George B. McClellan, of Civil War fame, served as governor of New Jersey from 1878 to 1881 and was boomed for the position of Secretary of War in Cleveland's cabinet.

[5] Thomas F. Bayard of Delaware became Cleveland's Secretary of State; Augustus H. Garland of Arkansas headed the Department of Justice; L. Q. C. Lamar of Mississippi was Secretary of the Interior.

29

Chicago, March 8, 1885.

Dear Friend,

I was quite terrified by your request to select a drama for your club. Why I do not know the first thing about what constitutes a good play. Yesterday I went to the chief dramatic agency here, and although they have dramatic works by the thousand, they had very few military dramas. "The Virginia Veteran" seemed about the best of them. There was another, "The Veteran of 1812," which I thought might be good, but it required such a large number of performers, I feared you could not make use of it. You see, mon ami, you gave me no idea of the strength of your dramatic corps. I went to the Western News Agency and found about the same selection.[1] I sent you two from that place. If you did not want anything military, "David Garrick" would be good. I saw Lawrence Barrett in the title role. I marked it on one of the lists. "Engaged" is lively and entertaining. . . .

You are pleased of course by the realization of your hopes in regard to Col. Vilas's appointment to a cabinet position. I notice that he and Mrs. V. were among the first callers at the executive mansion.

The first concert of the Motette Club is to occur on the 24th of this month. Each member is also pledged to sing six Sundays at Prof. Swing's services at Central Music Hall.

. . . Just two blocks east of Humboldt Park a large new school has been built and I am there. I hadn't an idea of such a thing happening, but I suppose "the powers" had. Do you recollect a short time ago when you thought I did scarcely right in refusing No. 2, and what you said about getting into a position where there would be no room higher than? Do you recall my reply? Well, there is no room higher than mine at the Von Humboldt School. I have No. 1.[2]

Len.

[1] The Western News Company, described by Bessie L. Pierce as a

"news depot," must have provided some other services as well. Pierce, *A History of Chicago*, II (New York, 1940), 421.

[2] From 1882 to 1885 Ellen taught at the Wicker Park School, a grade school, which she described as "one of the best in the city." This was a brick building, located at Evergreen Avenue between Robey Street and Hoyne Avenue. The enrollment on September 6, 1882, was 1,058; three years later it had risen to 1,831; by 1886 it had dropped to 728, apparently because of new construction. The Von Humboldt School, to which Ellen moved in March of 1885, was another brick building, newly completed. It had three stories and fifteen rooms. The enrollment in March of 1885 was said to be only 78, although in 1885-86 it went up to 642. The city of Chicago obviously was straining to keep up with her growing population. See Department of Public Instruction, *Report of the Board of Education for 1886, passim.*

30

Redfield, March 15, 1885.

My dear Ellen,—

. . . No I shan't confess myself at all surprised that you have been asked "to go up higher." I told you so a long time ago but it is a little inexplicable to me how without a great deal of "Fine work" it could come about that you should all at once have taken that "single Bound," been freed from the domination of and association with "the adorable Eliza," got right into the neighborhood which you preferred above all others and met there the friends you most desired should be with you. You must have had the "pins set up in great shape." (That's another Dakotaism supposed to be very expressive.) I trust your new labors will prove agreeable as I know they will be valuable.

I tried my first Jury case about ten days ago and much to my surprise won it. It was a rather desperate one too, but we never call a jury on any other. . . .

We are much in love with "Allatoona" and think of trying it. As a matter of course the farce we contemplated producing will be dispensed with or materially modified.

So adieu a little.

Tom.

31

Chicago, March 22, 1885.

Dear Mr. Walsh,

In your summary of all I gained by my last stroke of diplomacy, I recognize the skill of the lawyer. I admit all the "gains," but plead "not guilty" of any "fine work." In saying that I must have had the "pins set up in great shape," you must surely have forgotten that I told you it was all a complete surprise to me. . . . I think they have in some incomprehensible manner received the impression that I am somewhat successful in the schoolroom, and that may account for their unasked kindness. . . .

E. C. M.

32

Redfield, March 29, 1885.

My dear Ellen,—

I rejoiced with a wholly unselfish joy at your success as I believe you would at mine, and if my words conveyed any other idea the blame is theirs and not my intentions. Begging pardon for differing with you, I fail to see anything open to criticism in seeking preferment or in getting it though I had not a thought but that your late success was achieved entirely without solicitation on your part. I know well it pays principals and superintendents to accommodate their teachers in those matters. Why Mr. Howland should take an interest in advancing you is no more "inexplicable" to me than it is to you. It has been a very simple matter to me that you should rise, ever since I visited your schoolroom in Sheboygan some years ago.

Business has been somewhat brisk this month. Criminal law seems to flourish just now. I have no love for criminal law and no ambition to be known as a criminal lawyer, but these are cases which attract crowds and give a young attorney an opportunity to "make an impression." The opinion is very prevalent that glibness of speech is the one requisite of a good lawyer. Extensive learning tells after a long time but it's rather useless in the business of building up a practice. . . .

One of the members of our club is a young man who has until recently lived for a great many years in Washington where he was connected with some daily and reported dramatic news. He has heard nearly all the great living actors and, as you may suppose, is something of a critic. He converses well and is always entertaining when he talks of them which he delights very much to do. I think I should enjoy very much spending a winter or two in Washington. Were you ever overtaken with a desire to listen to the debates in Congress? I am frequently when reading of the stormy time they sometimes have these days such as in the recent Sherman-Dawes controversy.[1] The reading of Macaulay's "Trial of Warren Hastings" always awakens this feeling. I suppose that as a general thing though, it is very dull listening.

Very penitently,

T. J. W.

[1] An allusion apparently to a dispute in the Senate over rules of procedure, involving Henry Dawes of Massachusetts and John Sherman of Ohio. See *Cong. Record*, 48 Cong., 2 Sess., pp. 2385-89 (March 2, 1885).

33

Chicago, April 3, 1885.

Dear Friend,

I'm sorry my last letter "grieved" you. That's the worst of it. I'm always sorry when I've done anything wrong, and that isn't pleasant at all. By the way, you don't differ with me at all when you see nothing open to criticism in seeking preferment and getting it. The former is necessary in nine cases out of ten, and I am a devout believer in the latter. It was the means to that end that I referred to.

Do you know that I agree with the Dakota opinion that "glibness of speech" is an essential requisite of a good lawyer. Not the one requisite however. You have some ridiculous notion that you do not talk well, but it is all nonsense. I have not had the opportunity to hear you speak in public often, but, judging from what I have heard, together with my knowledge of your education, I should say that speaking well would be one of the things you could do perfectly and with the greatest ease. . . .

Mr. Tomlins thinks of going to New York. I hope he will not. There is no one like him. He is the personification of music, and his enthusiasm communicates itself to his choruses. Mr. Thomas has resigned his leadership of the Philharmonic Society in New York and they want Mr. Tomlins to take his place. If Chicago lets him it will be a mistake.[1]

Of course the post-office is mine. Did not you present it to me long ago?

E. C. M.

[1] Chicago had the good fortune to retain Tomlins and also eventually to attract Theodore Thomas (1835-1905). The latter had a distinguished career beginning with his performances in Germany as a child violinist and continuing in New York, Cincinnati, and Chicago. See notes for Nos. 25 and 200.

34

Redfield, April 10, 1885.

My dear Ellen,—

. . . Did you find the Easter services at the Jesuit church impressive? I can't lay claim to much piety but I do love to hear vespers sung when they are well sung.

Adieu.
Tom.

35

Chicago, April 19, 1885.

Dear Friend,

In today's Inter-Ocean I notice that the woman's suffrage question is again abroad in your land. Guess you'll have to come to it so you might as well submit gracefully. Why are you opposed to allowing women to vote in Dakota? Is it because most women are not democrats—or is it true that they are not? . . .

Bye-bye.
E. C. McC.

36

Redfield, April 25, 1885.

My dear Ellen,—

. . . I noticed that the woman's suffragists and the prohibition people are both organizing to "capture" the coming constitutional convention at Sioux Falls. Henry was out west about forty miles this past week and spent one evening with the redoubtable champion of the women's rights ladies—the gallant Major Pickler. Mrs. Pickler acquired a reputation at Bismarck last winter for being a shrewd and effectual lobbyist.[1]

Our dramatic enterprise seems to have fizzled out. Nobody seems to desire to mention the matter for fear of being made the butt of a joke about the farce that was to have been made a feature of it.

I think your sister expresses the situation properly when she says I am not much of a woman suffrage man.[2] Do you know that it makes a vast difference whether a man forms his political opinions in his study or in a debating school, severed entirely you may say from the world as it exists, or whether they are the growth of a mind necessarily unschooled, but which has become keen and comprehensive by meeting and resolving these questions in the practical work? . . . My friend, Sterling of Huron,[3] says he will lose all faith in Spink county if they don't send me to the Sioux Falls convention. The boys at the law school thought I knew a few things about constitutions. I can go if I want to. If I go I'll have to study up the woman suffrage question and a few others of less importance that are likely to arise.

Adieu.

Tom.

[1] Walsh's tone may have been affected by the fact that John A. Pickler was a Republican member of the territorial legislature (from Faulkton). Also, his wife Alice was an advocate of woman's rights and probably had been lobbying in the territorial capital for the cause of prohibition—which Walsh at this time opposed. The Picklers gained more than a local prominence. When South Dakota was admitted as a state, Major Pickler was elected to Congress and served in the House of Representatives from 1889 to 1897.

[2] This was probably a reference to Ellen's sister Mary. Walsh later changed his mind about woman suffrage.

[3] William B. Sterling, a resident of Huron, had been in Walsh's law

class at Wisconsin. In Dakota the two developed a close friendship. "Will" Sterling is not to be confused with Thomas S. Sterling of Redfield, later a U.S. senator from South Dakota. According to one source, when Walsh left Redfield in 1890 he did not see Thomas Sterling again until they met in the Senate. Harlow, *Prairie Echoes*, pp. 357-58.

37

Chicago, May 3, 1885.

Dear Friend,

I am a firm believer in "men's rights" in taking charge of baggage. I hate to do it and usually victimize some one. That's one reason why I will not exert myself in advancing women's rights. I hate to hear women rampaging about their "rights" and then asking special consideration because they are women. Though for many reasons I do not approve of woman's suffrage (that is where her "rights" begin is it not?) I think the time not far distant when that right will be hers. In mentioning her right in that way, I do not mean her right to vote as compared with that of the ignorant negro or illiterate immigrant; but the mistake of allowing the privileges of the ballot to a class of men ignorant even of the law which allows them that privilege, cannot be rectified by another mistake. Women's right to vote being gained all else follows. That she may fill a man's position I do not object to on the supposition that she cannot fill it as well. With the same training she will do as well or better, and many men, realizing this probability, realize also the danger of a social revolution. An exchange of duties will be impossible, or at least impracticable and ridiculous, and of the work which both can perform there will not be sufficient. There are positions, formerly filled by men exclusively, that women can occupy with grace and dignity, but these are not the positions that will be sought by the woman politician. If my ideal woman is not the successful lobbyist, the haranguer of the mob, or the expert "fine worker," neither is she the weak, half-imbecile nonentity which Dickens sometimes portrayed. She is more powerful, but far less dangerous to society as at present organized, than is the lobbyist, the haranguer, or the perpetrator of "fine work." . . .

L. N.

38

Redfield, May 10, 1885.

My dear Ellen,

Everyone is more or less apprehensive that injury will result to growing crops from the recent cold spell. You are, I am sure, unable to appreciate the anxiety universally felt here as to what the harvest shall be. I never felt it in the east. If I ever questioned my granger friends about the condition of crops it was more because I opined that that would be to them the most interesting subject of conversation rather than that I had any real curiosity to know. However they turned out, it did not occur to me that my physical or financial well-being would in any way be affected. It is quite different here. Our dependence on the fruits of the soil is so exclusive, immediate and apparent that the least discerning must see that his prosperity and that of the farmer have a common basis. Cheap statesmen rise to eminence out here by professing great love for the interests of the farmer. They only parade the intensity of their own selfishness and usually betray it, their own stupidity, and their constituents as soon as they are trusted, by working against those interests. There is a vast deal depending on the ensuing harvest—on it hinges in a great measure the future of Dakota for several years to come. The partial failure and low prices of the past year have compelled many to encumber everything they have and they are completely ruined unless helped out by a good crop this year.

. . . I could never content myself to stay in a town as small as this, only—well I expect to live outside of it some day. I'll tell you, though, for whose lot in life I believe I feel the sincerest compassion and he of all men seems to desire it the least. It's the fellow that follows the star of empire with a "prairie schooner" —a canvas covered wagon in which are all his earthly effects, the wife of his bosom, divers hopefuls, and a mongrel dog.

. . . The Illinois democrats, like the Dakota republicans, depend too much on "fine work" rather than an honest campaign and straight, hard work at the polls.

Your remarks on the woman suffrage question interested me greatly. . . . In reaching a conclusion, the question of whether any considerable number of our educated women are anxious for the franchise or would exercise it if granted them, must receive careful consideration. We can hardly afford to extend any further the franchise if it is to be exercised only by the vicious and ignorant of the favored class. So far as Dakota is concerned the movement is confined to the prohibition people and a few politicians who hope through their advocacy of it to attain notoriety for the present and a perpetual lease of office when the scheme carries.

Adieu.
Tom.

39

Chicago, May 17, 1885.

Dear Friend,

You're an immense fraud, aren't you? What did you once say to me for liking a large city and now you say we are the only people who "live." Now that you have said that, it's my duty to go over to the other side, isn't it? . . . I am not one who "would rather rule in h—— than serve in heaven," but I would rather be first in a wide-awake small town than an "unknown magnitude" in a large city. The fact of the whole matter is that the place has very little to do with the case. A person is content where he is happy and vice versa, and the place is always nice. . . .

Nell.

40

Redfield, May 24, 1885.

My dear Ellen,—

Flowers are blooming in profusion and peeping out in clusters as they usually grow from under the rank grass and they lend a great charm to a drive just now. Most of them are strange to me, that is I know them only by their family names. I've regretted a number of times having left my botany at home. Many of them excite my curiosity not a little. I used to think and am not yet entirely disabused of the idea, that for a man to profess a fondness for botany was an indication of a mind of little vigor or at least virility. Proficiency in mathematics, I thought, betokened intellectual strength and penetration. Latterly though serious doubts have arisen in my mind as to the correctness of this opinion. I should endure though the reproach of my "high blown pride" of intellect and do some botanizing for pastime if I had my outfit with me. Even the flowers though, aren't half as charming to me as a piece of green woods. There's a small patch of very scrubby underbrush with here and there something we dignify by calling a tree, along a rather infrequented road between here and Ashton. I always drive that way when going to the county seat for the pleasure of seeing the green leaves and hearing the birds sing.

It's just a little like self gratulation but do you know that the democrats out here are an exceptionally manly and intelligent set? Natural enough too. Those who have no opinions and those who are too weak to maintain them all train with the other crowd. We shall lose caste though as we gain power and the recent large reinforcements are of very indifferent material. . . .

Yours,
Tom.

41

Chicago, May 31, 1885.

My dear Friend,

. . . I should think you would long for the sight of "a forest verdure clad." Long ago I learned the definition of the word prairie, but I think its full significance never occurred to me forcibly until I read your last letter. Imagine going out of one's way to see some shrubs! You must indeed miss the trees you've always been accustomed to see. No, I do not think it ever occurred to me that a love for flowers, a fondness for the study of botany indicated any mental weakness in a man. On the contrary, I think its indications all good. Like a love for the beautiful in anything, it indicates a refined taste. If a man were to make a life work of the study of plants, the calm, unexciting character of his occupation might, in time, make him appear indolent, full, or a trifle slow, but that would be the result of and not a reason for his pursuit of the study.

I do not think I could exist very contentedly without flowers, but I never feel any desire to "analyze" them. In my limited field of observation I've generally found an over-brightness in mathematics more than counter-balanced by a dullness in something else, or in all things else. It may be hazardous to say so, but I think a mathematical prodigy is rarely likely to be a great man. Don't ask me why I think so, because I don't know.

I am quite ready to believe all you say of the democrats of Dakota. I know it is not always safe to judge by a sample, but I shall do so just this once since your opinion is also on the side of the "sample."

E. C. M.

42

Redfield, June 7, 1885.

Dear Ellen,—

I was forcibly reminded last Sunday evening that it was the anniversary of the night we went to the Festival—an occasion I shall, for many reasons, not soon forget. Owing chiefly to the extreme kindness of yourself the short visit I paid to Chicago a year ago proved very enjoyable indeed. The year just gone by has been an eventful one to me and though it embraces that period, the first year of a lawyer's practice, when time is supposed to lengthen out into eternity, to me it has flown quickly by. A large measure of the distrust and uncertainty which troubled me a year ago has been dissipated and at comparatively little cost I have crowded a great deal of experience into, and, I hope, gained some wisdom in, the last twelve months. However justly or unjustly, I can view the coming year with very much less anxiety and apprehension.

. . . I am not at all in sympathy with the avowed object of the Sioux Falls convention, namely to hurry admission. I don't want statehood until the democratic party grows so strong that it will take something more than a nomination by a republican caucus to get an office.[1]

Bye-bye.
Tom.

41

¹ The Sioux Falls Constitutional Convention did not meet until September, 1885. Dominated by Republicans, it had the aim of achieving prompt statehood for South Dakota. As Howard R. Lamar has shown, this was less a people's movement than a fight for power between two factions of the Republican party, with their influence centered at Bismarck in the north and Yankton in the south. Yankton Republicans and many "southerners" were bitter, having lost the capital to Bismarck. They proposed to escape the dominance of the territorial capital by a movement for separate statehood. Lamar, *Dakota Territory, passim.*

43

Chicago, June 14, 1885.

Dear Tom,

. . . Do you know one class of theory-illustrators that I always shun? Writers on educational subjects. I do detest the sight of an educational paper. The writers seem almost uniformly conceited and dogmatic. I like to teach and I like my school, but anything else pertaining to the business (except pay-day), I do not like.

Sincerely,
Ellen.

44

Redfield, June 21, 1885.

Dear Ellen,—

. . . Such delights are denied to us here in Dakota—when it's hot we swelter. Our evenings though are delightfully cool always and in this way we are in a measure compensated for the absence of the shade you find so grateful. It is slightly paradoxical but doubtless true that our cool evenings are owing chiefly to the fact that we have so little shade to interfere with radiation. Now a stoic might draw complete consolation from that reflection but I'll resign philosophy and take a hammock under the trees as a panacea for hot weather. You spoke of roses. Wild roses grow every where here. Some of the bushes are so tiny that there is nothing visible but the blossoms blushing in the grass. The cactus plants are beginning to bloom too. It seems very strange to see those plants reared as exotics with so much care in Wisconsin growing here wild.

Ever yours,
Tom.

45

Chicago, June 28, 1885.

Mon cher Ami,

Our "circus" went off splendidly. We had an excellent Steinway piano, and the singing and instrumental music added a good deal to the programme. We had recitations and readings in English, German, and Norwegian. The scene after the exercises were over was really amusing. The people up there are easily pleased and very demonstrative. I would not attempt to say in how many dozen different ways my hand was shaken. I did not object to that at all, but the osculatory part of the business I do object to. I draw the line at that.

They are very proud of their school. The "handsomest" school in the city will be opened, not far from here, next September. It is named after Hans Christian Andersen and is certainly a lovely building. I've never been in it, but Mr. M. says it is fine. . . .

E. C. M.

46

Redfield, July 5, 1885.

My dear Ellen,—

I was glad to learn that your closing exercises passed off so pleasantly. Is Norse taught in the Von Humboldt, or was the attempt in that direction sporadic, so to speak?

Our [Fourth of July] celebration yesterday was a great success. We were marched down to the Milwaukee [railroad] depot about 9 A.M. to escort a company of Aberdeen militia coming on the train due about 9:30. Then came an exhibition drill with the mercury at 110. It is to be hoped the spectators enjoyed it. No one in the company did and most of them felt that as the Aberdeen company are not at all proficient it was slightly discourteous to them as visitors to compel comparisons to be instituted. Then we played ball and we were beaten though with a good record and largely by accident. The sham battle was a decided sham to anyone at all acquainted with military affairs. . . .

Ever yours,
Tom.

47

Sheboygan, July 14, 1885.

My dear Friend,

Your letters were promptly received and would have been answered sooner but I was waiting for something. The Chicago Daily News, which I sent you this P.M., will explain what I was waiting to hear. I am greatly pleased with the prospect of going into the Andersen School. Do you think there has been any "fine work" going on? I shall not say there has not, but I didn't do it—directly. If I had not been put in the Andersen school, I think I should have been assistant special teacher of drawing. I was asked by the teacher of drawing how I would like the position. I prefer my present position, however, as the drawing teacher is constantly going from school to school superintending the work. . . .

Very truly yours,
E. C. M.

48

Redfield, July 19, 1885.

My dear Ellen,—

I am delighted at this new and signal indication of the appreciation in which your services are held by the Chicago school officials and tender you my sincerest congratulations. I trust your new situation will prove in every way agreeable to you. You acted wisely, I am sure, in taking the first assistantship rather than the position of special teacher, though that ought certainly to have many pleasant features, one of the chief of which seems to me to be that you can see the progress made by pupils.

The grand jury spent a half a day in investigating the removal of the county records to this place last fall but nothing came of it and so the matter is probably consigned to oblivion. It isn't entirely as agreeable to the Redfield people to go up there to attend court as it might be, but a great deal of the animosity of last winter has already passed away and we shall be neighborly now—at least until another election comes around....

Au revoir once more.
Sincerely yours,
Tom.

49

Sheboygan, July 26, 1885.

Dear Friend,

Received the "Court Calendar" last Wednesday. Was much pleased to read of your victorious cases and sorry for the one you lost, since losing it seems to have pained you. Why should you feel so deeply about it? No one is always successful, and in this case the cause of the failure was not with you. I think you have all reasons for satisfaction with yourself. You are evidently appreciated by the people judging by the number of cases in which you are interested as compared with the number to be tried and the number of attorneys.

Thanks for congratulations on my change of position in Chicago. I promise to send mine along when you are elected—well, we'll say, Governor of the State of Dakota. Is that satisfactory? ...

You are so much in love with nature that you'll be sure to enjoy yourself if the militia goes into encampment, Snakes! Mosquitoes! Bugs! Spiders! That's the programme, isn't it? And won't you say something eminently pious when the reveille rudely breaks all the slumber the mosquitoes have left you; and won't you think something "a-little-more-so" when the tattoo warns you it is time to stop flirting with the pretty girls who drive out to see "how the campfires look at night"?

Good-night.
E.

50

My dear Ellen,—

. . . Tuesday night about 10 o'clock a hot wind sprang up that was almost stifling. Nothing of the kind was ever known here before and I never experienced anything like it until then. It felt as though coming directly from some great furnace and yet the heat seemed less active and more oppressive than any originating from artificial sources. Occasionally the wind would grow violent and then a dead calm would intervene. Everyone expected it to culminate in a cyclone and we retired after midnight still expecting it.

I contemplate starting tomorrow morning on an extensive jaunt over the eastern and northern portions of the county, said to be the finest portion of Dakota. You see I had the honor a short time ago to be elected treasurer of the Spink County Agricultural Society—not Governor of the state of Dakota—and we are making a special effort to induce the farmers of that section to attend and bring exhibits to our fair. As much of this territory lies tributory to Ashton and they are to have a fair the task which is deputed to me is a rather delicate one and not altogether promising. I have an invitation to spend one night with a gentleman who has the reputation of being the most extensive and successful farmer in the county. He has 700 acres of wheat on his place besides corn and other grain. He is an Ashton man to the core, but he has been very friendly to me, is a radical democrat (to which fact is partly due our acquaintanceship) and was once sheriff of Dane County, Wis. I anticipate a good time even if the practical results of the trip should not be great and I shall see harvesting done on a larger scale than I ever have.

. . . That victory insures to us a client whose business is in such condition that he is in almost constant need of an attorney and being a man of considerable means his cases are usually large and important. He is a very intelligent man too, was once Surveyor-General of Louisiana and appreciates that the preparation of such a case requires a large amount of study and investigation. In looking up this case I found very smooth sailing until I struck a decision of the Supreme Court of the U.S. rendered about April 1 on a question almost identical and directly opposed to our theory of the case. I hoped that the other side would fail to get it—the decision was so recent—but through the assistance of some outside attorneys they found it and worked it as well as they knew how. I succeeded in convincing the judge, though, more thoroughly than myself, that the opinion was not exactly in point. I knew the case from beginning to end and "my learned friends" on the other side were more astonished at my familiarity with it than I was at their knowledge of its existence. But if I hadn't seen it and studied it carefully it would probably have "rattled" me. Of course the law business here is still very inconsiderable but it will grow very rapidly hereafter and in about three years hence, if I mistake not, support a strong bar.

Your letter suggested a number of charms that will attend the encampment of which I had not theretofore thought. What a magnificent opportunity there will be—to study—natural history!

The editor (of the local "Democrat") is a particular friend of mine and very much of a gentleman and an able fellow. By the way he wanted me to allow my name to be presented as a candidate for Territorial Secretary. I answered that I came to Dakota to practice law.

Yours sincerely,
Tom.

51

Sheboygan, August 16, 1885.

Dear Friend,

. . . I have always thought that if I could choose one field in which to find my life-work, I should choose to be an artist, a painter. As I looked at the sky that night, and thought of the joy it would be to be able to imprison upon canvas the fleeting beauties of that sky, the old longing came back to me, and it actually took a good deal of what has been called my "philosophy" (to be defined "want of feeling") to keep me from feeling "blue," and thinking some rather unfemininely harsh things about the vanity of all things in general and youthful aspirations in particular.

You must have quite extinguished the editor when he had the audacity to make the proposal about the Territorial Secretaryship. I can fully understand your distaste for anything of that kind for I've always thought that if I were a man I would rather be the humblest mechanic than an office seeker. If I were wealthy and felt strongly "called" to some office "of distinction," if I thought I might do some good in the position, I should, doubtless, accept, but to gain a living by holding office I would as lieve be a slave.[1]

E. C. M.

[1] To explain this attitude is not easy, but middle-class people of intelligence and culture wished to distinguish between themselves and a rising group of plutocrats, nondescripts, and grubby politicians. Ellen McClements and T. J. Walsh were affected, to some degree, by what one writer has termed the "best society virus," by a tendency to categorize people into the "acceptable" and "unacceptable." A "most charming" and influential writer with this point of view was Oliver Wendell Holmes, autocrat of the breakfast table. See Edwin H. Cady, *The Gentleman in America: A Literary Study in American Culture* (Syracuse, New York, 1949), pp. 147-49 and *passim*.

52

Redfield, August 23, 1885.

Dear Ellen,—

I shall have to choose between a democratic convention at Fargo and the militia encampment at Aberdeen,[1] both beginning on September 22. My present intention is to take in the convention and then offer my services to the military authorities for the last two days of camp. There will probably come up for consideration the question of the constitutional convention, admission as a whole, the division of our judicial district and the appointment of two additional judges, with other questions of more or less significance. . . .

Your friend,
T. J. W.

[1] As revealed in No. 56, Walsh had his towns reversed. The convention met in Aberdeen, while the militia encampment occurred at Fargo.

53

Dear old Fellow,

Didn't exactly contemplate addressing you in such a manner and am doubtful as to the propriety of so doing. There also exists in my mind a doubt as to the appropriateness of the second adjective. Guess I'll let it stand just as it is however; there is something so venerable and respectful about a formal address like the above. . . .

You know the Germans visit a good deal on Sunday and several of our friends thought they would spend that Sunday with us. I couldn't leave them in order to write letters could I? You see, I sing a little, like most people and I can talk a good deal of nonsense when I exert myself and those people seemed to like those things, and so—and so—I was indispensable to their happiness (so to speak) that day.

E.

54

Redfield, September 1, 1885.

My dear Ellen,—

They are having no end of trouble with the school here. Another protest against a male teacher employed to manage the grammar department was unfortunately defeated by a majority vote. The object of this marked attention is something of a curiosity as a pedagogue. He might not attract notice as a "hewer of wood," but when it becomes known that he is a "teacher of youth" his appearance becomes peculiarly striking. He has a hatchet face, a high forehead, gray eyes and a spare mustache of that variety of red sometimes spoken of as "carroty." He wears a gingham shirt, a paper collar, no necktie, ready made clothes that fit vilely and pantaloons that display two-thirds of the legs of heavy cowhide boots. He walks with his toes turned inward and a considerable bend. If he had the wisdom of Socrates I'd never employ him as a teacher. There is something wrong in the system by which such a man is certificated. It has been intimated to him that under all the circumstances he ought to decline to serve but he'll probably prove the one of that class of whom it is said "few die and none resign."

My friend, Mr. Seve [?], of the "Democrat," again urged me when I was in Huron to go seeking after strange Gods, but I did just as you told me, so that if I fail to become politically famous you must bear a share of the blame. Never mind, if I attain any celebrity as a lawyer, a distinction I prize much more highly, you may say you had a hand in getting it for me—and I will too. . . .

Good night.

Your dear old fellow,

Tom.

55

Chicago, September 13, 1885.

Dear Friend,

The Andersen School is fine. The building is the most ornamental in the city. It contains fifteen school rooms besides the principal's office, the library, German room, basement and gymnasium. . . .[1]

E. C. M.

[1] The Andersen School attained an enrollment of more than nine hundred pupils. Department of Public Instruction, *Report of the Board of Education for 1886*, p. 76.

56

Redfield, Sept. 19, 1885.

Dear Ellen,—

I have been very anxiously expecting the "History of a Title" but thus far vainly. "Ten Thousand Pounds a Year" is another work of a similar character which I have long desired and intended to read.[1] Vilas recommended it to us in terms of high praise. He is very familiar with choice bits of literature and along with a great many brilliant remarks entirely his own he frequently injected quotations into his lectures, all impromptu so far as the language went. In the course of the first lecture he delivered to our class, in commenting on the nature of law in general he used those lines from Pope's Universal Prayer,

> But binding nature fast in fate
> Sift free the human will,

with such peculiar aptness and so beautifully set off that it made a deep impression on me. It was the only occasion on which I ever felt my emotions overcome by the power of oratory. I should like to have heard Emery A. Storrs before a jury, not that I ever admired the man but it seems to me so strange, almost incredible, that one man should attain so complete a mastery over the passions of others.

The militia company starts this afternoon for Fargo. I shall be detained in Aberdeen for at least two of the four days the encampment lasts. Of course there is no compulsion in the matter of my stay at Aberdeen but one of the prime objects for which the meeting was called was to injure some of my friends and I'll remain until that is abandoned or defeated. They seem to think I can be useful to them in some way and I shall certainly try to be.

I send you today a copy of the Globe containing an account of some recent proceedings of the Sioux Falls convention. Campbell's resolution expresses nothing more than the logical conclusion of the theory of government upon which the convention is based. It is a complete vindication of the theory which I held from the start, that the movement is purely revolutionary in character and justifiable only under circumstances that would excuse an appeal to arms.[2] Campbell has a history. He was connected with the famous Louisiana returning board of '76 [3] and for meritorious work on that important tribunal was rewarded by his party with the position of U.S. Attorney for Dakota. He handed in his resignation very promptly after the 4th of March last and is now surmised to be ambitious to represent the state of Dakota on the floor of the U.S. Senate. . . .

Ever your
Tom.

[1] *Ten Thousand A-Year* (1841), a novel by the English lawyer Samuel Warren, must have been the work referred to. The *History of a Title* has not been identified.

[2] The Sioux Falls convention met without authority from Congress,

and Hugh J. Campbell of Yankton led a minority of the convention who were prepared to proceed independently to statehood. They would make South Dakota a "state" and force Congress' hand. However, such a radical course was not adopted. See further references to Campbell in No. 71 and accompanying note. Also see Lamar, *Dakota Territory*, for an analysis of Campbell's role in the statehood movement.

[3] A reference to the Hayes-Tilden disputed election of 1876.

57

Redfield, September 29, 1885.

Dear Ellen,—

I have been very much alarmed all day at failing to receive your customary letter. Came in just a few moments ago after a tedious all day drive to be again disappointed. Do write, please, and relieve my suspense. . . .

I have been requested to take the stump next week and have signified a willingness to do so but I shan't go until I hear from you. Let the excuses already made suffice for the infliction upon you of this letter. I shall have little heart to prepare a political speech until your answer comes.

Tom.

58

Chicago, Oct. 4, 1885.

Dear Friend,

Your last has remained for a terribly long time unanswered, considering the promptness with which I usually write. I have been so very busy.

Last week the Superintendent of singing visited us and informed me that the committee on music had appointed me "local supervisor of singing" at the Andersen. I scarcely understand their motive yet, as I have been unable thus far to learn of any other school having a similar arrangement. I was really annoyed by the intelligence and would have refused had it been possible, for I have plenty of work already. . . . I am expected to visit and hear sing, the whole fifteen rooms every two weeks. I'm about as fit for the work as I am to hear a Latin class recite.

Your friend,
E. C. M.

59

Redfield, October 11, 1885.

My dear Ellen,—

I return you today "The History of a Title." I venture to say after a cursory examination of the records that one-third of all our real estate is held by the most uncertain tenure. . . . Our attorneys here do not appear to be very well informed on this branch of the law. It formed a very lucrative branch of practice in Door Co., Wis. and I have always paid considerable attention to it.

It pleases me very much to learn that you get on so nicely at school and that your surroundings are agreeable. I can readily understand why your school directors should desire to have you direct the exercises in singing but like yourself, question the wisdom in assigning work that will render necessary putting your department for a greater or lesser period under the charge of someone else.

Did you understand from the papers sent that I was defeated for chairman of the Aberdeen meeting.[1] I told the boys not to present my name and insisted, as the event proved was true, that I should be of more service to them on the floor, but they said they had numbers enough to elect me and were going to do it. I guess they had, but they hadn't skill enough to use their forces. It is no inconsiderable honor, however, to be defeated by [Bartlett] Tripp. He is one of the finest lawyers in the West, has lived in the Territory about fifteen years, and though a life-long democrat he is so universally esteemed that it would not be strange to see him sent to the U.S. senate by a republican legislature. He is to succeed the present chief-justice of our supreme court in December and will give that tribunal a character for learning in the law that it now sorely lacks. You can understand that my diffidence in entering the lists against such a man was entirely sincere.

Yours with love,
Tom.

[1] A Democratic territorial convention.

60

Chicago, October 23, 1885.

Dear Friend,

No, I did not think it was you who were Mr. Tripp's rival for chairman of the Aberdeen meeting. I have for some time been laboring under the impression that your name is Tom, and if I am not vastly mistaken, that gentleman was mentioned as George. Now George is a very nice name, but if you have adopted it you must not expect your far-off friends to know about it.

For my present position I am sincerely thankful. I would not have one thing about it changed. We are to have our first exercises in the hall tomorrow night and I am to have the distinction of conducting the singing. It will not be an enviable task as there will be about 275 singers who are not in the habit of singing together. I think I will have to join the Arion Club, as we will need their services later. It is a very good musical club, for the time they have been in practice, and they are very anxious to have me join.

This is the first evening I've been home this week, and I declined an invitation to a "musical soiree" tonight. I heard a very amusing opera Tuesday night, "The Mikado," [1] with Emma Abbott as Yum-yum.[2] It is a Japanese extravaganza, but, as is customary in Gilbert and Sullivan's operas, it contains a vast amount of solid wisdom served up in an exceedingly ludicrous manner. One solo, by the "Chief Executioner of the Empire," referring to those whom he has "upon the list" for decapitation, is laughable indeed, but one cannot help agreeing with him that they'll "none of them be missed." . . .

Your friend,
E. C. M.

[1] This Gilbert and Sullivan production had just appeared, in 1885.

² Emma Abbott (1850-91) was a Chicagoan who had studied at home and abroad and attained fame for her performances in *Romeo and Juliet, H. M. S. Pinafore,* and other operas or operettas.

61

Redfield, October 25, 1885.

Dear Ellen,—

. . . It must be a source of great comfort to live that way instead of boarding. I'm very, very sick of it myself. A private boarding house even would be preferable to our unsocial surroundings. All the influences that go to make life at home pleasant would not be wanting as they are about the office and hotel. We see so little of life in a family here that I sometimes fear I shall forget how to conduct myself amidst such surroundings.

Your school work seems to be anything but unpleasant or laborious. I am glad to hear you talk in such a cheerful way about it, to know that you are so much interested without being worried. It occurred to me the other day that considering how the petty annoyances of my career as a teacher used to trouble me, I endure defeats in my practice with a degree of composure that is quite surprising to myself. I thought when studying that a defeat would quite use me up but I notice that my recovery in such cases has never been very long delayed.

I have been reading Bulwer's "Siege of Granada," a novel that struck my fancy because of the concluding chapter which was found as an extract in one of my old readers. The selection was always a favorite of mine and it must have appealed to my sense of the beautiful in language before I was eleven years old. I have no recollection of ever having attempted to commit it but the words were as familiar to me as those of some old song. I am unable to perceive any error in my youthful fancy for the description still seems to me sublime. That same mysticism that is employed to heighten the interest of "The Last Days of Pompeii" permeates the work in question.

. . . You can hardly imagine how many people we have of literary tastes. There is every prospect that a good strong organization will be perfected.

Not George but
Tom.

62

Dear Friend,

. . . I can appreciate your feelings in regard to hotel life though I never tried it myself. Would it not be pleasanter for you to board with a private family, or are there no private houses in Redfield? Do you know you never told me what kind of a place Redfield is? Are the houses all "dugouts" or have you palatial residences? Are your "lands all houses and roads all stone" or do the prairie "grasses, low and sweet" grow in the middle of every street? When you are in your office, looking out at the windows, which way are you looking? You see I want to get you located if possible.

Your club will doubtless be a success. It must be pleasing to find so many interested in the project. Still, I say still, as I said last year, I think a dramatic society, would be sure to be pleasant and give a great deal of pleasure during your long winter evenings. You doubtless have local musicians, and your programme could be part musical. A social dance after your entertainment would be quite the proper thing and would no doubt receive the hearty approval of the young folks, or are you all old people out there?

I almost forgot to tell you that I am quite consumed with anger about something very unkind which you said in your last letter.

Yours "no more,"
E. C. M.

63

Redfield, November 9, 1885.

My dear Ellen,—

I send you today some stereoscopic views of Redfield and vicinity that will probably convey to you a clearer idea of our surroundings than anything my lame discriptive powers could depict. If your imagination grows active on this subject, I'll give you this pointer. Don't picture us as surrounded with "under-done-pie-crust-colored [book] covers." Our supply of these, I regret to say, is much more limited than we wish it. It doesn't suffice to surround us. You will believe me though when I say that what we have are pretty well thumbed. Our district attorney has a very fine library, an exceptionally good one for this country. . . . I beat him in a justice court case last week, rather gratifying too, as my clients were wealthy farmers living near Ashton and very partial to that town. They labored very earnestly with us to move up there but promised us all their business whether we went or not.

I long very much to form the acquaintance of your whist club. Our office is headquarters for lovers of the game here. We have some very good players and I am usually very fortunate myself.

That was hateful the way I closed before. I'll confess without reservation and am

Yours contritely,
Tom.

64

Chicago, Nov. 15, 1885.

Dear Friend,

Your letter and views arrived Wednesday. I enjoyed looking at them immensely. Mary pretended to believe she recognized you in the granger [1] under the trees. She said the only reason she doubted its being you was the fact that the man mentioned had a "frying pan in his hand" and she knew better than to suppose you would make yourself so useful as that frying-pan would seem to indicate. . . . I further assured her that although western life would doubtless change you awfully, it would never make you so far forget your regard for the feelings of your friends as to permit yourself to wear a beard.

The Arion Club of this vicinity are good enough to earnestly desire my services and I think I shall join the club and if I do that to please them they will do something to please me. . . . We had quite a nice meeting in the Hall last Friday night. I have charge of the musical part and rather enjoy it. There is a chorus of about three hundred voices, alto and soprano.

I wish you had my chance of consulting the works in the public library. Remember what I once said about any book you may desire to consult that can be found in the library. It was a "standing offer."

Sincerely your friend,
E. C. M.

1 Meaning apparently a farmer.

65

Redfield, November 22, 1885.

Dear Ellen,—

I am pleased to learn that you found the views in any degree interesting. What led you to believe that I occupied a conspicuous position in some of the pictures[?] My vanity doesn't usually manifest itself in that way. Your sister must certainly have been indulging her mirth at my expense as she is perfectly aware how ineffectual for any good would the homely household utensil that "got to the front" in the picture be in my hands, how dangerous even it would be to myself and to all who should be foolhardy enough to partake of anything I might prepare in a culinary way. The matter that settled your belief is most laughable though. Didn't you know I wore a beard the winter I was in Madison? Outrageous, wasn't it? In a town too where people are expected to be somewhat precise in appearance. I was a picture and no mistake. One half of my jaw seemed to put forth a growth with which its fellow seemed unable to keep pace and the moderate darkness of my mustache was exchanged for a decidedly ruddy brown. Out of consideration for my friends, as you say, I shed it before going to Chicago and the same consideration enabled me to resist the temptation last fall to raise another crop. I haven't the dread of a Dakota winter with which I was filled a year ago and don't think I shall make any effort in that direction this season. I don't think you will recognize me in any of the views, unless it is in the Nimrod and it would be impossible for me to remain impassive under your gaze, so that theory is exploded. Your remark that western life must have changed my appearance made me wonder if you do really conjure me up in buckskins and sombrero, high boots and an arsenal in my belt. I want to go down this winter very much and let you see that I'm still the same harmless, insignificant chap who bid you adieu when he started west as long as fifteen months ago, but I'm awful, awful afraid that winter will be verging on spring before it will be possible to get off.

It can be easily gathered from the Manitowoc papers that Joe Rankin will never survive his present sickness. His illness for some reason, seems to me particularly sad. Rankin was no statesman but he was a brainy politician and uncommon honest and straight-forward for the business he was in.[1]

We are really going to make an effort to do something in the dramatic line this winter and you may yet hear of my "strutting, the monarch of the boards." The affair will be under the management of the militia company who are now endeavoring to make a selection from the plays you kindly sent me some time ago along with some others. An instrumental concert by home talent will also be an event in our social life this winter....

Good-night.
Tom.

[1] Joseph Rankin (1833-86) was a Democratic representative from Manitowoc, adjacent to Walsh's home town of Two Rivers. He had formerly been a city clerk of Manitowoc, occupying the same position that Walsh's father had in Two Rivers; but Rankin went on to the state legislature and finally to the U.S. Congress.

66

Chicago, December 1, 1885.

My dear Friend,

Is that truly a picture of you? You did wisely when you visited your barber before coming to Chicago. I certainly should not have recognized you, and I certainly would not have walked around with that beard. I don't object to side-whiskers—burnsides—rather admire them on some people, but I seem to naturally detest a man who wears a beard on his chin. If a man has a good chin—sufficiently prominent and slightly dimpled (as have two of my friends) he is mad to cover it up.

Upon meeting a person for the first time, does not everyone particularly notice some feature? One will be able to tell you just what color eyes the stranger has; another will talk of his Roman nose or "snub"; another will criticise the cut of his hair, and I will give you an accurate description of his mouth and chin. Don't you think people differ in selecting different features, and forming their estimate of new acquaintances in a measure according to the impression these features make upon them? . . . I did not, however, intend to subject you to so lengthy a discussion of the subject when I started out, but upon your own head (or beard rather) must rest the blame.

This place is at its worst, as a thing of beauty, when the snows of winter have been changed into mud or into almost black snow by the traffic of our streets. The theatres offer the chief attraction during the winter months, though at present there is absolutely nothing worth going to see at any of them. The season thus far has been bad in that respect. I do hope Booth will be here this winter.[1] I've been waiting for him ever since I came to Chicago. It seems a pity McCullough should die so young. His acting in Virginius alone was enough to make him insane.[2] I'm not very easily moved to any extent, but, in that play, where Virginius is represented as losing his mind I was deeply moved. I cannot recall any other piece of acting that made me thoroughly forget that it was acting.

About two hundred of the teachers have been "selected" to attend a course of training under Mr. Tomlins. I am one of the "selected" and we meet Wednesday evenings.

Sincerely,
E.

[1] Edwin Booth, the brother of John Wilkes Booth, was famous for his Shakespearean roles.

[2] John McCullough had a breakdown on the stage at McVicker's Theatre in Chicago on September 29, 1884. His acting career was at an end, and he died on November 8, 1885. See notes for No. 6.

67

Redfield, December 6, 1885.

Dear Ellen,—

Really I appreciated your last letter highly and was amused beyond measure, so much so that I could almost wish you would get angry again. I'll consent always to be the butt of my friend's wit (provided it be good and racy) rather than that he, or she, should be as dull and uninteresting as myself. Chins are an unmistakable evidence of character. Now if there ever existed a maxillary of less decided mold, more featureless or less striking, it has escaped my observation. If my chin be an index (and it must be as your logic shows) then my virtues and vices are alike negative and inconstancy is the only distinguishing trait of my character. And then to insist that I should parade it devoid of the covering which nature, evidently with kindest intentions, designed should hide the defect, is another one. But that I should show in my conversation and letters, so little permanence has my character, whether I read law or fiction, poetry or history, is the hugest joke of all, only you shouldn't twit so closely on facts. . . . The picture of the man in the river scene is not I.

We have had some very nice skating on the creek for the past few weeks. There is no large field but the pleasant weather has made the exercise a most agreeable relaxation. Comparatively few of our young people seem to know or care anything about it, though, and the lack of company makes it a less charming pastime than it was in Wisconsin. Are there not opportunities to skate on the ponds in your parks? St. Paul, you may have noticed, is to have an ice palace this winter and a round of sports adapted to the season after the style of the Montreal carnival.

No, I have never since coming west had any desire to go back to Manitowoc to live, or even to visit, except that I should like very much to see some friends in Chicago, only a few in Sturgeon Bay, and my folks at home. I am perfectly content to abide here for a while at least and sincerely wish that matters may so shape themselves as to make this my permanent residence. . . . I should not leave this place to practice law at any other point in the Territory and I have no desire whatever to quit the territory or the practice of the law either.

The newly appointed secretary of Dakota is a friend of mine. My commission hasn't arrived yet. Was it not you who said I was to be Governor?

Tom.

68

My dear Friend,

I was amused last Wednesday night, when Mr. Tomlins in speaking of the expression of the face in singing and its effect upon an audience made a statement somewhat like mine which so amused you. He spoke of the common idea that expression lies chiefly in the eyes as an erroneous one, and stated that they borrow their expression from the lips. Just try it yourself and see. Then smile with your lips and the eyes immediately follow suit. They are secondary in the expression of all the pleasanter emotions. Now, since the mouth expresses so much, must it not be indicative of character since the expression is merely the outward sign of inward grace or the lack of it? The chin and mouth go hand in hand (so to speak). Perfection in one cannot exist without perfection (or near it) in the other. You and I do not read chins alike. The "inconstancy" you mention was suggested by the dimple in your chin, was it not? It suggests nothing of the kind according to my reading, but I shall not overwhelm you with confusion by telling you what it does suggest. I wouldn't advise you to let the subject "harrer up your soul." I guess you're quite a nice little boy all around. . . .

E. C. M.

69

Redfield, December 19, 1885.

My dear Ellen,—

. . . Now a little more chin. I didn't think of any dimple, if anything of the kind exists, but of the regular contour, the lack of angularity that is supposed to indicate force and perseverance. What does a dimple signify? and a double chin?

May I go along with you to southern France? We shan't stay there, of course, so near the Bay of Naples. When I long for some place to rest, to dream in, next to the hereafter Naples is the place uppermost in my mind. My ideas of the place are perhaps borrowed rather from De Stael and Lytton than from the sager writers and travelers and are likely incorrect,[1] but in such a clime and on such water the "midnight serenade" must be enrapturing. Some of our young men out on a lark the other evening awoke me after midnight. They were singing some senseless song, but were so far away that the strains came in so mellow as to be positively beautiful. As they receded the effect heightened until the sounds were no longer audible. Soft stillness and the night certainly become the touches of sweet harmony. I still retain a vivid recollection of the rapture with which I listened to the singing on the river of popular patriotic songs during the early days of the war.[2] . . . I wish I might wish you personally a Merry Christmas but must content myself with the only substitute. Hoping it may be such to you and your friends, I am

Yours devotedly
T. J. W.

[1] Bulwer-Lytton was a particular favorite of Walsh, and he had also read Madame de Staël.
[2] During his childhood in Two Rivers.

70

Chicago, December 28, 1885.

Dear Friend,—

Did you get your little calendar and was it badly "mashed" on the way? I saw it in one of the book-stores one day and it immediately occurred to me that it was just the thing for an office and I forthwith cast around in my mind for the friends of mine who own an office. Don't subject the above sentence to any grammatical analysis please. I'm afraid it would be "found wanting."

I think I detected a vein of sarcasm in all you said about the "gathering of the clans" (fair schoolma'ams and valiant Knights of the rod and spelling book). . . . Wasn't the dancing the best part of the performance? and bye the bye, do you dance? It is one of the few things I do pretty well. . . .

No, I'll not tell you one word more about "chins." You are a heathen, and unbeliever in all I say.

E. C. M.

71

Redfield, January 3, 1886.

My dear Ellen,—

What a charming letter that was I got Thursday. No, I didn't wonder why you didn't write earlier guessing that the bustle of the holiday season had something to do with it. But I did inquire rather anxiously for my mail on getting in about ten o'clock Wednesday evening from a sixty mile drive. Santa Claus brought the pretty calendar in due time and perfect order though the envelope was sadly demoralized. Thanks. It is a gem and does much credit to your taste. It attracts universal attention and is admired by all who come into the office of which it is most decidedly an ornament.

I dance very little and only indifferently well. About thirty couples went from here by special train to a party at Frankfort Thursday evening. Political reasons influenced me largely as they did most of those who went. We do love Frankfort very, very dearly just now, and if she will only return our affection so far as to stay out of the race next fall Redfield will be the county seat of Spink County.

Court convenes a week from tomorrow and we are extremely busy getting ready every case which may by any possibility be reached. We have been more driven by work for the past ten days than ever before. All new cases must go over. There isn't much encouragement in practicing under those circumstances, though the bill providing for the appointment of two additional judges in this district now pending before Congress and likely to pass, will give us much relief.

. . . Do you know that a great many of those same carpet-baggers have emigrated to Dakota? One of our clients at Frankfort is ex-surveyor-general of Louisiana. An ex-judge of the Supreme Court of Arkansas has been elected to a like position in the to-be state of Dakota. Hugh Campbell, the father of the revolutionary state movement, was judge in Louisiana during the ever-memorable campaign of '76. It is such men as these who have made Dakota politics despicable in the eyes of many.[1]

I've grown desperately interested in a novel I've just started reading entitled "The Three Guardsmen" by Dumas. The interest is in the plot and adventures so thrilling that you scamper along to see how the thing will come out, which by your leave I'll proceed to do. So au revoir.

Yours faithfully,

T. J. W.

[1] Efforts to identify the carpetbagger judge from Arkansas and the ex–surveyor general from Louisiana have been unsuccessful. The subject is an intriguing one, and fuller investigation is warranted. Hugh Campbell has been discussed earlier in the notes for No. 56.

72

Redfield, January 17, 1886.

Dear Ellen,—

I send you today a calendar for the term of court just closed. You will notice that we continue to get our share of the cases. We stand at the head of the list, I believe, in the matter of new cases originating in the District Court. . . . We don't feel very dissatisfied over the week's work at court though we lost a case in which we felt a considerable degree of interest. We shall appeal it, however, and feel confident of ultimate success.

Good-night.

T. J. W.

73

Chicago, January 31, 1886.

My dear Friend,

Do you know I am learning to skate on rollers. A large rink has been built not far from here, by Mr. B——, the banker. He skates himself and he and about thirty of his friends have formed a club which meets every Monday night. No outsiders are allowed. Each gentleman can bring a lady or ladies and I, fortunately, have friends among them. It is just splendid. . . .

E. C. M.

74

Redfield, Jan. 31, 1886.

My dear Ellen,—

. . . We're laboring hard to cultivate the little dramatic talent our town possesses, with success that is, thus far, not marked. I always gave you a great deal of credit for singing when asked without demanding a tribute of flattery and coaxing as many who sing well delight to exact.

I'm waiting with much impatience for that long, long letter you're going to write me some time soon, but I must kiss you goodnight now and confer with my colleagues on the work of the morrow.

Devotedly yours,

T. J. W.

75

Chicago, February 7, 1886.

My dear Friend,

Let me here remark, mon ami, before I forget it, that you have at least one thing to be thankful for and that is that you were some seven hundred miles away when I finished reading your last letter. To say that I was shocked at the light manner in which you concluded that epistle is to put it rather mildly. I'm sure my letters have always been models of gravity, sobriety, piety, etc., and how your natural spirit of levity has survived the many applications it has received at my hands, and that might have reformed a less wayward spirit is a puzzle to me. . . .

There is one more date I know, and that is that Washington's birthday falls on Monday this year. Do you think I know it because I'm glad I won't have to teach that day? Not a bit of it. I like to teach. But there is to be a grand ball which I expect to attend. How I envy you gentlemen who have no trouble about your toilet. A dress suit is so easily gotten and is always au fait. No dressmaker to say, "Oh, Miss So-and-so, I was been so busy, I cannot of a possibility have make your dress."

I notice in today's Inter-Ocean that southern Dakota will be the State of Dakota if the Senate's lead is followed. You, I believe do not favor admission. Will you tell me why? . . .[1]

I kept my promise about a long, long letter even at the sacrifice of that most necessary "beauty sleep" which is so rarely possible in the land of Carter.[2]

E. C. M.

[1] According to the *Chicago Inter-Ocean* of February 6, 1886, a Dakota bill had just passed the Senate, providing "for the admission of the southern portion as a State under the title of Dakota, and the organization of the northern portion into a separate Territory under the name of Lincoln."

[2] Carter Harrison had been mayor of Chicago since 1879 and was a liberal, benevolent "boss." He was a Democrat, originally from Kentucky. See Bessie L. Pierce, *A History of Chicago*, III (New York, 1957), 61, 355-56.

76

Redfield, February 14, 1886.

Dear Ellen,—

The examination of Mr. Basford, contrary to my most sanguine expectations, resulted in the dismissal of the defendant on Wednesday last.[1] T. V. Eddy of Watertown and I argued the motion for dismissal on the part of the defendant. Eddy made a fine speech and closed with an eloquent peroration. It sounded better than it would look on paper but the justice was moved by it, visibly, and as that was the purpose of the speech why criticise its grammatical or rhetorical construction. I was the recipient of some compliments on my effort too, but an audience pleased is no impartial judge. The result was naturally learned with much joy here. An ovation was tendered Basford in the evening. Cannons were fired and bells rung in the outlying towns of the county in every one of which, with the exception of Ashton, the examination was looked upon as malicious and political. The proceedings have materially strengthened our position in the county seat fight and we hope this week to complete arrangements which will almost ensure our success. A committee of five from this place meet next Thursday, another from Frankfort of a like number at the solicitation of the latter to arrange some plan by which the two towns will work harmoniously in the coming campaign. Your humble servant is one of the committee from this place. . . .

You labor under a mistake as to my position on the question of the admission of Dakota. I am not opposed to admission but in common with the great bulk of the people of Dakota as distinguished from the politicians I am in no great hurry about the matter and it has never been demonstrated very clearly to me how my material interests would be advanced thereby. To be sure, the restrictions on our legislature are very inadequate but this evil is to be remedied by a more honest public sentiment and a better choice of delegates rather than by constitutional restrictions which are easily evaded. The republicans insist on division and admission of the south half. The democrats will concede nothing more than admission as a whole. Should this be refused, as it is likely to be, and the democrats should offer division on the river as they may at no greater sacrifice than in voting for admission as a whole, the republicans would be forced to assent or confess that votes in the Senate are what they seek rather than to right the wrongs of the suffering Dakotaians.[2]

Sorry I can't concur with you in the delights of rollerskating. I made progress enough in the art to determine satisfactorily to myself whether there was any fun in it and my decision was adverse to the popular roller. The rink here is under the management of the band and is a popular resort in the evenings when our musicians come out.

Please report if you find any levity in the foregoing and by studious endeavor I promise it shall in time be eliminated.

Gravely yours,
T. J. Walsh.

[1] O. S. Basford was among those accused of stealing the county records on December 5, 1884.

[2] Democratic Senator George G. Vest of Missouri had recently proposed a division of Dakota along the 101st meridian of longitude to the Missouri River and south from there along the river. This would have meant a division of Dakota vertically into eastern and western states and is probably what Walsh had in mind. In such a case the western half might have become Democratic. *Cong. Record*, 49 Cong., 1 Sess., pp. 980-84 (January 29, 1886), pp. 1169-71 (February 5, 1886).

77

Dear Tom,

Don't mean that at all—merely write it so for a change. Your last letter was simply horrid, or at least one sentence was. It displayed bad temper, a thing I hate. I think there is nothing quite so utterly lovely as a perfectly amiable person. The idea of you being Offended because I referred to the levity with which you had spoken of a grave matter, viz.—kissing a person good-night even at a distance of several hundred miles. You know yourself that was perfectly awful, though, to be perfectly honest, I didn't mind it a bit (at that distance) and was only jesting when I wrote. I suppose I'll have to forgive your grave and heartless letter. "Hope is the anchor of the soul" someone has said, I believe, so I'll try to exist in the hope that when we have corresponded for another score of years, more or less, you'll understand correctly the spirit in which I write.

Your last letter was very proper and quite legal. I am thinking of resuming(?) the study of law when the skating rink closes and in the meantime any assistance you can give me through the medium of your letters will be appreciated. (For fear you might miss the opportunity, will say that there is a possible chance given in the above to take offence).

I have no doubt Mr. Eddy made a fine speech, but I have equally no doubt that yours was a good deal better. Wouldn't say so, would you? Now I call that nonsense. This is not taffy. I say it honestly and see no reason why, with added years and the experience they will bring, you should not rank among the very first (if not the first) in your profession. To do this, of course, oratorical power is a high trump card. . . .

I haven't room to write my name gravely in full.

E.

78

Redfield, February 28, 1886.

My dear Ellen,—

I received your last about ten P.M. on Thursday on returning home from Frankfort where I had been all day trying a law suit. The case attracted much attention and drew quite a crowd. The subject matter, an action for a farm hand's wages against which was interposed a defence that the plaintiff had broken his contract by leaving before his time, was one in which nearly everyone in this county is more or less interested. The distinguished counsel on the other side accused me of talking to the galleries but I didn't mind that as, whether it was true or not, I knew the audience to be with me. He did say something which I resented though, namely that I knew nothing of manual labor myself as I had always been "held up" by my friends who were still assisting me. For the kindness he did my friends though and considering that I won the suit I freely forgave him. We can't try a law-suit against each other without quarreling all the way through. Now, I'm not wholly to blame for this, really, I'm not. I can preserve my usually good humor when opposed to any of the other boys, but this man never.

. . . It's a rather important case [*Fuller & Johnson Manufacturing Co.* v. *Foster*], involves about $1,000 and two or three years interest and I naturally look with some anxiety for the ruling of the court.[1] The law point involved is a very interesting one and since you have resumed the study of that fascinating science I'll propound the question to you. The plaintiff sues upon two promissory notes. We answer that the notes are void because when executed the plaintiff, the payee in the notes, a foreign corporation, had not filed articles of incorporation with the secretary of the Territory as by law required. The plaintiff replies that the law is unconstitutional and void because it contravenes clause 3 of Section 8 of article I of the Federal Constitution which says "Congress shall have power to regulate commerce—among the several states." By construction this has been made to read "No state shall pass any law which shall interfere with commerce between the several states." We claim that the clause quoted as well as the decisions refer only to acts of state legislatures and in no manner limit the powers of a territorial legislature, that the territorial legislature is the hand-maid of Congress and that the acts of the former until disapproved, are the acts of the latter. That because Congress cannot annul a state law the judiciary was empowered to prevent the passage of local legislation interfering with commerce. But as Congress may at any time annul an act of the territorial legislature there was no necessity for extending this power to laws passed by them. My friend on the other side hadn't anticipated this course of reasoning and was entirely unprepared to answer it. You will doubtless, however, be able to expose the error in it if it is not logical. I trust you will not take offense if I say that you may render me some assistance in so doing. You see I've taken seriously your remarks about your law studies and your desire for assistance through the medium of my letters.

You were mistaken though in thinking I was ill-tempered when I wrote last. No, you didn't say that, only that my letter displayed bad temper. Really I was in quite a cheerful mood at that time, only I wished sincerely that that plaguey seven hundred miles would grow beautifully less. That's "perfectly awful" too, I know. I'm sorry though if my letter gave you the idea that I took offence at anything you wrote, for your letter pleased me mightily and I did smile on reading it. So there.

I make my debut in the theatrical line on Monday evening, the eighth, as Bob Brierly in "The Ticket-of Leave-Man." [2] I wish I might get even with you for spurring my ambition in that direction by making you sit out the play. No, your judgment erred once, of that I can assure you.

I had a chance last week to go to Washington. Some Huronians who were going there to advocate division on the 46th parallel offered me transportation if I would agree to work with them for the bill. I had no over-weening desire to commit myself to the measure or to leave my business either just at this time and so didn't go.

I'll mend my (closing) ways and say this time only

Tom.

[1] See further discussion in No. 80 and the accompanying note.

[2] By Tom Taylor, an Englishman, whose best-known plays were *Our American Cousins* (1858) and *The Ticket of Leave Man* (1863). The latter had as one character the relentless detective, Hawkshaw. See Winton Tolles, *Tom Taylor and the Victorian Drama* (New York, 1940), pp. 197-202. Walsh gives a further description of his performance in No. 179.

79

Chicago, March 7, 1886.

Dear Friend,

Don't I wish I might have seen you as Bob Brierly! Now don't be silly, confess you did well. That piece is being given here by the Florence company at McVickers. I have not seen it. How did a performance of that kind take up there? When I say "up there," you must not think I imagine Dakota any nearer "the above" than we are, though Sam Jones and Sam Small do say Chicago is not very near heaven. Don't think for a moment, please, that I've been to hear either of those "slang slingers" preach(?).[1]

I heard Moody some time ago and I think I've been somewhat moody myself ever since.[2] He never could preach to a really cultured audience. He may do good in his sphere, but I have no faith in a creed that makes its converts by means of nervous excitement.

. . . Looking back over all that has been done for me since I came here I realize, thankfully I trust, that I have been very fortunate. I cannot suppose that any teacher in the city has a pleasanter position than I.

Now about that law question. I am flattered that you thought it worth while propounding it to me, and, though I fear my opinion is not worth much, I give it honestly as I think it was requested. I do not see how the decision can be against you in regard to the notes being good. They are so without doubt. I do think, however, that clause of Sec. 8 of Art. I of the constitution covers not only the State but the Territory as well. I would not say that you could not prove the contrary, but I would be convinced against a pretty settled conviction on the other side. Has Congress ever made more than a couple of attempts to regulate commerce between the States? I know very little about territorial laws, but cannot see how the law in reference to filing articles of incorporation with the secretary of the territory contravenes the clause in the Federal Constitution before mentioned. Even if that clause refers to all divisions of territory within the boundary of the U.S. would not your statement still hold good, that the acts of territorial legislatures, until disapproved by Congress, are the acts of Congress? And has not Congress the power to annul territorial law only because the territorial government—or means of government—is not so complete as in a State? Let me know how the matter is decided, won't you?

Did I ever accuse you of being bad tempered? How strange! Perhaps I was so at the time and merely tried to be hateful, or perhaps it was only in fun, or perhaps—well no matter. I won't do it again till I forget this promise.

E. C. M.

[1] Two southern evangelists, sometimes associated in joint campaigns. Samuel Porter Jones of Alabama was a Methodist minister of great popular appeal. Samuel W. Small was a journalist turned evangelist.

[2] Dwight L. Moody had a notable career as an evangelist and supporter of religious education.

80

Redfield, March 15, 1886.

My dear Ellen,—

The [Redfield] Journal which I shall mail you tomorrow contains a notice, (criticism isn't quite the word) of the play we tried to render a week ago. Although, as you will notice, no one who appeared upon the stage is allowed to retire without an approving nod at least, the article reflects on the whole the general feeling in regard to the performance. Ahem! just pat me on the back a little. That's a modest young man. No, we are not going to take the road at all. I was going to send you a picture of Bob Brierly but I had to leave town before I could gather together my costume and now I hate to sacrifice a week's growth of my new mustache. 'Tis true, 'tis pity. Really the fall of my mustache was as great an event as the play itself. There were hardly three in the audience who recognized me until I had been talking quite a while. Putting modesty aside though we surprised ourselves as well as the audience by the smoothness with which, with the most indifferent settings and scenery, the play went off.

Am sorry to say that we lost that case involving the question of corporation law concerning which we have both written. The judge apologized in a manner to me for his decision, said the question seemed to him a very doubtful one and that as the equities were on the other side of the case he gave them judgment. "I knew you would appeal," he continued, "and the question ought to be settled." He's right about our determination to appeal but that kind of a ruling seems to me to do little credit to him as a judge. He evidently decided on "general principles" and with little regard for the real questions involved.[1] You do me a real compliment, my dear, in saying that I can prove some things. I've had an ambition in that direction. Really though and candidly, I think of following the stage business some more so that I may perchance acquire a little of the knack of moving men. I don't think the power is so much a gift as it is the result of study—the study of how to kindle emotion. Once aroused it is easy enough to control or guide it and the simplest remark is often sufficient to start the blaze.

How pleasant your school must be. It is very gratifying to me indeed to learn of your success and none the less so because I anticipated it.

The gentleman who was dean of the faculty of the law school perpetrated a joke on me the other day. He is at present probate judge of Dane Co., Wis. I wrote him the other day concerning a claim we have against the estate of a decedent of his county and incidently told him I was doing pretty well. He used to insist that my initials stood for Thomas Jefferson, which they don't. He answered the letter briefly to the firm and then added, "Tell T. J. to call and see me when on his way to Washington." The old gentleman is beginning to succumb to the ravages of time, and then Dakota never will be democratic you know.[2]

Yours,
Tom.

[1] The local judge in question was Louis Kossuth Church, soon to be appointed by Grover Cleveland as governor of Dakota Territory. The case was *Fuller & Johnson Manufacturing Co.* v. *Foster*, 4 Territory of Dakota, 329 (1886).

[2] Jarius H. Carpenter was a professor of law and contracts at the University of Wisconsin and probate judge of Dane County from 1886 to 1891. As it happened, he lived long enough to know of Walsh's election to the Senate (1822-1913). See Merle Curti and Vernon Carstensen, *The University of Wisconsin: A History, 1848-1925*, I (Madison, 1949), 452. A letter from the Division of Archives, University of Wisconsin, has been of assistance in establishing beyond a doubt that Carpenter was the "gentleman" whom Walsh referred to (J. Frank Cook, Assistant Archivist, to the editor, September 7, 1965).

81

My dear Friend,

. . . Katie actually asserts that I have been going out too much, that I'm never quiet a moment and that I'm growing thin and pale. Quite enough to make me resolve to reform, isn't it? I am invited out this afternoon to meet two musical celebrities lately arrived from Europe. Mr. Thoesen is a violinist and Mrs. T. is one [of] the finest pianists I've ever heard.

Thanks for the paper you sent. Didn't I say you'd do well and then, just to rob me of my glory as a prophet, you tried to make me believe you didn't carry off the laurel wreath. I should judge that the play gave universal pleasure and you are wise in deciding to continue your efforts in that line, though your last letter would suggest you have another reason for following in the footsteps of Booth. I fully agree in what you say about the power to "move" men. It is not so much what you say as the manner in which you say it. I read lately in the Century Magazine an article that pleased me much. It was on the life and work of Castelar "the glory of the Castilian rostrum." [1] I would give a good deal to hear such a speaker, and yet, did his eloquence accomplish much? Had he ever a lasting triumph? In the same book are some "Reminiscences of Castelar," which contain a reason for the inevitable reply to the above questions. It will recall something which I said some time ago in regard to chins and which amused you so much. To quote, "Castelar's chin, too, is inadequate. It is delicately rounded, but there ought to be more of it. If he had possessed Serrano's forehead and chin,[2] the Spanish Republic might have been a living thing today." So you see, mon ami, that there is something in a chin after all.

In reference to one of your reasons for continuing the stage business "some more," I think the end you aim at may be easiest reached by thorough earnestness in what you say. Let a speaker thoroughly believe himself in what he says, or let him make himself believe that he believes thoroughly in all he says, and his audience will agree with him, for his every tone will carry conviction and establish between himself and his hearers the affinity he desires. That's what I think. I cannot talk at all myself, but I notice a great many things and find that most teachers who fail do so through their lack of belief in themselves, in what they know, or in the success of whatever effect they are trying to produce. I think that last—a belief in your own likelihood to succeed —is a great assistance in reaching success.

E. C. M.

[1] Emilio Castelar y Ripoll was professor of history and philosophy at the University of Madrid and foreign minister in the short-lived Spanish Republic, 1873-74. He is said by Alvey A. Adee to have become the "embodiment of the republican idea." See Adee, "Reminiscences of Castelar," *Century Magazine*, XXXI (March, 1886), 792-94, and William J. Armstrong, "Castelar, the Orator," *ibid.*, pp. 785-92.

[2] Francisco Serrano y Dominguez (1810-85), Spanish general, premier, and political leader.

82

Aberdeen, April 4, 1886.

My dear Ellen,—

Redfield promises to be the scene of considerable activity ere long. A large elevator is about to be erected, the contract has been let for the digging of an artesian well and within sixty days the Chicago and North Western Railway proposes extending their road west to the Missouri river. It will give us a temporary boom and a considerable increase of voting population which we can turn to good account next fall. . . .

Ever yours,
Tom.

83

Chicago, April 11, 1886.

My dear Friend,

. . . What a wonderfully cheering thing sunshine is! Here at home, when I get the blinds arranged so as to admit a roomful of "merry sunshine" (do you folks annihilate people who quote from the Mikado?) my happiness is blighted by the appearance on the scene of my big sister [Mary?], who likes a room just light enough to insure a safe progress among the furniture. The gloom of this day is somewhat lightened by the contents of the window at which I am writing. We have some very nice plants and I can just see the street through the bloom of pink primroses, geraniums, heliotropes, fuchsias, etc. The heliotrope is my favorite bloom because it is so fragrant. Speaking of flowers, as I turn my head and glance at the mantel, I see [a] dish of cut flowers whose history I must relate to you. Among them are some tea roses, and, if you were here, you should have the nicest in the lot. They were presented to me by my pupils who have just given me a "surprise party." It was indeed a surprise. I think they enjoyed themselves for they stayed till 2 A.M. I do not approve of such late hours for pupils of their age but of course if they wished to stay I was willing. We had music and dancing and games, and a "bountiful repast." The boys escorted the girls to the table quite like grown up dudes. One asked in such a pretty way the honor of, for once, leading his teacher. Mr. Morrill [?] in his courtly manner,[1] escorted our little crippled girl. I almost forgot to mention what seemed to be an important feature of the program from the satisfaction displayed by the pupils in performing it. It was the presentation to me of a silver fruit basket, at one side of which are the words "Presented to Miss Elinor C. McClements by the class of '86."

Sincerely,
Ellen.

[1] Probably Donald L. Morrill, principal of the Andersen School.

84

Redfield, April 18, 1886.

My dear Ellen,—

. . . Here I've written nearly a half a dozen pages and haven't said a word about the posies you sent. They're beauties and have retained both color and perfume. What a pity those tea roses should blush unseen on my breast! They won't keep five or six weeks, will they? Never mind, I'll feast my eye on the prettier ones in your cheeks.

Your "surprise" must indeed have been gratifying. I have felt more real pleasure from little insignificant (in themselves) indications of regard from my pupils when I was teaching than I have from the most substantial "honors."

It was distressingly dull at this time last year, but there is no ground for complaint on our part this season. . . . I had quite a faculty in physics and mathematics for referring problems and phenomena to general laws. It serves me a good turn in law too now and then.

Ever yours,
Tom.

85

Chicago, April 25, 1886.

My dear Friend,

The receipt of your letter convinced me that you have not come to grief in one of Dakota's pet cyclones. How awful seems the fate of those unfortunate Minnesota people!

I think, though I could not be certain about it, that I in some way gathered from your last letter the intelligence that you contemplate visiting this city in five or six weeks. That will be a very good time to see the place in its spring attire. You will find many changes in this part of the town, if you remember just how it looked two years ago. . . .

I do not read very much lately. I am trying now to get something suitable in the way of songs, declamations, subjects for essays, etc., for our closing exercises. Can't you help me? Please do suggest something that would be nice.

It is very late so good-night.

E.

86

Redfield, May 2, 1886.

Dear Ellen,—

I sent you on Friday a copy of our brief in Fuller and Johnson Mfg. Co. vs. Foster, thinking it might be of interest to you. It will not commend itself to you as a particularly powerful document though it may appear concise and lucid. . . . The fact is, he (the judge) didn't consider the matter at all, and as a consequence he is going before his colleagues on the supreme bench in a light that reflects little credit upon his ability as a judge. The case will present an excellent opportunity to "open up" on him, towards which I confess a slight inclination that must be repressed.[1] A shrewd lawyer never quarrels with the judge but you will admit that there is much provocation in such an arbitrary act. My friend, Mr. [William] Sterling of Huron, who was at the law school with me, and I went out to Faulkton last Thursday. Sterling has a talent for conversation and is always entertaining and agreeable. Politeness was born in him and decorum thoroughly cultivated in his training. Sterling's partner is attorney for the Chicago and North Western Ry. Co. and he himself is on intimate terms with most of the officials of the road. We went out to utilize, if possible, some information that has not yet become common news.[2] I never before realized the immense power which a railroad may unscrupulously wield. . . . One cannot live in Dakota and give any credence to the common fallacy in economics that all wealth springs from labor. Much of the land of Faulk Co. will double in value in consequence of the construction of this road. A much smaller quantity will depreciate. I'll have to give some attention to these questions by-and-by. A man who is unfamiliar with them will be out of place in public life soon. He is now, even.

Your devoted
Tom.

[1] Another reference to Louis Kossuth Church, who along with other district judges would form the supreme court. In spite of Walsh's confidence, he and his brother lost on the appeal.

[2] If Walsh was thinking of speculative investment, he apparently did not carry through with the idea.

87

Chicago, May 9, 1886.

Dear Friend,

I received your brief and read it with interest from beginning to end. Yes, I noticed that you confined yourself pretty closely to a statement of the facts in the case. Unkind to your opponent! I'm afraid your version of the old saying reads "All's fair in love and law."

. . . Dozens of the elect have begged me to join, but when I won't I most generally won't. It's bad enough to sing in any chorus, but in a poor one I will not sing as one is nearly certain to fall into line with the majority, and, in this instance, the singing of the majority is far from perfect.

Sincerely,
E. C. M.

88

Yankton, May 15, 1886.

My dear Ellen,

Your twice welcome letter was received on Wednesday and the Arion concert programme yesterday. I'll make this epistle very brief because I shall leave here for Chicago on Monday morning, arriving in that city some time next, unavoidable accident alone preventing, and then I'll tell you how horribly tedious it has been to sit around here all week waiting to get a chance to talk. . . . As there are no trains out of here on Sunday I am delayed two days in consequence.

Faithfully yours,
T. J. Walsh.

89

Two Rivers, May 23, 1886.

Dear Ellen,

I reached my quarters on Monday night, or [early] Tuesday morning rather, without difficulty, left the next morning and arrived here according to program. I have felt guilty ever since at allowing you to go out that cold night. If nothing interferes with my plans I shall arrive in Chicago on the boat Thursday evening and shall try to see you before retiring. . . .[1]

Au revoir,
Tom.

[1] Lake steamers of the Goodrich Transportation Company departed daily (except Sunday) for Milwaukee, Manitowoc, and other points on Lake Michigan. *Chicago Tribune*, July 25, 1887. According to one newspaper, the Goodrich company had nine steamers in operation, "models of elegance," the "finest fleet of boats on the Great Lakes." *Manitowoc Co. Chronicle* (Two Rivers), Special Edition, September 20, 1892.

90

Redfield, June 1, 1886.

My dear Ellen,—

My faith shall ever hereafter be pinned to clover leaves, tea cups are a delusion and a snare. I had a most fortunate trip out reaching here without mishap at eight this morning. You know I had little time to lose after leaving you. Made close connections and reached the depot just about ten minutes before the train pulled out.

You will notice by the map that that portion of my journey made during the day time lies in immediate proximity to the Mississippi and the Minnesota. The scenery along these streams is in many places strikingly and beautifully picturesque. On Sunday morning in particular the huge bluffs along the great Father of Waters, clouded by a haze which seemed different from either smoke or mist, seemed peculiarly sublime. . . . Abundant rains have fallen and crops wear a healthy aspect. Coming directly from Chicago and the "Twin Cities" our little town seems very small and hum-drum but that feeling will doubtless wear off rapidly.

I trust you will pardon my abrupt and unceremonious leave taking at the avenue. I was very loath to go and yet the evening passed so rapidly I didn't appreciate until getting down on the street how imminent were the probabilities that I should be left. Attribute to my anxiety in this matter any unseemly haste I may have displayed about getting away. I needn't tell you how thoroughly I enjoyed my visit with you nor how much you contributed to make my stay in the city a season of brief though complete enjoyment.

Yours,
Tom.

91

Dear Colonel,

I was rejoiced to learn that you reached home so safely —overcoat and all. When you left here that night I had no idea you would have any difficulty in making your train. If I had thought about the distance you had to go it would have occurred to me that you might be late, and I'd have made you hurry. Now I am going to scold you. When you did think of it, and when you so much desired to go on that train, you should have mentioned it. We could have walked to the car in half the time it took us. Your apology about your haste in leaving us at the car was unnecessary. I certainly noticed no "unseemly" haste. You shook hands and took off your hat, wasn't that sufficient, or does western etiquette add a postscript or two? By the way, I think a gentleman has the best of it in appearing polite in public, and his most effective coadjutor is his hat. I've amused myself this afternoon by studying the subject some. Do you see those girls coming along Robey St.?¹ I wonder if they know the two gentlemen they are about to meet. Yes, and with just the result I anticipated. The girls are young and embarrassed and nod in the most jerky manner. The gentlemens' hats carry off the salutation gracefully. There are hundreds of carriages out today for it is lovely. The smiling old lady in that one evidently knows the blond gentleman on the sidewalk. The carriage stops—let's watch his hat. That was very nicely done; he shakes hands with both occupants of the carriage in a very deferential manner; his hat is still in his hand, and still—. Now that might be slightly exaggerated were the lady young but I've come to the conclusion that she is his prospective mother-in-law. Let me see, what was I saying before hats were mentioned? Oh yes, about your leaving. You are forgiven since you request it, but I don't know for what.

I don't know when I enjoyed anything so much as I did our drive that evening. I am like King Richard. I would give my kingdom for a horse only I like a good horse and I'm afraid I would not be satisfied with the result of my barter.

By the way, some one who looks like you went by a short time ago. You need not laugh, it is a fact. He's a regular dude. He is very dark, that is his hair and mustache are, and he is dressed in the lightest of grey suits. He has on his head the very dearest and whitest little straw hat. I like to see dark men dressed in light clothes. Don't you remember a white hat you used to wear that was so becoming? If I recollect correctly it was also becoming to me, and you kindly offered to give it to me remarking that you never saw a becoming hat on me before. Please say something real sweet about my excellent memory.

Do you know why I am writing all this nonsense? Well, it is to please you. Don't look so astonished; it isn't polite. Didn't you ask me to write you a "nice long letter"? Well I knew I couldn't fulfill the first half of your request, about the nice, so I am trying to fill the second part of the bill. . . .

Bye-bye, Col.
E. C. M.

[1] Ellen's home address was 588 N. Robey St.—later changed to Damen Avenue.

92

Redfield, June 13, 1886.

Dear Ellen,—

You ought to have allowed me to criticise your letter [?] since I insisted on its possessing two qualities often irreconcilable but which you so well know how to harmonize. Let me commend its frankness at least. You were displeased, you say, because I didn't hurry away fast enough. I have no apology to offer. Even the knowing that I was in danger of losing the train wouldn't have induced me to shorten that delightful walk. The route seemed annoyingly direct and short.

You remember my telling you of a lady who studied law with me at Madison. Her husband who gained some celebrity by taking the prize at the inter-state oratorical contest some years ago, was elected to Congress a year ago last fall.[1] She went to Washington with him and has been taking the lectures at the Columbia[n] law school.[2] But it isn't she I started to tell about. Mr. La Follette, her husband, has recently been distinguishing himself by an oration which he delivered to the graduating class at Columbia[n]. His speech won such praise that the faculty have ordered it printed. . . .[3]

Notwithstanding this is Sunday, I arose at six this morning, rode forty miles and got back in time for dinner. I never before saw wild roses in such profusion. Most of them were of the conventional rose color but many had a deep red dye, a richer, more sumptuous color. Occasionally a breeze wafted over a bed of them came to us as fragrant as any that ever blew even in the vale of Cashmere.

Where did you get the military title for me? Colonel—me no colonel. I'd rather be your

Tom.

[1] Robert M. La Follette. His wife, Belle Case La Follette, was a very able person and Walsh may have been deeply impressed by the possible accomplishments of such a couple.

[2] Columbian University, later known as George Washington University.

[3] Walsh was apparently mistaken in one of his details. On May 31, 1886, La Follette had delivered an address to the graduating class of the Howard University Law School, located in Washington, D.C., as was Columbian College. Belle C. and Fola La Follette, *Robert M. La Follette*, I (New York, 1953), 69.

93

Chicago, June 27, 1886.

Dear Friend,

. . . Everything on the programme went off splendidly. There were many who could not see, or hear a portion of the literary part of the entertainment but in such an assembly it could not be otherwise under the circumstances. "Our Carter" [Harrison] was rapturously received and his speech was a decided success.[1] He was graceful, witty, pathetic, and, in his reference to the anarchists, diplomatic. If his speech were reported verbatim the parenthetical (loud applause) would often occur. The little crippled girl was highest in general rank for the year and took the Foster medal. When Mayor Harrison placed the medal around her neck she began to cry and leaned her head against him. He was really affected, said some soothing words to her, and stooping down kissed her. There was a perfect hush throughout that packed house. And now I'll tell you something about the singing as I believe it may interest you and you will know I do not say it boastfully. They did sing well. . . . The Flower Queen was a success though I tremble[d] for it. The twelve girls of the flower chorus were dressed in low necked, short sleeved white dresses, the bodices being covered with flowers. One with roses, one daisies, etc., etc. Each carried a bouquet of the same flowers. The queen was dressed in a trained dress of white mull, with wide flowing sleeves, and she came upon the stage with the air of a Nilsson.[2] Yes I was satisfied, and I was prepared to be critical. You will pardon so much school, won't you? I'll not do it again. Katie says my head is full of school, but it is not strange that it is.

Good-night.
L. N.

[1] The *Chicago Inter-Ocean* of June 26, 1886, described the closing exercises at Andersen School held the evening before (Friday). Some 1,500 people had completely filled "the spacious hall." Mayor Harrison and others were mentioned by name, but not Ellen McClements. The little girl who received the Foster medal was Sadie A. Willard. Department of Public Instruction, *Report of the Board of Education for 1886*, p. 161.

[2] Christine Nilsson, Swedish opera singer.

94

Redfield, July 6, 1886.

Dear Ellen,—

It isn't as a matter of retribution that this letter has been delayed. We've been celebrating [the Fourth] so vigorously that I haven't before found an opportunity to apply myself to answering your last letter.

Earlier in the week I was out to Faulkton and called on Mrs. Pickler, the Major was away. She had just returned from some political gathering and was rather more talkative than usual. Evidently she had been making good use of her time as there was hardly a gentleman of any prominence whom she had met of whose sentiments on the suffrage question she was not able to inform me. Her household duties do not seem to suffer in consequence of her attention to public affairs. They have a very nice, comfortable home and a number of bright children. It does seem so odd though to drop in for a call of a few moments and be regaled with a discourse on practical politics by the hostess. It was through no fault of mine or my friend either that the conversation took that turn. She was wholly responsible herself, and to do her justice she showed much familiarity with the subject and discussed it liberally and intelligently, much more so than a gentleman of some local prominence politically who talked at us after we got back to the hotel.

We celebrated at Northville on Saturday where a base-ball tournament took place.[1] The town turned out en masse, not because any one here is particularly interested in the great American game but Northville is an important factor in the county seat campaign. We downed the Ashton club of which their papers have done much boasting by a score of 12 to 2 and took third money. That "we" is used advisedly. I caught behind the bat twelve innings and that circumstance, together with the fact that the mercury rose to 106 on Sunday will excuse my not writing on that day. Yesterday for like reasons everybody went over to Doland. They wanted us to play there but my enthusiasm had quite died out and we didn't. I disported myself in a new military dress uniform but always turned up missing when there was any drilling or marching to be done. . . .

We haven't any very important cases for trial this term but in numbers we still maintain our place and usually the interest we feel in a case is measured by other considerations than the amount involved.

Your
Tom.

[1] Baseball "tournaments" became a tradition in Dakota; that is, a competition similar to the basketball tournaments held in many states in the twentieth century. When the editor visited Redfield in the summer of 1962, a baseball tournament was in progress.

95

Chicago, July 16, 1886.

Dear Friend,

. . . I can fully appreciate your astonishment on hearing Mrs. Pickler (a woman!) discuss political questions "intelligently," even though she probably has studied the subject carefully. It was even more astounding when you add that she talked more intelligently than "a man" at the hotel. Now it would be strange enough if she could talk better than any man one might happen to meet (anyone of the intelligent voters of this great republic) but when the man is of some "local prominence" politically it is high time the matter should be looked to. Mrs. Pickler must be shown her sphere.

O yes, I have learned something else I wanted to know, but not from the paper. I sometimes wonder why folks admire (ahem!) my singing, you among them. Your explanation of your admiration for the quartette of Chicago ladies who visited Redfield lately, clears up the mystery as far as you are concerned. Time's up. I must start for the park.

L. N.

96

Redfield, July 18, 1886.

Dear Ellen,

We still continue to swelter in a temperature ranging from 80 to 110 though the heat is less oppressive today than for some time past. We sent you no rain. Unlimited quantities of it might fall upon our parched prairies and fields and they would still absorb. If half an average crop is harvested we shall be fortunate enough. . . . The signal service officers all over the northwest have been wrestling with the problem of accounting for the hot wind we experienced some weeks ago, without arriving at any satisfactory theory.[1] It is still therefore "a freak of nature."

. . . I went merely to accommodate two Sisters of Mercy who were desirous of getting out to a convent about ten miles from here. I felt well paid for my exertions in their behalf too. They were particularly bright and intelligent, good conversationalists and quite willing to talk. One is a teacher of painting and music. The other had traveled extensively and had a fund of anecdotes which she related well and with an occasional gleam of humor. She had been to the head of navigation on the Missouri and on the Yellowstone, had seen buffalo swim the rivers and scamper over the plains. There is a sublimity in the sacrifices of these women born and reared to lives of comparative ease, if not luxury, voluntarily devoting themselves to the severest drudgery without a hope of earthly reward, which I can and do admire but fail to fully comprehend.

You didn't say you didn't like to hear men talk politics so I'll tell you that the democratic county committee of which I have the honor to be chairman meets at our office tomorrow for the transaction of some important business. It's a pleasure to meet my colleagues at any time. Really our committee averages up much better than that of our opponents in point of influence in the county, as well as in intelligence. I am happy to state that Ashton's prospects for retaining the county seat are at the present writing most slim.

I wasn't astonished to hear Mrs. Pickler discuss politics intelligently. Some folks would be. Did I say I was? It amused me and seemed odd, that's all. You could do better than she, but I cannot recall the time when you made that the first topic of conversation upon my calling on you. So even my astonishment might be excused. See?

Ever yours,
Tom.

[1] A weather service had been established in 1870 and was placed under the Signal Corps of the United States Army.

97

Chicago, July 25, 1886.

Dear Friend,

In regard to Mrs. Pickler, I am not prepared to state that you said in so many words that you were surprised "at the familiarity" she showed with the subject (politics) and "the liberal and intelligent" manner in which she discussed it, but every word you wrote showed your surprise so plainly that to have stated it would have seemed like tautology. But I found no fault, did I?, with what you said. You had a right to express your opinion and the nature of it did not surprise me in the least. As to my "doing better" than Mrs. Pickler, that's all nonsense you know. I do not "talk politics" at all. Still I forgive you having said so. It was quite the thing for you to say since of course you were aware that I would look upon it as the Chinese do upon an invitation—the one giving it does not mean it, the receiver knows it is not meant, and the giver knows that the receiver knows it. Lots of "knows." Now do you know?

Shall I tell you why I never introduced politics as a topic of conversation when you called? I rarely introduce topics of conversation for anyone who calls upon me. That is the privilege of the visitor, I take it. Of course if I saw a poor fellow overcome by his natural bashfulness or his great modesty, I should say something about the weather probably, but I never saw you in either of those situations, so I've had no chance. When I have an opportunity, I'll even promise to try to say something politic.

. . . When I go to Europe I shall stay more than two months. Some friends of mine are going next summer and they have invited me to go with them. I do not expect to be able to do so but I wish I could.

Ellen.

98

Redfield, August 1, 1886.

Dear Ellen,

Henry is extremely anxious, while in the east, to attend the trial of the anarchists.[1] That would be something of an attraction for me. Were it in progress while I was in the city I should have tried very hard to prevail upon you to attend, because, you see, I couldn't reconcile myself to "skipping" it and it would have been equally hard to cut short my visit with some of the folks in the Wicker Park neighborhood. . . . I suppose the jury will feel compelled to sacrifice a few of them to the demand for more blood. Does that remark shock you? Allow me to remark further that I should have attended the meeting of "sympathy" were I in Chicago when it was held. Not that the defendants get from me any compassion that is born of weakness, though I am conscious there is enough of that questionable virtue in me to spoil me as a prosecuting attorney. But I have not the least doubt that the press reports of the trial are . . . [*editor's omission*] unfair and prejudicial to the prisoners. Don't you know that it's a desperate case to get a jury to acquit after the reporters have condemned?

How delightful it would be to get a letter from you from the effete monarchies.

Tom.

[1] The first of several references to the violence in Haymarket Square on the evening of May 4, 1886, and to the trial of eight anarchists that followed. A number of policemen and other persons had been killed, and more than one hundred were injured.

99

Chicago, Aug. 8, 1886.

My dear Friend,

So you would have asked me to attend the anarchists' trial, would you? . . . Who are these anarchists? A lot of rabid, half-civilized foreigners who are unfit to be called American citizens. Do they expect to bring their old world barbarisms here and parade them with impunity? The interest felt here in the trial is very great, and I think a majority of our people are united in their hope that punishment may be as severe as possible.[1]

. . . You went to accommodate the two lovely Sisters of Mercy. I was much interested in your account of them. I don't know much about them, but have always looked upon them with respect amounting almost to veneration, and believe that all the good they do (and it is doubtless a great deal) is not nearly all they would do if their efforts were properly rewarded.

I would like to write you a longer letter but I am going out riding this afternoon and it will soon be time to start. I am going out to Cheltenham Beach some evening soon. Wish you might go too and see the destruction of Pompeii.[2] I remember your admiration for Bulwer's "Last Days."

Sincerely,
Ellen.

[1] The views expressed here were typical of the times. See Henry David, *History of the Haymarket Affair* (New York, 1936), pp. 206-18.

[2] A fireworks display. See No. 101.

100

My dear Ellen,—

The papers sent with your last letter were duly received.
. . . See how incorrigible I am. Positively, I am only confirmed in
the opinion that the defendants are not having a fair trial. I tried
to get a paper containing the arguments in full but couldn't. All
of our western papers printing the associated press reports tell of
the scathing arraignment of the anarchists by attorney Walker.
Then follows a brief notice to the effect that he was followed by
Zeisler for the defense.[1] Walker's speech seemed to me a rather
dry affair for the occasion, one which even in a much less inspiring case, a country lawyer would receive little credit for. You
think I'm half an anarchist. I believe the testimony in the case
is such that every one of the defendants deserves hanging, only
I should like to see the jury instead of the newspaper[s] convict
them. I was surprised at the allusion in Walker's speech to the
finding of combustibles in the Wicker Park neighborhood to fire
the city. I don't remember your saying anything of it nor did I
notice the fact in the testimony. They are a bloodthirsty set without doubt. I had no idea that you were ever in any danger. I have
a very fair idea of the manner of people they are. We used to
have some of them in Wisconsin. Their principal occupation was
drinking beer. They felt particularly proud of their atheistical
ideas, considered Tom Paine (whom they did not understand)
as a model philosopher and man, and themselves as the pioneers
of a great social revolution. Their leader was a young man of
some ability but extremely vain. He held some local office in a
town adjoining ours and at a joint meeting of the town boards,
at which my father was present, he was consuming considerable
time in haranguing the meeting on his pet subject (marriage as
the greatest obstacle to progress) when my father terminated his
speech by remarking that he had evidently mistook the object of
the meeting, that the question before the house was not one of
religion or social statics, but to determine [on] which side of the
road the ditch should be built.

Isn't Cheltenham Beach the place of which McVicker lately
assumed control?[2] I wish very sincerely that I might go with
you to see Pompeii. Is it a panorama or a real pyrotechnic display?

Our political campaign opens actively this week. Everyone is to hold himself in readiness to go where directed this week and to use any means in his power to secure favorable delegates from all the precincts in the county at the caucuses to be held next Saturday. Next week occurs the county convention to send delegates to the legislative convention in which will be represented this county and Clark. At the primaries next Saturday delegates will be chosen to the county convention. If Redfield is able to control that convention it will go a long way to render certain success at the polls in November. . . . No one knows party lines in this struggle.

Yours for success,
Tom.

[1] Francis W. Walker was an assistant to the state's attorney. Sigismund Zeisler was one of the counsel retained for the defense by the Central Labor Union of Chicago.

[2] James H. McVicker was a successful actor and theatrical manager who made Chicago his home and in 1857 built McVicker's Theatre at large expense. After the fire of 1871 it was rebuilt, and in 1885 it was completely remodeled. Walsh's letter would indicate that McVicker also turned to other fields of entertainment. See John Moses and Joseph Kirkland (eds.), *History of Chicago*, II (Chicago, 1895), 568-69, 573.

101

Chicago, Aug. 22, 1886.

Dear Friend,

The anarchist trial is over. I need not ask what you think of the verdict in the case. It is terrible, of course, but so was their crime. Few expected so sweeping a decision I think. I look upon their death as a necessary piece of brutality and barbarism, and trust that the papers are right in their opinion that anarchism has received its death blow in America.[1] Anarchy may be uprooted, but the labor troubles are yet to come. Besides there is only a short step between ignorant socialism and anarchy. . . . I was greatly amused by the droll way in which your father took down the eloquent speaker you mentioned.

The destruction of Pompeii is not a panorama but a grand

pyrotechnic display, and each rebuilding of the mimic city costs $1,000.

You don't know the latest sensation around here, do you? Well, there is a——ghost in the Andersen School. Hundreds have seen it, even the police. Do you [know] the absurd folks down stairs would not tell me of it because it happens to "appear" near my room. I'll tell you all about the nonsense next time. . . . I'm going over to school now, I have a pass key, to see if there is anything around the rooms that could produce some reflection on the windows. Tonight I am going to try to see "the ghost."

Yours,

E.

[1] As implied here, the philosophy of anarchism was on trial, no less than the eight defendants. They were not accused, specifically, of throwing the bomb that had killed seven police officers but rather of an anarchist conspiracy that resulted in *someone* committing the murderous act.

102

Redfield, August 29, 1886.

My dear Ellen,—

Accept my kindest thanks for the papers sent. I read the arguments with much interest and concur with you in the belief that Ingham's was the ablest. His peroration was eloquent and the diction elegant.[1] Undoubtedly the trial is the most celebrated in our history since Burr stood before the bar charged with treason.

The convention at Frankfort on Wednesday was a most decided success. It does begin to look as though failure could only occur by the most improbable accident. . . . Yes the republicans do rule generally in Dakota but the democrats are no longer an insignificant factor as the newspaper item you quote might seem to indicate. If we elect a member of the legislature this fall I shall not be greatly surprised and in certain contingencies we may elect one or two county officers. The reasons why Dakota should send a democratic delegate to Congress are so convincing and their nominee is likely to be personally so superior to the nominee of the other party that I expect to see a great many break away from party prejudices in the matter. Wilson, our candidate of two years ago and who will probably make the run again is known throughout the territory as a lawyer of eminent ability and a successful business man. I met him at Yankton. We went out together to see a ball game. He's a perfect gentleman, polished, but by no means vain. I'd like to take the stump for him and will probably be called upon to do so, though I don't see how I can.[2]

I anticipate a very pleasant trip to Deadwood. All but 45 miles of the journey can be made by rail. The remainder is made by stage through the Hills over a route said to be very picturesque. Mountain streams of marvelous purity abound and the atmosphere is rare and bracing.

We have a nine days wonder as well as you. Our artesian well began throwing a stream of water of excellent quality last Thursday morning with a pressure of over 150 pounds.

Your own,
Tom.

[1] George C. Ingham was a special assistant to the state's attorney. Excerpts from Ingham's speeches and those of other principals may be found in John D. Lawson (ed.), *American State Trials*, XII (St. Louis, 1919), 174-98 and *passim*.

[2] This was John R. Wilson. For his actual role in the later convention see No. 108.

103

Chicago, Sept. 6, 1886.

Dear Friend,

School opened this morning very pleasantly. I have a class of forty-five.

We were all so pleased to meet your brother [Henry] and enjoyed his little visit. I came near not seeing him at all. I was dictating to Katie when the bell rang and I never thought of your brother. I thought he had gone home; so I said, "Katie, if it's an agent (a book agent has haunted me lately) I'm not at home." I went into my room and could hear voices presently in the next room. I thought they would call me if it was anyone I knew, but Mary just didn't. She's hateful to me some times, and I suppose

I should have been sitting there yet if your brother hadn't laughed.
I knew him in a minute and appeared on the scene. . . .

Sincerely,
Ellen.

104

Redfield, September 12, 1886.

My dear Ellen,

I have just returned from Huron where I have been attending the territorial fair and the court at chambers. I saw little
of the fair except the races and some paintings of a lady friend
of mine. A lady rode a five mile race against a gentleman jockey
who beat her most ungallantly; but as she wasn't pretty no one
seemed to care much.

Saturday of each week is motion day, the court sitting at chambers. I enjoy attending very much. Questions of practice are the
principal ones coming up and having a good set of practice works,
I am usually pretty well prepared to meet my opponents. The
attorneys gather in from all portions of the district and we have
quite a social time.

. . . While I'm talking politics I may say that our county seat
matters are not near so placid and promising as they were a week
ago.

I went to see a play at Huron, given by the Chicago Comedy
Company, can't say whether for euphony or because they really
came from your city. The play was a vile thing, such a one as,
if put in a book would be known as a "dime novel." They shot
people on the stage and drew revolvers promiscuously and all
that sort of thing. The manager doubtless committed the mistake
of supposing that such "doings" as were carried on on the stage
were not uncommon in our every day life. I am not sure that he
doesn't reflect the general opinion entertained regarding us in the
east.

Ever yours,
Tom.

105

Chicago, September 19, 1886.

Dear Friend,—

. . . The Exposition does not please me as well as in other years that I have seen it; that is, the pictures are not as good as usual. I never care much for the other exhibits. There is the usual display of elegant jewels, costly fabrics, impossible machinery, musical and unmusical instruments, etc., etc., etc. There is quite an exhibition of grains from Dakota but not from your region. The pictures, as I said before are not to be compared to those of other years, if I am able to judge. One of the best is "Know ye the land?" Describe it please, will you? I am quite sure you can. "Low tide at La Vallette France" is very fine. The most expensive picture in the collection, but one which cannot be admired from a purely artistic standpoint, is a scene in Wall Street—"The Bulls and the Bears." The "animiles" are being let loose on the street. It is a wonderfully fine caricature of course, but I don't think I should give $6,000 for it. You will begin to dread exposition time won't you? I know I always give you a pretty large dose of it.

Bye-bye
E. C. M.

106

Redfield, Sept. 26, 1886.

My dear Ellen,—

Do you really think it would have been better for me to go to the temperance lecture? Perhaps you reasoned that because I didn't go I stood in need of the lecturer's teaching. That's usually the case I believe. Few except those in whom temperance principles are confirmed ever attend these temperance meetings now. . . .

Don't be alarmed about your description of the pictures at the exposition becoming tiresome. Why didn't you go on and tell me about the "know you the land" picture? When I was a very small boy and they put me to bed before I grew sleepy I used to revel among fancied cities of magic splendor and in gardens filled with flowers of fabulous beauty and luxuriance. But imagination has actually grown to be the most laggard of all my slow faculties so you'll get a very poor picture I fear. Of course I should put the "virgin as soft as the roses she twines" in the foreground. No, she isn't there at all. The sun is just sinking over the tops of the mountains in the distance. That's where it usually is in a picture. A path or road leads down a hill not very steep and then along the shore. The chief feature is luxuriousness of color and vegetation. Roses on one side rise into prominence with flowers of minor importance filling up the spare space, on the other wild shrubbery in profusion. The mountains prevent the sun's rays from striking the water which is at one side. I told you my imagination is unreliable. I've been jumbling together in the above a half dozen pieces of natural scenery which have made an impression on me. I know my landscape isn't anything like the copy, but I've guessed my best guess. Now tell me about it.

I'm going to Aberdeen Tuesday as a delegate to the democratic territorial convention. There will be a lively time when the clans assemble and probably something very much like a row. You see the South Dakota people will come up nearly united in favor of division. The North will present a solid front against this position. Occupying a central position our delegations will probably hold the balance of power and be likely to dictate the nominee. One of the aspirants for the nomination as delegate to Congress, attended our county convention Thursday. He made a speech to the convention. And let me tell you something in strict confidence. I could have done much better myself and you know I can't talk well enough to go to Congress.

You didn't think of putting off writing three weeks, did you? Really they would lengthen out into as many years.

Good-night.
Tom.

107

Chicago, October 6, 1886.

My dear Friend,

I did not intentionally delay answering your last letter, and write tonight for fear my three days delay may seem like a longer period to you. By the bye, what will you do when I do not write to you for "three years" nor for ten times three years? Never mind answering that question; you'll very sensibly do as I shall—write to somebody else.

No, you were not in the remotest degree in need of the teachings of the enchanting [temperance] females you described I am certain. You are very forgetful. Haven't I told you before that I think you quite a nice little boy all around. More slang, but I can't help it. I've been bad all day.

It breaks my heart (figuratively speaking) to be compelled to tell you that you did not describe "Know ye the land" quite exactly. Your first start off was nearer right, the "maiden fair to see" is there. Thanks for guessing so obediently, you may go to the head of the class.

O, Booth is here. I have been waiting for him ever since I came here. He plays Hamlet Friday night and I'll give you my opinion of him as the "melancholy Dane." I expect a rare treat. . . .

Thanks for the papers, one of which was received today. Did things go as you desired? I believe your heart was not set upon division, or rather that you favor division in a certain manner. Tell me all about it when you write. I read faithfully all the papers said about the convention but you see I don't always know just where you are in the proceedings and then I am all at sea and don't know which way is best.

L. N.

108

Redfield, October 10, 1886.

Dear Ellen,—

Yes, I shall be very busy today but I have no thought of demonstrating the fact by deferring the answer to your last letter.

I received official notification this morning that I should be called upon to edify the Dakota voters from the stump and must set about immediately to prepare myself for the occasion. I am not apprised yet where I am to go nor when I shall speak. The occasion is one which properly improved must ultimately be of much value to me, and realizing the importance of this step into a field in which I have never yet ventured I desire naturally that such mean abilities as I command may be displayed to the best possible advantage. I doubt seriously whether I shall be able to rise to the necessities of the occasion but I am reassured by one circumstance. The tariff is now the one great national issue. It will be a feature of the debates of the campaign. I have considerable matter already worked up on the subject which may be conveniently used. I have spoken on the question as you know several times and always managed to entertain, if I did not convince, my audience. You did me the honor on several occasions to request me to assist some of your enterprises by suggestions. It is from no desire to reciprocate the compliment but because I recognize that they would be of value to me that I now request you to lend me your aid in the same way. I wish I might submit my manuscript to the criticism of your sound judgment and excellent taste.

Yes, the Aberdeen convention went off quite to my satisfaction. Mr. Day requested me to make his nominating speech but I begged off and he consented upon my agreeing to second.[1] The newspaper man was over kind to me although I had no acquaintance with him as might be inferred.[2] It was long past midnight before the work of selecting a nominee was begun. . . . It was quite a victory though, as the older heads in our delegation kept assuring us that we had tied up with the wrong crowd, that Day was downed, etc., etc. I knew all along that he was the strongest man in the convention though I didn't suppose that he could poll a majority on the first ballot as he did. It wasn't for that reason I supported him though. He is the representative of the younger and better elements of the party. Wilson of the Black Hills who was the nominee of the party two years ago supported him with all the strength of that region. I met him the first time at Yankton last spring. He is a young man of much culture and the most refined manners, a gentleman in every true sense. He was chosen temporary chairman you may have noticed, and gave me a place on the committee on resolutions. The planks on the question of division, on the tariff, and on pensions are my work. The territorial central committee was also reorganized on a new basis suggested by myself. Altogether it was a great convention and as important, perhaps, as any ever held in the territory.[3]

It may have occurred to you that as the nominee is doomed to certain defeat an unnecessary ado is made over the convention, but you must consider that whether elected or defeated he will have a powerful influence with the administration and the majority in Congress. He will also have the distribution of the federal patronage in the territory which with all our land offices and Indian agencies is a matter of great significance. The aspirations of rival candidates for these positions gave a degree of asperity to the debates that made them interesting and lent an additional importance to the result. Well, you've had enough of the convention but before quitting the subject you must be assured that I was not the only man there, an error into which the preceding pages may possibly lead you.

It would be one of the rarest pleasures to me to hear Booth with you in Hamlet. You must write me all about him. . . .

I'll tell you of the crowds that hung breathless upon my words when next I write. Also of the vaster multitude who will go to sleep over them.

Tom.

[1] M. H. Day of the Black Hills already represented Dakota on the Democratic National Committee. He now sought the nomination for delegate to Congress.

[2] Walsh may have referred to an article in the *Sioux Falls Daily Argus* (September 29, 1886) praising his "fine speech."

[3] Some twenty years later Walsh would begin to play a similar role in the national Democratic conventions. He was particularly proud of his influence in the platform committees.

109

Chicago, Oct. 17, 1886.

Dear Friend,

. . . I did notice the pencil note upon the first paper you sent, but, mon ami, I guess you wrote with a dull pencil for I did not clearly make out the first one and so did not know that Mr. Day was your man. He certainly stood well with the convention. I am quite certain the editor only did you justice when he said you made a "fine speech." Remember this, my friend, a man's confidence in himself is half the battle. You know, of course, I do not mean a silly vanity, but a calm belief in one's power must be a fount of strength in time of need.

I notice lately in one of the papers that Theodore Roosevelt is a candidate for political honors in New York.[1] I thought, during the last presidential campaign, that he would probably soon be heard from again. I do not know, however, as he will be a great political success. I do not mean especially in reference to the next election, but as a politician. He is not cool enough. He lets the enemy see when he is wounded, and they will use the knowledge to his disadvantage.

I promised to tell you about Hamlet, didn't I? Well 'tis needless to say that he was fine. In looking on the play one forgets that it is Booth. In the scene where the mimic play is performed, it was quite wonderful to watch the changing expressions on Hamlet's face, as he watched the king. And when at length the king rushes from the throne, followed by the queen and their attendants, and Hamlet leaps to his feet exclaiming "Why, let the stricken deer go weep," etc., he was grand in his exultation. Booth, in some scenes, reminded me strongly of Napoleon but not nearly so much as an actor I saw last week as Claude Melnotte in "The Lady of Lyons." I am not at all familiar with his name, Mr. Frederick Paulding, but his acting was excellent to my mind.[2]

E. C. M.

[1] Roosevelt had returned from his adventures on the Little Missouri River in far western Dakota Territory. He was now campaigning for mayor of New York, and doubtless his versatility helped to keep him in the news. See Theodore Roosevelt, *Hunting Trips of a Ranchman: Sketches of Sport on the Northern Cattle Plains* (New York, 1885).

[2] Claude Melnotte, a romantic youth, appeared in Edward Bulwer-Lytton's *The Lady of Lyons* (1838). He also appeared in what seems to have been an adaptation by Henry James Byron (1859?). Frederick Paulding has not been identified.

110

Redfield, Oct. 26, 1886.

My dear Ellen,—

It was reported here today that business is practically suspended in Ashton and the same might truly be said of our town. I have been out in one of the doubtful districts all day myself. The same precinct was being worked by five resident adherents of Redfield—all men of influence in the community. My trip has reassured me somewhat but there is no disguising the fact that if we pull through it will be by a remarkably close vote.

I spoke last Monday night for the congressional ticket at Volga, Tuesday at Brookings, and Wednesday at Estelline, the former home of the Bell man.[1] At Estelline a meeting of the republicans had been called for the same evening of my engagement and the local manager arranged for a joint session. It was understood that the meeting was not to be in the nature of a debate, but it naturally took that course. I sustained our side unassisted. Mr. Matthews of Brookings who was district attorney for this judicial district when I came here was the chief speaker for the opposition.[2] We have always been friendly and the greatest good feeling prevailed. I enjoyed the occasion very much, particularly as our people flattered me with the assurance that I scored the greatest number of points. I have invitations to speak at Huron and Aberdeen one of which I shall probably accept. . . .

Tom.

[1] In all probability this is a reference to Hayden Carruth, who edited the *Estelline Bell* from 1883 to 1886. See Notes for No. 207.

[2] George A. Matthews was running for a seat in the territorial council, and was elected.

111

Chicago, Nov. 3, 1886.

My dear Friend,

. . . The election went off very quietly here it seems. Henry George was defeated in New York I'm happy to see.[1] I'm sorry your plans are not prospering as you would like them. Thanks for the paper. You just saved yourself. Honestly just before receiving it I had been thinking thusly: "There, he (meaning you) has been making speeches all through the country, and I (meaning me) know the papers must say lots about how good they are, and yet he (meaning you) never sends anyone (meaning me) a paper." I would have so liked to see all the papers said about you and I hope you know me better than to suppose I would misunderstand your motive in sending anything said in your praise. Now tell me all about it won't you[?]

Good night.

E.

[1] In the mayoralty campaign of 1886 in New York City, Henry George ran as a labor candidate, with some socialist support, and was defeated by the Democrat, Abram S. Hewitt. Theodore Roosevelt ran third. See Harry Thurston Peck, *Twenty Years of the Republic, 1885-1905* (New York, 1907), pp. 131, 733-34.

112

Redfield, Nov. 7, 1886.

My dear Ellen,—

My brief note of a few days ago informed you that the object upon which we had all set our hearts and for which we have labored so unceasingly was triumphantly accomplished at the polls last Tuesday. The official count made yesterday increased our majority to 102. Immediately after the canvass the commissioners by a unanimous vote ordered the removal of the records to this place and two of the officers have already arrived. The vote on the county offices is very close. The treasureship, an office paying from $4,000 to $6,000, will be contested. Altogether it was, as the result shows, one of the hottest campaigns ever known in this section and the like of which we shall not see for many years. It cost our people upwards of $6,000 and the Ashton people spent more than that. Both sides made a canvass of the entire county and had or thought they had the name of every voter, his residence marked on sectional maps, and just how he was going to vote. These maps showed further who were influential men in their respective neighborhoods and information was at hand as to the most effectual way to "work" them. One permanent good at least will result from the campaign. It has enabled the people of our vast county to become acquainted with each other more thoroughly and extensively than almost any other means could. And in this connection Redfield has cause to congratulate herself on the use of none but respectable means from the beginning to the close of the campaign. A large share of the people in remote districts looked upon us in the beginning of the fight as a lot of thugs and outlaws. This feeling may be considered as virtually dead now. We have to regret that a few of our supporters went back on us at the most critical moment, but as to them we can afford to be magnanimous should the spirit so incline, or, if the occasion demands they can be made to feel their folly. The result is a source of great satisfaction to us I can assure you. It will practically center the law business of the county here and, we hope, largely increase our patronage as well as enable us to dispose of business entrusted to us more satisfactorily, with greater accuracy and dispatch, and at considerably less expense.

I am afraid your illness has some more serious origin than malaria. Has it not occurred to you that this is an unusual time of the year for malaria? Don't people have typhoid fever more than once? Couldn't you try, particularly if you are feeling better, to write before Sunday this time? It is really too sad about your friend. The dread disease [tuberculosis] is comparatively little known here. Many of our people who were afflicted with bronchial and lung trouble in the east find entire relief here.

You expressed pleasure at the defeat of Henry George. I was likewise pleased, although I regret Hewitt's abandonment of Congress at this critical juncture in the tariff reform movement. Cox will be back from New York and will more than fill Morrison's place.[1] I said that George's defeat pleased me, not because I consider him, as many do, a socialist or an anarchist, but because many who are socialists and anarchists believe him to be of their ilk. They would certainly regard his election as a triumph or vindication of their "principles." I should regard it as a calamity if George were elected to Congress. . . . [M. H.] Day cut the republican majority in the territory from 56,000 to 20,000.[2]

I shall have to let politics alone hereafter and attend more strictly to business. . . .

Tom.

[1] As might be surmised, the leaders named by Walsh were Democrats. Abram S. Hewitt had served as a representative from 1875 to 1879 and again from 1881 to 1886, when he resigned to become mayor of New York. Samuel "Sunset" Cox had served in Congress first from Ohio and later from New York. He was re-elected as a representative from New York in 1886, after his return from a mission as envoy to Turkey. William R. Morrison of Illinois was an unsuccessful candidate for re-election in 1886, after serving eight terms in the House of Representatives.

[2] That is, in the race for delegate to Congress.

113

Chicago, Nov. 10, 1886.

My dear Friend,

I received your letter at noon, and, like an obedient child, answer "before Sunday." No, mon ami, I am not a bit sick, I am thankful to say. I just glance in the mirror over my dressing case to see if my looks corroborate my words, and I assure you, if intensely red cheeks are a sign of good health my words are proved. It does seem a strange time to have malaria, but Chicago is a wonderful place you know. . . .

Ellen.

114

Redfield, Nov. 21, 1886.

My dear Ellen,—

You didn't say you were leaving the city for a visit but I inferred as much. Hope you had a very pleasant time. It used to seem to me when I was teaching a great treat, almost a necessity, to get away out of town of a Saturday, now and then. I am seldom conscious of the same yearning now, perhaps because opportunities come oftener, but more, I think, because there is less monotony in our business—the routine is not so oppressively regular.

. . . I have always taken a lively interest in real estate law though I thus far have had little occasion to use such knowledge of the subject as I have been able to gain. Titles are ordinarily so simple out here that the assistance of a lawyer is seldom needed.

By one of the strange chances occasionally exhibited in politics one of the democratic nominees from this legislative district has been elected. There is every probability that his seat will be contested. In case it is I shall go to Bismarck to defend his case for him.

The St. Paul papers give very brief but sad accounts of the many wrecks along the lakes in which Two Rivers point occurs with unenviable frequency. It ought to be made a high crime to sail the lakes after the 1st of November. The account given by the sole survivor of a Frankfort, Mich. wreck of the lashing to the mast of their woman cook recalls vividly a similar catastrophe that occurred on our shore when I was a boy—in both cases only adding horrors passing the power of conception to the death that finally relieved them.

Henry and I were invited out last evening and the conversation turning in some way upon the opera I entertained the company with an account of "The Flying Dutchman" as we saw and heard it.[1] Everyone seemed interested in my recital not because of any skill of mine as a story teller but because of the thrilling character of the scenes narrated. . . . You will probably have another opportunity to hear Patti this winter.[2] It is considered likely that she will be in St. Paul during the carnival season. Should she I shall endeavor to go down to hear her.

If I should get a letter before next Sunday what would I do? Why, I'd waive the insufficient notice, accept service nunc pro tunc and file my answer forthwith. Wouldn't you?

Tom.

[1] Wagner's opera, *Der Fliegende Hollander* (1843).

[2] Adelina Patti (1843-1919) was a coloratura soprano who became, in the 1880's, the most popular singer of the day.

115

Chicago, Nov. 28, 1886.

My learned Friend,

You see I have had to borrow an introductory expression, and, though it is, I believe, occasionally used somewhat sarcastically by legal gentlemen, I must beg my "legal" correspondent to believe that it is not so used here.

It is suggested by the closing lines of a letter received last Wednesday, and penned, so far as I can judge, by yourself. By those lines, I can imagine, you desired to convey to me, by means of written characters constituting words, some idea—some beautiful thought doubtless, but, alas, mon ami, you spoke in a foreign tongue, and your less learned friend comprehended not your words. So you will excuse, will you not, any failure on my part to comply with any suggestion made in the closing lines of your last, if indeed they carried such import.

. . . Did I tell you I have commenced taking vocal lessons again? The lady was highly recommended to me, and I think I shall do well with her. She has had a large experience, was formerly teacher of vocal music at Vassar College and is a pupil of Marchesi (Professeur de chant au Conservatoire de Vienne).[1] Do you know—of course you don't, but can you credit it—she thinks my voice a little out of the usual run, very clear, very sweet, very resonant, and all that? Don't imagine I want to brag about it. I guess she means it even though she is likely to be a little mistaken about it. I am going to continue my lessons now for a long time just to see what I can do. I shall not be disappointed however, if I never rival Patti.

E. C. M.

[1] Probably Mathilde Marchesi (1826-1913), a German mezzo-soprano, who taught for a time in the conservatory at Vienna. Her husband was also a famous singer and teacher.

116

Redfield, December 5, 1886.

My dear Ellen,—

You see I'm not so much given to facetiae as yourself or I should have commenced this with "My dear Diva" or "My precious Prima" or something of that sort. Really you're mistaken though. The use of the foreign expression to which you must refer is no indication of erudition on my part. I learned its significance, as I did most of my Latin, in the back part of the spelling book. . . .

I find no difficulty in believing everything your instructor says of your voice. It has been all that and more to me always. You know how charmed I was the first time I heard it in song—that is, if you found the occasion as pleasant as it was to me—I have no doubt you remember. I have no doubt your progress will be rapid if you set your heart upon becoming an artist. My best wishes for your success.

Tom.

117

Redfield, Dec. 19, 1886.[1]

Dear Ellen,—

I have just returned from my weekly pilgrimage to Huron to attend chambers. I got two important cases wound up yesterday in a manner much more gratifying to myself than to my opponents, one of which will probably go to the Supreme Court. I got judgment in another case a week ago from which an appeal was promptly taken. That will make three cases for us at the next term of the Supreme Court. . . .

A project is on foot with very fair prospects of success to make Redfield the seat of a college which the Congregationalists are about to establish somewhere in central Dakota. I had rather see a public institution of learning of a high order here, but there seems to be no immediate prospect of such a thing and it does seem as though with the proper effort on the part of our citizens, which by the way they seem willing to put forth, we can get this.

We are going to make an effort to induce Judge Church's successor to take up his residence and sit at chambers here.[2] We are almost at the geographical center of the district, on both lines of road and trains run so as to accommodate attorneys from all quarters. It is not improbable that this place will be made the seat of the United States Court by a bill which congress will probably pass this winter to divide this judicial district and give us another judge. Getting the county seat didn't satisfy our ambition, you see.

That long apology, on the latin question, won't do at all. I was grievously, mortally offended and supposed you were in downright earnest. No I didn't either. I knew all the time that you knew more about the tongues dead and living than I ever pretended to know.

I shall say "I told you so" with much pride and satisfaction when the possibilities at which your music teacher has hinted are realized, as I doubt not they will shortly be—that is, I will if I may still be considered one of your oldest and best prized friends.

T. J. W.

[1] Walsh has two letters in a row. Apparently one of Ellen's is missing.

[2] Judge Church was about to assume his new office as governor of Dakota Territory. His successor in the fifth judicial district was Judge J. S. Spencer.

118

My dear Friend,

I continue writing on this sheet of paper to let you see that my intention was to write yesterday. I had just seated myself beside a cheerful fire, writing material at hand, when the Boeses came to get me to go to the theatre. Yes, on Sunday night too. Will tell you about the theatre anon as I have a much more important topic to speak of now.

On Christmas eve I received your "trifles." My friend, how dared you send me such an extravagant present? I should have considered two of them almost more than I ought to accept, but twelve, mon ami, I must reiterate you are an extravagant boy. They are lovely, exquisite, and no one could value your gift more highly than I do, but you ought not to have sent me so much.[1] I have shown them to everyone who has come in and the verdict is always the same as to the beauty of the pictures and the perfect taste shown in their selection. One lady who came in yesterday made this remark: "It is not everyone who could fully appreciate such a gift." I think I forgot the compliment intended for me in her remark, in thinking that it is not everyone who would think of selecting just that gift. It occurs to me now, also that there probably are not many who would do me the honor of believing I would appreciate these lovely works of art. I thank you. I shall have two of them framed as soon as possible to hang above my piano. I shall see them oftenest there. Accept my best thanks for your lovely present—perfect except in its magnitude.

When I become "a star," may you call me friend? I make no rash promises. If, in making a tour of the world, our company should come to grief, for lack of funds at Redfield, just call around to cheer us up, won't you? But if we are very successful I intend to cut all my old friends—that's my way. Now you didn't think I really believed in what I said before, did you? I know I have quite a nice little parlor voice but I'm not a whit deceived by it or by my teacher. Do you remember the night Mrs. Throop had her organ taken away? The look of disappointment on your face when you found out you could not therefore hear me sing flattered me more than all Miss Smythe has said.[2]

. . . Thanks again for your gift. I suppose we shall have "to receive" on New Year's Day. We cannot reckon on seeing you, I fear.

Very sincerely,

E. C. M.

[1] The reference is to etchings, some of which later hung in the Walsh home and in Walsh's office.

[2] Lily E. Smythe was Ellen's music teacher, mentioned previously in No. 115. She had taught at Vassar College before moving to Illinois.

119

Redfield, New Year's Day 1887.
25° below

My dear Ellen,—

The above refers to the state of the weather and not to the elevation or depression of my spirits, though even the visitor whom I have just bowed out and who left a retainer hasn't saved me from a certain degree of moodiness this afternoon. I don't know how much regret at my inability to be one of your New Year's callers has to do with it but I assure you you can not deplore my absence more deeply than do I. The calendar and cards you sent were duly received. Henry begs me to express his acknowledgements and thanks for your kind remembrance. I have hung the calendar where it will be likely to engage my attention on rising each morning and, to use an expression that may be peculiar to our vernacular, "I'll go you" on your proposition to commit the extract on each leaf. The next time we meet we'll recite them alternately and the first one who misses will have to —will you name the forfeit? Seeing that I have the better memory, (by the way you didn't say how you found that out) it wouldn't be fair for me to fix the penalty. Come, pass judgment.

What a queer coincidence about those pictures. I had actually selected the two you talk of framing to adorn our "rooms." (I think its . . . [editor's omission: illegible] [a] Curiosity that a certain young bachelor always talks of his "rooms" or his "apartments" though the singular would be the more truthful expression.)

Our legislature begins its session in about ten days. The senator from this district is a client of ours.[1] He spent Thursday evening with us talking over a number of proposed measures and

A farm three miles southeast of Redfield.
Spink County Historical Society.

The Foster House, a hotel run by Gene and Fred Dodge, in which the Walsh brothers lived.
Spink County Historical Society.

A view of the James River, near Redfield.
Spink County Historical Society.

The Spink County Court House, constructed after Redfield's victory in the county seat fight.
Spink County Historical Society.

Redfield in 1898.
Spink County Historical Society.

The Central Hotel in the early 1880's.
Spink County Historical Society.

A picture of Walsh taken in Chicago, about 1887.
Courtesy of Mrs. Genevieve Walsh Gudger.

Elinor C. McClements, 1889.
Courtesy of Mrs. Genevieve Walsh Gudger.

Sturgeon Bay, 1882. Walsh is to the rear with arms folded. Henry T. Scudder is in front of him.

Courtesy of Mrs. Genevieve Walsh Gudger.

Tom Walsh, center, with friends of the Sturgeon Bay
years, perhaps a theatrical or literary group.
Courtesy of Mrs. Genevieve Walsh Gudger.

Tom Walsh when a high school teacher in Sturgeon
Bay, 1882.
Courtesy of Mrs. Genevieve Walsh Gudger.

Henry Walsh, center, with his son Dana, in front of the Bank of Redfield, 1897.
Courtesy of Mrs. Raymond T. Birge.

Henry C. Walsh, about 1890.
Courtesy of Mrs. Raymond T. Birge.

informing himself on some of the legal questions likely to arise in connection with them. I shall have an opportunity while attending court at Bismarck to see something of the way in which our laws are made. It will be entirely new to me. The legislature did not sit while I was at Madison. . . .

Bye-bye,
Tom.

[1] E. W. Foster of Spink County, a Republican representing the ninth district (Spink and Clark counties).

120

Chicago, Jan. 9, 1887.

My dear Friend,

Yours from 25° below was duly received. I always supposed, from tradition, that those lower regions were at least balmy.

Am sorry you did not find it convenient to "look in" on New Year's day. By the bye, did I wish you a happy, a very happy New Year? If not, I do so now most sincerely. . . . My first call was received between twelve and one A.M. and the last at eight P.M. Quite a day's work, you see. I was at the theatre the night before and we stopped for lunch which accounts for the extreme earliness of one call.

. . . I agree about the verses, only when we begin to hurl Shakespeare at each other's head let us get far away from the haunts of men. They might think us crazy. About the penalty of missing. Thanks for allowing me to decide it. I do therefore solemnly pronounce the penalty.—The first one who misses shall be compelled to accept from the other a box of candy—Gunther's best. But if either is found missing intentionally, that person shall—will you name the forfeit? Seeing that I would never do such a thing as miss purposely, it would not be fair for me to fix the penalty. How do I know your memory is better than mine? Dear friend, could it be worse?

L. N.

121

Redfield, January 16, 1887.

My dear Ellen,—

Didn't I tell you some time ago that Redfield was striving to become the seat of a college? ... The decisive vote stood 11 to 9 for Redfield. The projectors are known as the Midland Congregational Association. The denomination, it seems, is divided into three sections in the territory, the lines of which are geographical and not doctrinal or dogmatic. The northern section has a college at Fargo, the southern at Yankton and it was a desire on the part of the Midland section to keep pace with these remoter regions that gave rise to the project that has proceeded so far as above stated. Its influence on our social and intellectual life can not fail to be of a marked and beneficial character. We all regard it as an acquisition second in importance only to the county seat. I have been very busy for some time past and have been away a good share of the time owing to which facts I have learned very little of the details connected with the matter or the character of the work they will undertake.

We are just about to start a case that for the value of the property involved, the intricacy of the questions of law arising and the doubtful nature of the conflicting claims exceeds in importance any case in which we have yet been concerned. The fight will be between mortgages claiming priority of liens in property worth $6000. It came up while I was away and after Henry had detailed the facts to me he said, "Now we are getting into the practice of the law." I thought so too. It is an ideal case, one in which there is opportunity as well as incitement to study.[1]

Our local opera company will shortly produce "The Little Tycoon."[2] Mark you, I don't participate except as prompter.

I should say that, since we are to go "far from the haunts of men" and the punishment runs to sweets anyway, that anyone missing Shakespeare purposely ought to submit to the usual penalty in a game of forfeits, the inventor of each penalty to get the benefit of the doubt in every case.

Yours devotedly,
Tom.

[1] This seems rather clearly to have been *Kalscheuer* v. *Upton et al.*, 6 Territory of Dakota, 449 (1889). The Walsh brothers, representing

Kalscheuer, respondent, lost when the case was appealed to the territorial supreme court.

[2] *The Little Tycoon* (1882) was a comic opera in two acts by Willard Spenser. Violet, daughter of General Knickerbocker, "One of the Old Time Knickerbockers," was the little tycoon—as revealed by the cast of characters, *ibid.*, p. 2.

122

Chicago, January 23, 1887.

My dear Friend,

. . . I don't know as I have very much to tell you about Wilson Barrett except that I thought him a very good actor but a man toward whom I felt a natural antagonism. I cannot imagine why such a silly thing should be, but I hated him in every character he assumed. I saw him as the Rev. Richard Capel in "A Clerical Error," as "Clito" the Athenian sculptor, and as "Chatterton, the marvelous boy, the sleepless soul that perished in its pride"—saw him and admired his acting, but hated the man.[1] Mrs. Langtry is coming and I do want to see her if possible.[2]

Do you know, I was disappointed, about your Shakespeare punishment. I thought you would be selfish, like I was, and say something that you like. I was sure you would say the person would have to get a big bunch of roses. I know you like flowers. Instead of that you mention some indefinite punishment(?) or reward(?) but as I never play "a game of forfeits" I cannot in my ignorance agree to the proposition. Better make it roses.

Have you read "Ben Hur, a tale of Christ" by Gen. Lew Wallace? I am reading it now. It is quite a wonderful book.[3]

Goodnight.

E.

[1] Wilson Barrett was an English actor and author. He was co-author of the play *Clito* (1886).

[2] This was the "incomparable" Lillie Langtry, an English actress noted for her beauty. See a critical description by Ellen McClements in No. 126.

[3] *Ben-Hur* was published in 1880.

123

Redfield, January 30, 1887.

My dear Ellen,—

Your letter traveled no faster than mine. It was received but yesterday. We have ceased to expect trains on time or oftener than once in every two or three days. The storm raged so furiously yesterday that all trains were suspended and we have had no mail since Friday night. Your idea of a blizzard certainly does not accord with the sense in which the term is used here. Snow is a necessary constituent of our blizzard. It is usually quite fine and dry so that it is driven by the wind with great velocity and penetrates the clothing of those exposed to it causing much annoyance. Stories are told of large rooms being filled by snow blown through a key-hole, but they are not well authenticated. More snow has fallen here this winter than during any season, it is said, since 1880. Some pretend to say that it is the harbinger of a good crop but I take it that observation has not yet been sufficiently continuous to predict with accuracy although the increased moisture will necessarily have a tendency in that direction.[1]

We are just starting a suit that is a model case, such a one as when I was studying I was ambitious to manage. There is enough involved to incite one to study, enough doubt to make it necessary, and enough certainty to prevent worry. You said once that such matters interested you, so I will tell you about it. . . .

Our grand Army Post has arranged for a series of weekly public discussions by local speakers. They have me on twice. One night to discuss which has done most for civilization, the clerical or the legal profession, the second to talk on the tariff. If any of the audience live through the first night, I think I can entertain them the second.

I have been reading considerable fiction lately, to little purpose however, I regret to say. I have been desirous for some time to read Ben Hur but because of hearing so many in whose judgment I am unable to repose much confidence, go into raptures over it, I had almost abandoned my purpose. I shall persevere now however. I devoured Disraeli's "Young Duke" and [George Eliot's] "Daniel Deronda" recently but quite too rapidly as they are both works of rare merit. Of course the latter is the higher grade of composition but "The Duke" is filled with eloquent passages and characteristic epigrams.

Well roses it is.

Tom.

¹ This was the famous winter of 1886-87 in which thousands of cattle died. Ranchers had never experienced such a blizzard as that of late January.

124

Chicago, February 10, 1887.

Dear Friend,

Yes I do take an interest in questions pertaining to law. I don't know why it is so, because I know nothing about the subject, you know, still it interests me and I'll try to give an opinion in the case you state. You musn't laugh at me though because it will probably be wrong. . . . Do you refuse to act for anyone whose claim you consider faulty?

I am sure your discussion of the tariff will be interesting. I wish I might hear it. There does seem to be vital need of "reform" in that direction. I lately saw a list of articles with the duty charged on each and it does seem as if the luxuries are the most lightly taxed articles. I don't know from what paper it was clipped but if I can get it I'll send it to you.

Last Saturday night I attended one of the "grandest" parties I have ever seen. It was given by one of the wealthiest Scandinavians here and was attended by the elite of Norsedom, opera singers from down town, etc. One of the prettiest women there, and most unquietly dressed, was the wife of the Swedish Consul. She was in full dress, all black, even her gloves, the only relief being her complexion and great strings of pearls around arms, neck, and in her hair, which is also black. Miss Neilson looked very pretty too.

Good-night,
E. C. M.

125

Bismarck, February 13, 1887.

Dear Ellen,—

Today finds me at the capital. I arrived last Tuesday at the request of our member of the council who wrote that if the wires were properly worked the legislature might be disposed to do something for us. There are now three terms of the court, one of which is held here, one at Yankton and one at Deadwood. The central portion of the territory has been neglected by every party. There isn't a public institution within its boundaries. . . . I hope to get away by Tuesday but may be obliged to remain during the week. I'm not particularly fascinated with the lobby and my visit has in no measure heightened my ambition to shine on the floor. The major portion of the business is routine work of the dryest character but even that is recreation compared with being compelled to sit out the wordy, senseless speeches of some members who don't seem to recognize that their forte is voting and not talking. . . .

Gov. Church is expected tomorrow or next day. There is a horde of anxious place hunters here who await his coming with no little anxiety. He went to Huron the day I came up and stayed with us at the office for about two hours between trains. I told him he hadn't anything good enough for me. They think here pretty generally that I'm after something but I'm not, and it would be something particularly tempting that would induce me to quit my business now. The patronage of our governor greatly exceeds that of the governors of the states, you know. All offices of the territory are by provision of the organic act, appointed by him upon the advice and consent of the council. The treasureship and the auditors office are estimated to be worth $12,000 each.

I'm not at the end of my rope, but my paper,

Good-night.
Tom.

126

Chicago, March 6, 1887.

Dear Friend,

I should make some apology for not writing lately, but a letter more or less from me will make little difference I am sure. Really I have been rather busy and I neglect all my correspondents now adays. I don't suppose I write one letter now for ten I used to write. You once said, probably in a joke, that you keep my letters. I hope you do nothing of the kind. If you do their bulk must be wonderous size by this time. Do you rent an extra room for their safe keeping?

Did I tell you I saw Mrs. Langtry? I believe not as I've not written since. My expectations of seeing a great beauty were greatly disappointed. To me she seems actually plain looking, and she is too thin. Her cheek bones are too high and her cheeks are hollow. . . . I saw her as Lady Clancarty.[1] Her costumes and jewels are superb.

I must tell you of a nice present I had lately. It seems that a few years ago, over at the "Wicker Park," I entertained an artist unawares, but he says I told him he would be an artist some day. He left school after leaving my room and studied "art" down town. I met him by chance in a street car one night and he told me all his plans and asked me for a loan of one of my pictures. I had some new ones taken some time ago and I gave him one. The other day he brought me an almost life size crayon. It is very good and I was much surprised that the boy could do it. It is not one of the usual "solar prints" done up with a little crayon but a real free hand picture. I rather hate to parade such a pretentious picture of myself but he'd be so hurt if I didn't give it a place "on my walls." . . .

E. C. M.

[1] The historical melodrama, *Lady Clancarty*, was written by Tom Taylor (1874).

127

My dear Ellen,—

After nearly four weeks absence I arrived here on Friday. Your letter of the 10th ult. awaited me but I was disappointed in not receiving an answer to my last from Bismarck. It is probably snow-bound somewhere. Our bill went through the house all right and is now tossing about on the uncertain waters of the council. It is difficult to predict what will be its fate in the upper house. The combinations made during the early part of the session are rapidly going to smash as the day of adjournment approaches and the pet bills upon the passage of which ambitious members had builded their hopes of future political advancement are one by one killed off. Then it must run the gauntlet of the governor at whose hands I am much afraid it will meet defeat. Church never exhibited any particular love for this town.

I enjoyed my stay at the capital pretty well, though I am not particularly in love with the life either of the legislator or of the lobbyist. I rather anticipated that the debates on the floor would fire my ambition but they didn't. You see on nearly all important legislation a combination of some kind or other is put up which is sure either to carry or defeat the bill and the speaker can but feel that his talk is either useless or unnecessary. For myself I never care to talk in any body except to convince. . . .

I came home by way of St. Paul and staid over to hear Patti. It is useless for me to attempt to tell how she sang but it was indeed charming. Her program was much the same as I notice she will shortly present in Chicago. It included "The Last Rose of Summer." She omitted the second stanza of this, however, greatly to my disappointment. She also sang "Home, Sweet Home" and "A Mile from Edinborough Town" upon being re-called. Do you not sing the latter? I could not surmise from what other quarters it appealed so familiarly to me and so admired it doubly because of its associations. They presented some selections from "Semiramide," Patti taking the title role and Mlle. Scalchi the part of Arsace.[1] Patti looked very much a queen only she ought to have longer hair to take the part to perfection. Semiramide would lose half her royalty in my eyes if her hair reached no further than her shoulders.

No, unfortunately we haven't yet arrived at that point when we can always choose which side of a law-suit we shall espouse. I doubt whether any lawyers can always do so.

Tom.

[1] *Semiramide* is an opera by Rossini. Sofia Scalchi was an Italian opera singer.

128

Redfield, March 20, 1887.

My dear Ellen,—

I am a little uncertain as to the present status of our correspondence. I have been expecting a letter from you, though I am not sure that I am entitled to any. Seeing it's Sunday, however, I shall be a good boy and write you at a hazard. . . .

You no doubt learned by the Inter-Ocean of the fate of our court bill. Church is not a name to conjure with in this neighborhood or in any other. Nine members of the council besought him to sign the bill or return it with his reasons but he coolly dropped it into the waste basket and told them he had no time to write veto messages. He assumed a most dictatorial authority over legislation and never a Roman senate was more obsequious to emperor than that chosen from our remarkably independent people to their little Caesar.

I'll keep right on expecting a letter from you daily until it comes to make glad

Your Tom.

129

Chicago, March 27, 1887.

Dear Friend,

Our correspondence has been a little out of line of late, but I shall follow your example and not try to discover the wherefore of the why.

Are you going to flee that "great country" and come back to civilization? When I read about your last blizzard, I felt sorry for you indeed. I had strawberries for lunch yesterday, what do you think of that?

Now, mon ami, I'm afraid you are laughing at me—or trying to get a chance to do so—when you ask my opinion on some law question. You should well know I have no knowledge of the subject, whatever, and the most I can do is to make a guess at the possible or probable result. Still—since you ask me to do so—I'll try to guess. Let me remark, en passant, that some people make a terrible jumble of their affairs if your cases are samples. . . .

Does this effusion make you "glad"?

E.

130

Redfield, April 3, 1887.

My dear Ellen,—

Did my tirade against Church impress you with the idea that I had "soured on" Dakota or that I had builded any hopes on his action as governor? I hasten to correct the idea if you did really entertain any such, because I know it must have been anything but agreeable to you involving as it does a confession on my part that my success in the west did not meet my reasonable expectations. Nothing can be farther from the truth and you can't coax me back with strawberries and lettuce either.

Of course I was only seeking an opportunity to laugh at you in propounding foolish legal problems. My scheme utterly fails, however, I must say with Shylock "your exposition hath been most sound," because you construe the law as I would have it. I'll send you my brief as soon as it is out which will probably be in about three weeks. . . .

You may laugh at me now if you like. I was just about to telegraph and inquire after your health when your last letter came. Please don't allow that to hurry you about answering this though. I need not assure you, however, that your letters never come too soon.

Devotedly yours,
T. J. Walsh.

131

My dear Friend,

No, I did not laugh one bit when I learned that you had intended telegraphing an inquiry about my health. It was awfully good of you. Thanks. My health is very good as usual. I was amused at a remark of our engineer over at the school the other day. I had been putting some music on the board after school, and as it is a rather difficult song it took me some time to put it on, and he met me as I went through the lower hall. In a most ministerial manner he informed me that I "vork" too hard, that I "lose my red cheeks," and that I ought to leave school just as soon as it is dismissed and walk in the sunshine. Which was all very kind, only all a mistake. I don't work hard—don't feel conscious of really working at all—and I'm sure I walk enough. . . .

I did not misunderstand you in regard to your darling Dakota. Never for a moment thought you had ceased to worship at its shrine. Rest assured, my friend, I am convinced that you would die for "the land of your adoption" and regret that you had not two lives that you might try it over. Is that satisfactory?

Carter's dead. Long live the Mayor! [1]

E. C. M.

[1] An apparent reference to the popular mayor, Carter Harrison, who resigned in 1887 to take a trip around the world. His actual death occurred in 1893 when he was again mayor and was assassinated.

132

Redfield, April 17, 1887.

My dear Ellen,—

Your engineer is your true philosopher. Such a round of duties would banish the bloom from any cheeks, only that there is so much variety in it that it may bring a certain amount of rest in its course. I think I'm regaining some of my capacity for work which was rather sadly demoralized about the time I left Madison. I put in a good afternoon's work yesterday, argued six motions. . . . Came out ahead in four of the six cases.

Redfield is going to grow this season. The county seat is beginning to make itself felt. Work on the college and court house will begin at once. A hotel and a wholesale dry-goods house are said to be assured. Nearly fifty residences will be put up. There are a dozen in course of erection now. If we can only manage to capture another rail-road or two a veritable boom will set in.

While away yesterday a gentleman called to see me whom I met at the State Teachers Examination at Madison in '79. He still guides the erring youth, kind Providence pity him. Another young man whom I met at the same time is located at Woonsocket. He's a brighter genius—he quit teaching some time ago. The latter and I became quite intimate. Seven of us, all young men, boarded together on the bank of the third lake. 70% was the awful limit. Three sessions were held daily. At each session a report was made on examinations taken at the second preceding session. The lord high executioner seldom failed to decapitate at least one of our number at each session. Finally only Estee and myself were left and on that last day he fell. He pulled through the next year.

You asked me some time ago, if I had read Ben Hur. I have been reading it, with intense and sustained interest, it is needless to say.

Let me beg you not to think hereafter of answering my letters when you are "just tired to death" or anywhere near that state, even allowing for the hyperbolic expression and feminine exaggeration. Your letters never come too soon nor are they ever too long but pray don't again take time from "nature's sweet restorer" to write them.

Devotedly yours,
T. J. Walsh.

133

Chicago, April 25, 1887.

My dear Friend,

. . . See what an agreeable lawyer I'd make. I am ever so glad the court did not agree with me on the case you stated. Do you always agree with the court? I mean do you always feel that you are the champion of the right side?

Why were you so mysterious about Miss Reed? Isn't she engaged to your friend Mr. Sterling? Don't judge her light and gay manner too harshly. She can be serious enough should occasion demand it I've no doubt. And what if it is not in her character to be "serious"? Should we be judged because we are too grave or too gay, when that manner, like our complexion or the color of our hair, is doubtless perfectly natural? Learn to be lenient in your conclusions. . . .

I must go downtown now. It is almost four P.M. and we rehearse at five. Last Friday I was asked to be the soprano of a new downtown quartette and we hold our first rehearsal today. I have to sing for a while at least, but if I don't like the voices I will withdraw after a time. I know the tenor and alto but the bass I've never seen to my knowledge. The tenor and alto are both good singers in chorus but all voices do not blend well and that is what makes good or poor part singing.

Bye-bye.
E. C. M.

134

Redfield, May 1, 1887.

My dear Ellen,—

 . . . Spencer is becoming quite a favorite with the attorneys. He says that were our town a little larger he would come here to live, and he hasn't yet made up his mind not to. He recognizes that it is the proper place at which to fix his chambers and it would not be surprising if within six months we should become the legal center of the district. Tis a consummation very devoutly to be wished by us.

Large bunches of crocuses could be seen today from the car window growing quite close to the tracks. It robs a wild flower of half its beauty to pluck it, or rather it seems that no matter how unattractive in itself its native setting may be, there invariably arises a harmony, a perfection of arrangement that no human skill can equal. In other words, our flowers must be seen on their native heath in order to be appreciated, or expressed differently, "if the flowers that bloom in the spring have nothing to do with the case," the case has a great deal to do with the flowers that bloom in the spring. But talking of flowers, I am sure you would find them and our fields no less attractive for a short time at least than is "the busy town." I am afraid I shall find it impossible to visit your city before fall or late in the summer. Might it not be possible to entice you out to see them if any of your friends were coming west to spend their vacation?

No I don't always agree with the court. I had a very spirited debate with him the other day. He has a great advantage over a man through "Authority though it err, etc." See almanac. No, consult your memory.

Hope you found your quartette agreeable. Would they sing for me, think you, if I went down?

Good night.
Tom.

135

Chicago, May 10, 1887.

My dear Friend,

I think I shall like our quartette practice very well. The three other voices are certainly good. We sang at the meeting of the Aldini Council of the Royal Arcanum last Wednesday night. The Inter Ocean spoke of it; perhaps you noticed the item.[1] The people seemed much pleased with our singing. I had an invitation last week to join the choir of the M.E. Church, Cor. of Wabash and 14th St., but my teacher does not want me to and I don't care to.

"Couldn't I be enticed to come out to see your flowers?" My dear boy, I couldn't afford to much as I love flowers. I beg your pardon for the familiar mode of address used above. You see I often speak so to my boys at school so I forget myself occasionally. I have not the slightest doubt that your flowers are very lovely, but I think they cannot possibly be as beautiful as that trailing arbutus you sent me from Wisconsin. I never saw anything more deliciously pure in appearance and their fragrance haunts me still.

I had a strange book brought me lately, "The Strange Story of Dr. Jekyll and Mr. Hyde."[2] You ought to read it if you can. . . .

E. C. M.

[1] The notice appeared under a column headed, "Secret Societies," with a subheading for the "Royal Arcanum." It read: "The Aldini Council on Wednesday evening threw open its doors to its lady friends. There was a goodly number present. The programme included quartet singing by Bros. Collins and Marsh and the Misses Parantan and McClements; bass solo by Bro. Collins and recitation by Mrs. C. J. Edwards and Miss Mamie Butler." *Chicago Inter-Ocean*, May 8, 1887, p. 20.

[2] Robert Louis Stevenson's *The Strange Case of Dr. Jekyll and Mr. Hyde* was published in 1886.

136

Yankton, May 15, 1887.

My dear Ellen,—

I think I spoke to you a year ago of the beauty which an abundance of foliage gives to Yankton at this season. By the way, it's just a year ago today I left here for your city. Wish I could start again tonight. . . . They seem to have a passion for lawns too —particularly fresh and rich in color just now and frequently starred with beds of variously colored tulips. You know Yankton is quite an old town. It was made the capital on the organization of the territory in 1861. This brought here people of more or less refinement and though few of them were wealthy or enjoyed large salaries, the "perquisites" were evidently large as many of them have attained a competence and built elegant homes here. It's really funny. You don't expect to meet anyone under the grade of Colonel here. Such an array of ex-generals, ex-judges, ex-governors and ex-cuses, as some smart fellow has said, cannot, I venture to say, be found in any city in the country outside of Kentucky.

I'm reading "Middlemarch." [George] Eliot knew women pretty well and men too for that matter. Not only her reflections, which are always pointed and entertaining, but frequently a trifling incident in the plot or a side remark without which the text would be a matter of indifference to the ordinary observer, shows her wonderful insight into and power of analyzing human character and motives. . . .

I went to hear some music Wednesday evening. They sang

Flotow's "Martha" and to my feeble judgment and comprehension sang it well.[1]

Au revoir.
Tom.

[1] *Martha,* an opera by Friedrich von Flotow, was first produced in 1847 in Vienna.

137

Chicago, May 29, 1887.

Dear Friend,

. . . I am to sing at Oakwood cemetery tomorrow. Our whole society is to take part. We leave here by special train at 8:30 A.M. and are invited to dinner at Kinsley's when we get back. We practiced a good deal last week and that took up some of my time. Oh I must tell you something. I have a new piano, got it yesterday. It is a Chickering upright and has a lovely tone.— I intend to practice a lot this summer.

I am busy now on our graduating program and will soon have the final examinations to amuse me.

E. C. M.

138

Redfield, June 5, 1887.

My dear Ellen,—

Your letter was received but yesterday. I sent you Friday a cluster of prickly pears which may possibly blossom out if exposed to the hot sun. Henry brought them in from the valley about twenty-five miles west. I saw one in bloom yesterday in the same region and from this and what he says the bunch sent you must have been a charming spectacle when plucked from the barrens where it grew. Three of the buds, I think he said, were open when he found it.

I expect to "make a day of it" at Huron next Saturday. Have about half a dozen cases coming up, several of them of considerable importance involving questions of very great importance.

Had to send to Minneapolis for some books I desire to make use of. It's a pesky nuisance trying to practice law without a library. I've exhausted everything in town on one of these cases and am unable to find anything directly upon the point involved either one way or the other. I'm confident that my position is correct but you know an authoritative decision of a court is of so much more significance than the usually prejudiced view of interested counsel. . . .

Two Italians discoursed some very fine music for us here this week on the violin and a harp. We induced them to tarry a day and had them play at an impromptu party on Friday evening. Dancing was the chief feature but they interspersed a few selections so beautifully played that no one thought of dancing. Why is the harp left almost exclusively to these roving foreigners?

Yes you're pretty good to write when you had company but now you'll have to say something awful nice (that's the proper expression I believe) to me for writing the next day after getting your letter after waiting two weeks, and it's awful hot this afternoon too. That sentence is too awful.

So'm I.
Tom.

139

Chicago, June 12, 1887.

My dear Friend,

What do you suppose I've just been doing for the ever-so-manyeth time today? I've been looking at the cactus you sent me. Three of the flowers are fully open. They are very lovely indeed, almost crimson in color, with yellow centers. It was very kind, but just like you to send it. It was quite moist and just as fresh as could be when it reached here. I planted it in a flower-pot immediately and it grows nicely. I am going to take it over to school tomorrow to show it to my pupils for I'm sure they have never seen one like it. Thank you ever so much for it.

And this is your birthday, isn't it? I've been so very busy of late that I haven't even had time to think of my calendar. I hope [it] says something pretty for you. I must look the first thing in the morning. I wish you, mon ami, many happy returns of your birthday, and hope that the coming year may bring you everything it is good for you to have. By the way, have you been learning those quotations? If you have I give up at once and shall have the forfeit (the roses) ready on demand. I shall, however, learn your verse, whatever it may be, when I go over to school.

I spent a couple of hours at school last Saturday and the Saturday before practicing singing with the pupils. I have a chorus of one hundred voices. I will send you a program and an invitation to be there.[1] Wish you could be here. You should live in Chicago. No, you shouldn't either. You have ten times the chance where you are of becoming "famous." Too many striving for everything here. You know I have a very brilliant future in store for you and shall be disappointed if I do not have to "some day" send my congratulations to a future Governor of Dakota. As you are the only person I know who is likely to get there, you must see your duty clear.

You spoke of not having such books as you need at times. I wish I knew enough to consult books for you. I suppose the public library here contains what would aid you. Now vacation is coming and I'll have nothing to do but attend to my music and time will hang heavily on my hands; so if at any time I can be of use to you in consulting books here, let me do it please. If you will tell me as nearly as possible what you want perhaps I may be able to find it for you. . . .[2]

E. C. M.

[1] At Andersen School's closing exercises.

[2] The Chicago Public Library was opened in May, 1874, with a collection of 17,355 volumes. By 1893 it had over 189,000 volumes. Moses and Kirkland (eds.), *History of Chicago*, II, 137-38.

140

Redfield, June 19, 1887.

My dear Ellen,—

All right, I'll take the roses but you must let me buy the candy. I remember most of the January quotation, some in February and without much regard to order a few in March. From that time on, memorizing the tablets ceased to be "a labor of love" in some senses at least, and I got so far behind while away at Yankton that my courage has well nigh failed me. I was unable to find anything very apropos about the sentiment to which the bard treated me. Thanks for your very kind wishes on the occasion of my birthday and the expression of your conviction that I'll "amount to something" some day. Were I in need of an incentive to exertion there could be applied none more powerful than your words. A birthday, at one time, seemed an occasion for congratulation. It is with no small measure of regret I am compelled to reflect that aspirations then indulged are yet far from being reached and hopes which seemed shortly to be gratified still seem but little nearer of attainment. Of one thing perhaps I should be satisfied. I have doubtless reached a clearer appreciation of my abilities and though that knowledge is by no means flattering to them, it may serve to make my efforts to accomplish something more availing.

Believe me, your very kind offer to assist me through your city library is appreciated more than you can know. I shall certainly avail myself of your services as soon as you can spare the time. I can direct you so that in a short time you will find little difficulty in seeking what you are after and finding it if it exists. Your offer comes at an opportune time. I sent to Minneapolis the other day for an opinion in a Kentucky case but they report they are unable to find it. I'll write you about it tomorrow. You must tell me though if the work is tedious or annoying in any way. If you feel any interest in the work and you think I can give you any light on matters that do not seem clear to you, it will be a great pleasure to me to help you if I can.

It would be a great pleasure to me to attend your closing exercises, particularly as they seem to be not quite after the pattern to which such meetings are expected with great regularity to conform. Your music will, I am sure, be well worth listening to. . . .

Obdurately yours,
W. T. J.

141

Dear Friend,

I read your letter in reference to "the law" with great care and shall with the greatest pleasure try my "prentice hand" at looking up what you want. . . . Tuesday and as much more time as may be necessary I shall devote to your case. I only hope I shall be able to do it. I am terribly stupid in some ways.

I am pleased to be able to tell you that our graduating exercises were a perfect success if the comments of our audience are to be relied upon—and our own judgment. My right arm is actually a little lame I find as I reach for my ink bottle and I believe it is the result of the hand-shaking I underwent last Friday night. I wish I could show you my great baskets of flowers and other pretty things, among them a ring set with a ruby, six turquoise, and two pearls, from two of my boys.

E. C. M.

142

Redfield, July 3, 1887.

My dear Ellen,—

The work you sent arrived on Friday evening. The decision seems by its language to sustain our position though the fact that it was rendered on an appeal from the Probate Court instead of in an independent action in another court destroys in some measure its value to us. It must have been an interminable job to copy all that stuff, and not-withstanding your assurances I feel guilty in imposing it upon you. Not because you requested it but because they will be of great value to me I wish you would try to send me for use next Saturday the following: Trabue vs Harris, Metcalfe 597 and Rogers vs Mitchell Ib. 22. The subject in hand is discussed at section 420 as shown by my notes. If you find anything squarely to the point, namely that a presentation is ineffectual unless the claim be properly verified, please make a note of it. Never mind the California decisions. I have access to them and have searched them carefully. You may, however, feel interested to look at Eustace vs Johns 38 Cal. 3. If Zachary vs Chambers

Oregon 321 sheds any light on the question send me a brief synopsis of it. All of the above citations I obtained from the U.S. Digest.

. . . I fear I expressed myself too bluntly about his friend Church the last time we met. It's a weakness I have, but I never yet

Crooked the pregnant hinges of the knee

That thrift may follow fawning,

and I can't do it, nor can I bear to see anyone else do it.

Permit me to express the hope that your vacation may prove an enjoyable period of recreation, much needed I am sure. I had intended to devote this letter to some matters more particularly personal to ourselves but considerations that I shall refer to again moved me to defer for a short time.

You are very, very kind to do all that work for me and I'm more grateful than my language herein and my readiness to impose a new task might lead you to suppose.

Faithfully yours,

T. J. Walsh.

143

Chicago, July 10, 1887.

Dear Friend,

I hope you received the letter I sent you Thursday, in time. As stated in my note I do not know if there was anything of use to you in it but hope that there was. Thanks for your explanation of the difference between payments and offsets. I see my mistake. In writing to you I feel perfectly safe, you see, in expressing what are probably the most erroneous ideas, for I know you will not give them a moments consideration, nor does there exist the slightest fear of your being influenced by them. In this respect you differ greatly from another friend of mine who also is "vastly learned." He is inclined to be influenced by your humble friends opinion and so I am very careful about what I say. . . .

Did you want to get up a counter curiosity on my part when you said you had intended to tell me something (important I judge) about yourselves but decided to defer it. Now I shall be very much interested in anything referring to you and your brother, but I'm going to patiently wait till you unfold the tale. I shall buy out no news-stands.

E. C. M.

144

Redfield, July 17, 1887.

My dear Ellen,—

Your letter enclosing the result of your further labors in the law library came just before my leaving for Huron on Saturday, a week ago. Accept the sincerest thanks of our firm and myself for your very valuable assistance in this matter. We feel a special interest in this case and had no other convenient means of presenting the authorities in support of our position. I regret, though, that you put yourself to so much trouble in the matter. From the notes you sent and a few other decisions fortunately discovered at a late hour, I prepared and filed last Saturday a supplemental brief which ought to sway the court towards the proper conclusion.

We began suit against the Chicago Milwaukee and St. Paul R.R. Co. ten days ago for the modest sum of $10,000 damages for killing a man last spring. The case seems to me a very clear one, though I have learned to doubt the infallibility of my judgment in matters of this kind. At any rate I intend devoting to it every moment I can spare until our next term of court which will be held as soon as the court house is completed, probably about October 1. If you find the work of searching authorities a pleasure rather than a task I shall be pleased to detail the facts to you and call your attention to some works and decisions on the governing principles.

I'm sure you must have been joking when you accused me of treating your suggestions lightly, and if I did please do not allow the fact to deter you from offering any more or from attacking the positions I may take if you feel so disposed and they appear to you unsound. I alluded only a short distance back to the suspicions I entertain as to the soundness of my own judgment. I'm naturally sanguine and though I say it, given to being industrious and energetic. My efforts would be more fruitful had I someone at hand always ready to point out the difficulties of a certain line of action, the error of my reasoning, the obstacles unnoticed until after a fatal conclusion or precipitate action has been resolved upon. Henry is too apt to accept my ideas without question or to scout them without reason. Believe me no flatterer when I say that when you differ your arguments are very convincingly expressed. . . .

Truly yours,
T. J. Walsh.

145

Chicago, August 1, 1887.

Dear Friend,

. . . I am sure you don't really care much about knowing how the teachers looked and acted, but as a punishment I shall try to tell you, though I'm sure I've almost forgotten all about them. At the concert I got a position where I could see them to advantage—up in the gallery, not so near the stage as you sat the night you attended the May Festival. There were over ten thousand people to look down upon and the sight certainly was worth seeing. It was extremely warm, so pretty summer dresses and hats of all colors were out in full force. The ladies outnumbered the gentlemen greatly, so you can imagine the display of feminine toilets. What I noticed most, as something very beautiful, was the display of fans, every shape, size, and hue, and in their constant motion they looked like thousands of huge butterflies hovering among the bright flowers and ribbons that adorned the fair schoolma'ams. . . .

E. C. M.

146

Redfield, August 7, 1887.

My dear Ellen,—

Our common council did me the honor to elect me its official counselor but I promptly declined because the salary didn't suit. I was waited on by a committee last evening to know if I would accept in case the salary were doubled. Considering that there are two other prominent candidates who seek it at the figure I declined the offer is particularly flattering. Guess I'll take it this time.

We have been enjoying a visit of a week from two of our sisters. They admitted being very agreeably disappointed at the appearance of the west, its people, their mode of life, etc. . . .

Tom.

147

Chicago, August 14, 1887.

My dear Friend,

Will you kindly settle the dispute? Did you notice that I spelled your name correctly(?) on the last letter I sent you? What did you think of it? I ask because you said at one time that you had exhausted every device (in vain at that time) to make me spell it that way. Now why did I all at once change my method of spelling the name? [1]

. . . Did I tell you I intend to attend the equestrian school next fall? Quite a party of us are going and one great desire of my younger days will be attained if I become a good rider and I think I will. (Modest, as usual, you will remark.)

Your common council shows itself a very enlightened body. Tell it I think so, will you? I do not agree with you that their proposition is "flattering"—complimentary certainly—but you are never flattered by what you know you deserve.

E. C. M.

[1] One can mildly suspect that Ellen was looking for a proposal and giving a gentle hint. She had learned how to spell "Walsh."

148

Redfield, August 28, 1887.

My dear Ellen,—

Strangely enough I noticed the unusual spelling of my name on your last letter but one before opening it. I say strangely, because I had ceased to think of the matter, in fact notwithstanding anything I may have written it never occupied my thoughts seriously. My elder brother, however, who gets the mail about as often as I do except when in the course of events a letter from Robey St. is expected to be forthcoming, has done no end of worrying about it. I give up your conundrum in regard to your reasons for changing your views of the correct orthography of my patronymic. It would interest me to know however. They are quite as cogent and substantial, I am sure, as those which induced you in the first place to vary from the standard. There isn't any egotism in that remark. It's a privilege I maintain that every man has, to spell his name as he pleases—at least it's a privilege he has in Dakota and exercises with no little frequency.

Our people have taken to the unChristian habit of picnicking on the "Jim" on Sundays. Henry has gone off today to pick wild plums. The banks of the river are very attractive at this season. Wild grape vines hang in profusion from the shrubbery and trees making in many places a complete network. . . .

No, you said nothing about intending to attend a riding academy, though I remember hearing you once express a desire to ride. I've taken to riding quite a little myself this summer, though I'm told in confidence I might be more graceful.

Write me all about your trip and don't fear details.

Tom.

149

Chicago, September 6, 1887.

Dear Friend,

. . . Tell you all about our trip? I don't think I can tonight, but we had a delightful time. There were between one hundred and one hundred and fifty passengers. One of the pleasantest gentlemen aboard was going to remain North for several weeks to hunt and fish. Most of the dear particular souls aboard were afraid of him. They called him the "cow-boy," and of course he did look rather striking. His costume certainly indicated the "wild West," and a rifle and a revolver or two with a belt of cartridges were calculated to inspire awe in the gentle feminine heart. I found him a most interesting person. I don't think I ever laughed more in a given space of time than while talking to him. And do you know, mon ami, something in his looks (his face, I mean) and in the way he laughed and talked reminded me of T. J. Walsh. That reminds me. I am so sorry to have made your brother unhappy by my way of writing your name. It shows how thoughtless I naturally am. Annie noticed the superscription on an envelope one day and asked me if it would not probably cause some remark that you might not like. I resolved to do so no more; hence the change.

E. C. M.

150

Redfield, September 11, 1887.

My dear Ellen,—

You must have had a charming time while away. . . . Henry and a friend of his leave tomorrow for Minneapolis and St. Paul to attend the exposition and state fair and to hear the Booth-Barrett combination play "Julius Caesar." [1] Wish I might go too, but there will be an Exposition at Chicago this year, will there not?

I'm going to defend a case tomorrow which promises to furnish much merriment. It's the funniest affair I have thus far been connected with. Two swains from a neighboring village had made a "match" which didn't seem to please the old folks and to obviate this difficulty had everything arranged to come over here quietly today and wed. The old gentleman runs a hotel and the obnoxious prospective son-in-law boarded with him. The young people had stored the would be bride's trousseau in the daring lover's trunk for use in the emergency, but unlucky step! the old man coolly walked over to the justice's office and got out a warrant charging the youth with larceny of the girl's clothes. For this he must tomorrow still unmarried stand trial before his peers. It seems that as soon as the arrest was made the parties started on a race for my office. The younger man got here first as the elder gentleman learned more in sorrow than in anger about ten minutes later. My sympathies are with the old man. He's very honest and very feeble and his antipathy to my client is, I fear, much, only too well founded. But he's not likely to make much out of his larceny suit and I'll see that he makes no more than there is in it.

I was engaged at the same town Friday afternoon and all day Saturday trying a somewhat notorious case into which I was called after it had been started. It is one of the few cases I won knowing I should have lost. In this case however, the merits were with us but there was a fatal error in the proceeding which I discovered as soon as I took hold, but of which the other side seemed entirely oblivious. Should I have told the court of the defect? Quite a number of circumstances have transpired lately of a very gratifying nature, indicating a probability that at no distant day I may be able to stand on an equal footing with lawyers in the front rank here. I suppose I ought not to say so and there are few to whom I would.

Good-night.
Tom.

¹ Edwin Booth and Lawrence Barrett had been touring the country since 1886 presenting their Shakespearean repertoire.

151

Chicago, September 18, 1887.

Dear Friend,

A remark in your last letter suggests to me that I do doubtless oftener act upon impulse than reason. It had never occurred to me and it shocked me somewhat, honestly, for I do detest a "creature of impulse." I discover daily how more and more I am an erring mortal. . . .

You have doubtless often seen in the papers references to the concerts given by the Apollo Club. It is considered the best of its kind in the U.S. Admission to it is almost impossible to secure without a good deal of influence and yet I have "been accepted" without any influence whatever. Shall I tell you how it happened? I learned that a few voices were needed in the club, so a friend of [mine] and I thought we would go down and ask them to test our voices. It was not the pleasantest ordeal in the world, for each person had to [go] into Apollo Hall and sing before a committee of three. I had to sing a few scales and a portion of "Lohengrin." I didn't sing well at all because I was nervous, but Mr. Tomlins wasn't displeased apparently. Yesterday I got a letter informing me that "the committee" had reported favorably, etc. I am very much pleased for it is the club of the city and has of course the best training.

What you said about your rank as a lawyer does not surprise me in the least and I am glad you felt that your telling it needed no excuse to me. You need never feel that I shall misunderstand what you say. You are very bright, you have an excellent mind and I think it has been wisely guided. Now if I know this, who know you so little, how can you help knowing it yourself? And the knowledge will assist you to even better things. Consciousness of power is always likely to do that, I think, when the mind is well balanced.

Your brother will doubtless enjoy his visit to Minneapolis and St. Paul and he cannot help admiring Booth and Barrett. I've seen both and I think I admired one quite as much as the other. There is a delicacy, a refinement in their acting which is lacking in many players. Henry Irving's acting shows the same quality. Booth uses very few gestures it seems to me in my limited knowledge of him. I shall certainly see them together.

E. C. M.

152

Redfield, September 26, 1887.

My dear Ellen,—

Your letter didn't arrive on Tuesday, but as it was a "long" one and had many other even more meritorious and commendable features I readily gave you credit for your endeavor to gratify my whim. You suggested nothing of the kind, but please entertain no suspicion that I had any intention in anything that was said in my last letter of calling your attention to that impulsiveness of character of which you accuse yourself. Were there no better reason a wholesome dread that my own house might be shattered about my ears would be sufficient to deter me. I shall try to be wholly exempt hereafter from your merited criticism.

. . . Would you believe it, I have no recollection of having prepared a lesson out of school excepting of course the work I did at the University? That was doubtless due, however, to my being so very, very bright, etc., etc. Now isn't there just a little humor in that? I attributed it to the fact that I never disliked to study and always engaged in it with ardor. I never pursued any branch of study without acquiring a liking for it. You said something about a consciousness of power arising from a conviction of one's own talents. Your humble servant fears he is too apt to rate his own higher than they are. I don't know, though. I've never yet undertaken anything without feeling that I knew perfectly well the way I was treading. At least I am never awed in the trial of a case by the magnitude or intricacy of the questions involved or the weight of the counsel on the other side. I think I have another element of strength. I am no copyist—that is I can apply principles, and whether the path is a beaten one or not, the principles being no more involved I can usually see my way clearly enough.

That's certainly enough to say about myself. I'll try to find something else to write about now. Really, you must remember that I have ceased to think much about what would be appropriate for a school library or any other kind except a law library. . . . Make an extensive selection of historical romances. If there is such a book, ancient mythology written on the plan of the funny history of Rome would be read with great profit. You remember Saxe's modern version of some of the Greek myths.

Good-night.
Tom.

153

Chicago, October 1, 1887.

Mr. Walsh,—

It appears that in writing my last "long letter," and in endeavoring to have it reach you by a certain time, I was "gratifying a whim" of yours. Well, mon ami, I write this lengthy missive to "gratify a whim" of my own.

"Now isn't there just a little humor in that?"

I must warn you also against expecting me to "exhibit any repentance" for this act.

E. C. M.

154

Redfield, October 9, 1887.

My dear Miss McClements,—

After so far recovering from the shock incident upon the receipt of your brief note of a week ago as to be able to think consecutively and to reach a rational determination in reference to it, I concluded not to reply earlier than next Sunday, feeling that I should express myself in a manner more worthy after I had felt the full force of "the rod that chasteneth." Your letter left me free, if I read aright, to answer should I see fit, for which, in all sincerity I am humbly thankful. I have no upbraiding to give utterance to. Indeed my sense of my unworthiness and inferiority has been so painfully apparent to me all through the course of our correspondence that your decisive action was not unlooked for. Yet oppressed with this sense and half suspecting that some delinquency on your part might have occurred in order to give me an opportunity to terminate our correspondence, I persevered, much to your annoyance, I now fear, hoping by diligent effort to carve for myself a place in life that I might ask you to share without calling for sacrifice. This hope strengthened and chastened my every effort. I regret very much if it pains you that it should be mentioned and yet I could not leave it unsaid. I have advanced, O, how slowly!! until I almost dared mention my hopes to you. The coming term of court promised opportunities to establish myself in my profession, opportunities I had prepared to improve to the limit of my poor abilities. It promised more, that I should not thereafter be compelled to maintain an eternal warfare with the wolf at the door. I had begun to harbor the idea that the hope long since born, that we might labor together, might possibly reach its fruition. You said on several occasions that I was destined to become famous. I confess I entertained the same hallucination when a boy and in later years felt that if your prediction were to be verified it would be because of your assistance. I knew that you would be an apt student in the law, you said you liked it, and your clear judgment, your quick perception and your surpassing power of expressing yourself tersely and convincingly I recognized as elements that would go far toward making a lawyer of anyone who might draw on them at will and who was constantly subject to their influence.

Better than any other prospect in this day dream was the reflection that we should thoroughly understand each others work and aspirations, that should I advance on the pathway, even slightly, of fame you might justly feel that it was not alone my achievement. Surely I may be pardoned for venturing to lament over such an untimely destruction of most cherished hopes, fondest aspirations and ardent desires. I say untimely. Another reason concurs to make it so. For a long time my friends have been endeavoring to have me appointed assistant U.S. attorney. It has been a source of great gratification to me to see how spontaneous and general has been the demand for my appointment. In my own party everyone in the territory for whose assistance I in any way care, no matter what wing he belongs to, has endorsed my candidacy to which there is practically no opposition.[1] I was almost betrayed into telling you of it, and strengthened by the assurance that were I successful, I should be able to offer you a life somewhat better at least than comparative poverty. I had almost confessed to you that for years I had cherished the hope that you would honor me with your hand in marriage "when my ship came in." Reflecting on the proverbial uncertainty of politician's promises I was unable to muster the courage. . . . I shall now, however, in all probability, remain a private citizen. I wish you hadn't written that concluding paragraph. It has in it too much, much too much, of the utter despair of the motto over the gates Inferno. O, do retract. Say anything else. Do not ask me if I do not mistake my sentiments? They are not the exotic growth of an hour, a passion bred in a brief season to subside as quickly. If separated nearly one thousand miles and nearly two years at a time those sentiments only grow in intensity, how must they not develop nurtured by your immediate and constant presence. They are the necessary growth, permit me to say in humility, of an ardent admiration of your mind and habits. They have become a part of myself. I recognize that I have said but little in this letter. Attribute it in charity to the intensity of my feelings.

I shall await your letter long and longingly, though you said it should not come. Its coming will gratify no whim. It will arouse energies in me thus far only dormant. Ellen, fail not to say you repent.

Tom.

¹ Walsh had been interested in the position of federal attorney for Dakota Territory, or assistant attorney, almost from the time he arrived in Redfield. On February 16, 1885, he wrote to William F. Vilas of Madison, Wisconsin, seeking his support. Vilas had been Walsh's favorite lecturer at the University of Wisconsin and was at this time about to assume the position of Postmaster General in Grover Cleveland's cabinet. Walsh to Vilas, February 16, 1885, William Freeman Vilas Papers, State Historical Society of Wisconsin, Madison.

155

Chicago, October 13, 1887.

My dear Friend,—

Your letter has caused me the deepest regret, the keenest remorse. I could not foresee that you would take so seriously what was at worst but a little exhibition of pique on my part, due to an expression or two used by you in a recent letter. . . . I am as proud as Lucifer, as sensitive as the mimosa. I acknowledge it with regret—and for some reason your words, quoted above, jarred on me and I sent those blank pages as a mild punishment, doubting even that you would feel even a passing regret for having only half a page to read instead of the usual eight. That my action could possibly cause you the sorrow indicated by your last letter, I did not dream. I hasten to assure you of all you ask—that the senseless words are repented of, and that I do retract anything in which you see a meaning deeper than the unworthy aim spoken of above.

You wronged me in that you supposed me capable of wishing to terminate our correspondence in so despicable a manner, and in thinking I sometimes delayed my letters for a like purpose. I should have frankly stated my wishes if I had desired to end our correspondence. Why should I desire it? Our correspondence has been a friendly one; it has been a source of pleasure and profit to me, why should it not continue as long as we are friends.

That any action of mine could cause you a permanent regret, could deaden your ambition, make life worth less to you, I will not believe. If I did, I should indeed be most unhappy.

Of this I must assure you solemnly, you do not know me. How should you? And in the absence of such knowledge you have made for yourself an ideal in which I find no resemblance to myself.

From the tenor of your letter, I judge that your admiration, your conviction that I might in some way aid you in life, rests wholly upon the supposition that I am intellectual. Let me assure you, in all honesty, that the basis is a false one, no structure could stand on it. I am not dull I know, but my mind is only mediocre at best. For your good opinion I thank you but it is not founded in fact.

I can write no more tonight. We had company till a short time ago, and I had to sing of course. I have an invitation to a party tonight and shall go now. There I shall also sing, of course, people like to have their company entertained, but I'll own to you I do not feel in a singing mood.

Sincerely your friend,
E. C. M.

It would be madness for you to decline that appointment. "Your life is *your* life" and it is your duty to make the most of it and of the talents that have been given you.

156

Redfield, October 20, 1887.

My dear Ellen,—

Your brief letter of a week ago awaited me on my return from Huron on Sunday and I embrace this first opportunity to reply. I shall say nothing of the world of light and gladness your note let in upon my clouded spirits in assuring me that I had not forfeited your friendship and esteem, even though it failed to lend any encouragement to other cherished hopes divulged in my last. . . .

Another matter referred to in your letter I must notice, namely that I am in error as to your intellectual abilities a false admiration for which you assumed was the foundation of my devotion. Only a short time ago in the sweetest way, you did me the credit to say that I must be conscious of my own abilities. Why, pray, should I be less discerning as to yours, or my judgment be at fault in the one case and not in the other, unless indeed your other assumption that my admiration is founded on a conviction of your intellectual superiority is erroneous? It is. I assure you. It is only one of many traits that challenged my admiration since first I knew you, that have made you queen of every castle my matured fancy has constructed, where you have reigned supreme without a rival. Nor have I any fear that these are any more imaginary than your intellectual attainments. 'Tis true our opportunities for cultivating each other's acquaintance have been slight. Yet they have been amply sufficient to imbue me with an attachment, an affection ardent and uncompromising and a conviction that life's greatest possibilities are attainable only with your aid. Love seems a vulgar term to apply to such a faith. I dare not entertain a hope that I might so fill your thoughts, yet to hear you say it would be an inspiration. I have no right to exact any promises and I will not; but having spoken freely, even though an unfortunate misapprehension may have occasioned my confession will you not say at least that I may hope to win a place in your heart like that you've found in mine?

This may yet reach you by Sunday. If it does I'll get a long letter. My partiality for that vanity hasn't yet abated you see.

I should indeed feel sad if my letter should have deprived anyone of the pleasure of hearing you sing. After astonishment at a late unfortunate circumstance had been succeeded by the deepest sorrow, I said to myself "I wish I could hear her sing."

T. J. Walsh.

157

Chicago, October 30, 1887.

My dear Friend,—

Your letter did not get here till Monday so that is one of the reasons why you have not received your "long letter" sooner. Nor am I quite sure this will be a lengthy epistle. There is plenty to be said—too much—but I fear me I shall find great difficulty in saying it.

It sounds stereotyped, I know, to say that the contents of your last two letters took me by surprise, but it is true never the less. That I should have become to you all that you say, gives me both pain and pleasure. Pleasure, in that you have so honored me, pain, because I fear I shall have to give pain to you. It is only just that I should be perfectly frank with you and if I hurt your feelings you may rest assured you do not suffer alone.

I have no doubt that most young ladies give a good deal of thought to a probable settlement in life, but I can say truly the subject has never been of interest to me. A few times I have been compelled to contemplate the possibility of such a situation for myself, but I confess to you that it has been with an inward smile, almost derisive at the absurdity of the thought. Even mamma (that most quiet of little women) has chided me for my lack of seriousness in affairs of the heart. Why should it seem absurd, unless they are right who have pronounced me unfeeling, hard-hearted, heartless, cold, selfish, and all the other uncomplimentary things you can think of. Don't you see, you do not know me? What are you going to call me? I'll tell you one thing, as a secret you know, whatever you may decide upon, it will be the first time I've cared anything about the verdict.

That my last letter was some comfort to you makes me glad. How could you for a moment imagine that you had done anything to forfeit my esteem and friendship?

You say my letter was lacking in one respect. I knew it, and felt like apologizing when I wrote for not referring to certain disclosures in your letter. But how could I do so? You spoke of what you had intended doing. Could I take it for granted you were still of the same mind?

I scarcely know in what words to thank you for the honor you do me in giving me so high a place in your esteem and affections. I felt humbled by your words. What have I ever done to merit such a judgment from you? Talked to you in my customary common-place way for perhaps a half-dozen hours in my life? Written you an alarming number of letters, often in the most wretchedly careless manner? I will say no more, however, against your opinion. Do so many value me highly that I can afford to convince one that he is mistaken?

With my whole heart (if I have one) do I thank you for all you have assured me of, your esteem, your affection, your faith in the good you think I might be to you. Of myself, of my feelings toward you I know not what to say. I fear that my regard for you, great as it is, is not of the kind you desire. It seems brutal to say so, but I like you too well to deceive you. I will say to you more than I've ever said to anyone else, I wish I could conscientiously give you the answer that would please you. I would not wrong you by trying to impose upon you that which would be less than a full equivalent for what you give.

Do not, I beg, form any wrong theory in this matter. I fear you may do so because in a recent letter you said something unworthy of your intelligence—something about "feeling your inferiority, etc." I know no one whom I respect and honor more; no one who could honor me more than you have done in desiring my love.

You ask for no promise, nor could I make any, but I do want you to know that I like you ever and ever so much; that I think you good and kind and noble and that the woman of your choice will be fortunate. Don't imagine that I am that one irrevocably. You may perhaps congratulate yourself on your escape. I am scarcely to blame if I cannot love people upon demand. For once, I do consider it my misfortune, however.

Yours sincerely,
Ellen C. McClements.

158

Redfield, November 6, 1887.

My dear Ellen,—

For the frank, generous and inspiring words of your letter of a week ago I lose no time in expressing my sincerest gratitude. Whatever shall be your verdict they will ever abide with me as a comforting assurance of a passion not vainly spent, an ambition not wholly ungratified. . . . Shall I not also take comfort from my meagre victory? You see I have no hard names to call you. If those wild hopes of which my better judgment told me there was no foundation—that I might have inspired you with a sentiment tenderer than esteem—have proven to be vain, it argues my unworthiness rather than your lack of heart.

Hear then my verdict. For in so much as I can but consider the qualified love you express as more than the equivalent of my "all," as priceless as mine is unstinted, I ask that in your own time you pledge it to me at the altar and become my wife, accepting in return my deepest earthly affection and devotion. I had rather tell you this than write it. 'Twould be sweeter to hear you say simply "Yes" than to read it. If "No" is your answer I might persuade. But I could only protest my love and of that I know you are assured. It is all I have to offer.

My former letters disclosed how much your answer means to me. I feel that since the receipt of your last letter I may say to you freely that I am ambitious beyond anything which fires most young men, and I say with pleasure that my ambition does not take the vulgar course of hunger after official position. You once said my mind had been well directed. The compliment was greater even than you intended since I have always been my own teacher, if such a thing can be. However that may be, my ambition has been chastened until my energies have become centered in an endeavor to rise in my profession. If official distinction comes as a consequence it is welcome. It shall never be sought after. And one of the most encouraging signs that my ambition in this direction is not hopeless is that it is being begun to be recognized that therein lies my chief hopes and that I am making a determined effort in that direction. . . . Well all this means that I am hopeful as well as ambitious, and I recognize as my greatest need someone who can work with me, who can drive me by argument from untenable positions, and assist me to clothe in convincing language the reasons I can urge for my own views. You can not drive me from my conviction that you are preeminently fitted for work of this character. And it is such qualities as these, not meretricious or subject to decay, that gained my admiration and now command my love.

By your leave

I subscribe myself,
T. J. Walsh.

159

Chicago, November 13, 1887.
My dear Friend,—

Now that last letter was the result of serious thought and see how it failed to show you the error of your way. You are slightly terrible, are you not? Didn't I explain everything in a highly satisfactory manner and you reply by saying over again just what you said before—only worse—and you make me say over again just what I said before, only I shall certainly convince you this time. I'm sure I thought last week's letter would do so, but your evident non-conversion argues poorly for certain powers you say I possess. Don't you see?

O dear! O, dear! (I don't mean you.) What shall I say to convince you that you would be a most miserable "critter" with me for a "blessing" (?). You are, perhaps generous in being willing to accept my esteem and deep friendly regard in exchange for your "deepest earthly affection and devotion" (for the offer of which I am truly thankful), but did it occur to you that I am almost austerely just and that the compact might not come up to my idea of what is right? It seems to me that a deep and abiding affection on both sides is the only safeguard against unhappiness. Since I came to this city I have seen a few instances of what would be misery, if not death, to me if I were so situated. At home, my father and mother never differed, but at Mrs. ——'s the unfeeling remarks and bitter tones astonished me beyond measure and fairly made me sick. They laughed and jested over those unpleasantnesses afterwards as though they were humorous. I thought they were brutal. I made a remark then that has ever since been a subject of jest with my friends here—that if ever I married a man I should leave him the first time he ever spoke an unkind word to me. Don't you see what a terror I would be to undertake. Are you not intimidated? Of course this is all nonsense and has nothing to do with you or me, but, honestly, little things that I've heard friends of mine say to each other have led me to decide pretty definitely that the life of an independent school-ma'am is not the least enviable on earth.

I do agree with you that we have many tastes in common but there are some points upon which we should surely differ, some very dangerous points some would say. For instance you mention the altar. Did it occur to you that right here we should differ? Don't imagine I do not believe in altars in some things pertaining to them, but you are, I believe, a Catholic. I am not and could never be one. That you are one is all right, that would make no difference to me, but I have known some Catholics too well not to know it would make a difference to you that I did not profess the same belief. Don't think me a pagan. I have the greatest reverence for true piety, under any name; my faith is as calm as the deep sea, as fixed as the hills, but it is too catholic to permit me to be a Catholic. I believe, however, that everyone has a right to his own belief.

Another thought suggests itself. Long ago, when I first met you I heard Mary mention your age and am led to believe that there is too little difference in our ages. . . . Again do I feel constrained to refer to your hallucination in regard to my mental abilities. It strikes me, knowing my own attainments, that it would be rather a risk for me to undertake to fill the position of your advisor in chief, so to speak.

I began thinking and doing for myself when very young, and, to tell the truth, it would hardly suit me to settle down as the mere housekeeper of even the best and wisest man in the world. I never for a moment supposed, however, that you are one of those men who thinks a woman's mind is best and most fittingly employed in planning the bill of fare for the next day's dinner. Let me remark also that I think the woman who cannot get up a good dinner—should occasion demand it—must be an idiot.

Were I convinced that it would be best, there would be, I confess, a certain fascination for me in what you propose, but in the face of all I have stated, I dare not say the "Yes" that you would rather "hear than read."

Do you know, mon ami, I think your chances of a written yes were greater than of a spoken one. You, my correspondent, are my very dear friend; the you that your associates know, I hardly know at all. For that reason, I think I could not speak to you as familiarly as I have written.

I smiled in reading your last letter at your confession that you are ambitious. Did you imagine that a revelation to me? Why I have known that as long as I've known you, and it was due to that knowledge that I so often spoke what was never flattery. I, who have always been praised far beyond my desert, do know that appreciation so expressed has its value and I rarely withhold it. Herein lies both my fault (if it is one) and my excuse. When I predicted your future success I always thought of you as my valued correspondent whose success would give so much pleasure to his friend (myself).

Your friend,
E. C. M.

160

Redfield, November 30, 1887.

My dear Miss McClements,—

I believe I comprehend, indeed I am sure, I am quite convinced. Let me tell you how I analyzed your reasons next morning after receiving your letter, under the bracing effect of an hour's ride and a breeze characteristic of our country and the season. You wouldn't ordinarily consider these influences as very conducive to humor, would you? Not the circumstances. But it was so and I almost laughed aloud as I thought how you had urged.

1. I'm too religious.
2. I'm too fresh.
3. You'd rather be an old maid anyway.

Why didn't you mention our disproportionate avoirdupois or the lack of harmony in the color of our eyes or something really substantial? Don't be alarmed. I'm not going to attempt to reason you out of your determination. I had never thought of your supporting it by reasons. . . . Let me with these words dismiss a matter which for obvious reasons I dwell on with no pleasure. Should I ever reach such a station in life as nature and education fitted you to adorn, and you adhere to your determination as resolutely as I shall to mine, I shall assume the liberty of re-engaging your attention with the matter referred to. Although in many of the affairs of life—in too many—my character lacks that fixedness of purpose, that unbending resolution which makes men loved as well as honored, in those matters which give color to my life and awake my higher emotions there exists at least some of the Roman in me.

Now I'll try to write such a letter as I used to—not that there was anything very commendable in the matter or the style either, but you once said you derived pleasure and profit from them. Court sits on Tuesday. I have made every preparation that my limited opportunities would permit and feel reasonably well satisfied. It must be a source of great satisfaction to have access to a complete library in the preparation of the case, that you may know just what law your opponent is able to produce against you and not be continually harassed with the suspicion that there may be decisions directly in point while the adjudications at your command bear only remotely on the issues. . . .

Our college building is almost completed and presents an appearance far surpassing what I had supposed it was contemplated to build. Miss Gaff "of Cincinnati and Leipsig" arrived last week to take charge of "The Conservatory of Music." . . .[1]

I shall be delighted to read your account of the reception of the president and his wife—more than delighted—and there may be some conflicting emotions, because I shall read your letters no more—not now. I shall still hope to again in that uncertain future to which I have herein above referred. I now embrace the provision of our original agreement in reference to the termination of our correspondence. I shall find some means to communicate to you the outcome of your probate case should it prove favorable to us. Should I visit your city this winter as I expect to, you will not deny me the privilege of calling on you, I trust. Let me say in justice to myself that my Ellen is not a Marjorie Daw built up by your letters,[2] but were she so it would do them no more than justice. They have been treasures to me which I now abandon from a sense of duty to myself and to you of which I am unable to divest myself, whatever may be my feelings, and with regret made poignant with the severest disappointment of a somewhat unsuccessful life.

I am still
Devotedly yours,
T. J. Walsh.

[1] Efforts to identify Miss Gaff (or Goff) have been unsuccessful.

[2] A reference to *Marjorie Daw and Other People,* by Thomas Bailey Aldrich (Boston, 1873). The story concerned a wholly fictitious character developed by one correspondent to another, who was invalided, in the effort to fill his hours with pleasant images of a beautiful girl.

161

Chicago, December 6, 1887.

My dear Friend,—

I trust you will forgive me for making you read another letter of mine (that is if you do read it, you may return it unopened).

Your last letter surprised me beyond expression and wounded my feelings deeply. I now believe that language is intended to conceal rather than to express thought, since you so misconstrued my letter. Did it then seem a cold, calculating, selfish epistle? Yet as I have since thought over its contents, I think I can truthfully say that of myself, of my own interest, I thought very little. You remember three "reasons" which you said I "urged" in my last letter? Perhaps if I speak of them you may see my motive more clearly. I do not like to be misunderstood. 1st—You are "too religious." Did I say so. Strange! as I do not measure a man's piety by the number of services he has attended. I doubt not I am quite as religious as you.

Your severe rebuke in reference to my having given "reasons" for my "determination" (did I express any determination?) was perhaps a little hard—more so than you intended, I believe, or I should not be writing this, and it is hard, too, to have to explain. Do you know, mon ami, I at first intended to give you, in my last letter, the promise you asked for, and then came the thought "better not, he knows me so little, and there will be so many things to surprise and disappoint him." Influenced by that fear I wrote those reasons which unfortunately seemed to you almost out of taste. Had you replied that the differences I mentioned were immaterial to you, you might have had the assurance you wished by return mail.

My grandfather was a Presbyterian minister who preached for nearly half a century in the north of Ireland. He was a Scotchman, however, and was taken back to the Scotch highlands for burial when he died. So, you see, it is not entirely strange that I do or do not believe certain things. When you wrote, I am sorry you forgot that I found no fault with what you might believe in. The short-coming was in my self.

2nd—You are "too fresh." Is it possible I used that expression? It must have been in a moment of mental aberration for I do not even know what it means. Does it mean the same as that horrid slang "verdant"? or does it mean "young"? Surely you must have known I had no reference to your age as being not just right. I meant simply this. Suppose we are now about the same age. It is said a woman ages more rapidly than a man. Well, ten years hence, do I want any man to regret (when he looks upon my snow-white locks) that he did not marry a Miss of "sweet sixteen"?

3rd—I'd "rather be an old maid anyway." Not if I know it. I hate the species. I never had the remotest intention of remaining a member of that noble army.

Now I have "done up" your reasons. I'll try to write of something else, imitating your example, you see. First, however, I must give my "reasons" for forcing this letter upon you at this time. Knowing how much you dislike reasons, I ask your indulgence just this once.

Thanks to your last letter, since its receipt I have had before me an ever-present picture of you riding over that bleak prairie road, with the icy air around you, and at your kind, true heart the chill of the "severest disappointment" of your life—and I the cause. I cannot bear to think of it. It has made me terribly sorry, but I did not know you would take my letter as you did.

Another reason—and I'd like to know how you are going to explain yourself. You tell me that should you ever reach such a position in life as I am fitted to adorn (taffy) etc. you will speak to me again on a certain subject. What does the above indicate? That you have too poor an opinion of me or that I have too good a one of you. If you think me the kind of woman to be led to accept a man for his position, you do wrong me, Brutus; and if you are the kind of man to want such a woman, I have not so thought you.

Finally—the "something else" that I promised to write. My letters have often surprised you. Let me hope that this will not be entirely disagreeable.

Mon ami, I have tried to tell you how full of faults I am, how over-kind are all your estimates of me. I have not pretended that my affection is a "grande passion," as the French say. Perhaps, I am incapable of feelings so absorbing, or like the builders of old who "builded better than they knew," perhaps my love is greater than I know—certainly none of it has ever been wasted. I can assure you of this at least, and I am a severe critic. Of all men whom I know or have known, there is but one of whom I have not thought at some time, "You do not fill the niche in which I placed you." You are that one, and if you don't mind about the awful things I've warned you to expect of me, and if you wish it very much, why "some day"

> "I will follow thee, my Tom,
> To the land they call Dakota."

Yours,
Ellen.

162

My dear Ellen,—

My calendar for Friday, the day your letter arrived, says that "Fortune brings in some boats that are not steered." My ship I had supposed had gone down to destruction freighted with the dearest hopes I cherished. Surely the fickle dame must have seized the helm when I abandoned her. Strange, too. Fortune and I never were friends before. Only when I read your closing sentences did I fully appreciate how much I had asked of you and my conscience smote me lest your compliance might have sprung from the intensity of my desire rather than from your own choice. They reassured me however, and I've been supremely happy since, equally so from the fact that I had not as yet in your estimation fallen short of your ideal, as from the revival of the hopes crushed by your last letter and buried, as I supposed, in my own. For although I spoke of recalling your attention to the matter at some time in the indefinite future, there remained in my bosom hardly the ghost of a hope that I should be successful. And that suggests the desire you expressed that I should explain that passage in my last. 'Twas very kind in you to assume that I had an explanation and that it bore no connection to the suppositions you discard. I am sure though, that even were there some bitterness in the remark or in any portion of my letter you would not fail to find an excuse for it in my deep despair. But there was not—at least not in that portion. I was about to add to the sentence to which you referred something like this. "You will probably scorn my offer then as you do now, but I shall have made some atonement for presuming to thrust upon you such poor gifts as I can now offer." I didn't write it because I thought it might grieve you and I knew you would do me the justice to believe that the possible constructions at which you hint, and of which the passage was certainly susceptible, were quite impossible because beneath me. . . . So much for explanations which I hope will make some amends for the injury inflicted unwittingly by the langauge of my last which it seems did rather conceal than express my thoughts.

Self-made men are said ordinarily to have too supreme a regard for their maker. We are all somewhat prone to over-estimate our own works. I might answer with these remarks your saying that I had met your expectations, had you any reason for believing, as the fact is, that in that result you, yourself, were no unimportant factor. For the further assurances you require of me, I'll answer that if I shall find it possible to extricate myself from the labyrinth of referee trials motions, at chambers, and accumulated business generally in which I now find myself involved (and it now seems likely that I shall before the 22nd instant) I shall leave on that day for Chicago, and let my coming answer that "there is no terror in your threats." But whether I come or no they will still be regarded as the idle wind.

You didn't say in response to my request that I might call upon you when in the city, but applying the rules of legal construction to your letter, as much might be reasonably inferred and I shall act accordingly unless you direct otherwise.

O, you forgot to tell me about the president's reception. Do you know that I had no other idea when your letter was handed me than that it was devoted wholly or almost wholly to that subject. . . .

That was a pretty conceit of the rose. It is delightfully fragrant still, not more so however than the words it can not hide. I'll ever, hereafter, regard a rose with increased favor.

Time will be leaden-winged until I am able to get away. 'Twould aid its flight if I got another letter soon.

Devotedly yours,
Tom.

163

Chicago, December 18, 1887.

My dear Friend,—

Something in your last letter suggested that you would like me to write again before you leave Dakota. So you are really coming to the city again, and I "didn't say that you might call," in response to your "request." You didn't request, allow me to state. You said you hoped I would not deny you the privilege, etc. That was not an interrogation and I answer only interrogations. Being a legal gentleman I suppose I cannot prevent you from applying the rules of legal construction to my last letter and shall be looking for you. Of course you must take dinner with us on Christmas if you have not promised anyone else. And if you are in town on the 29th, I'd like you to go to the Apollo concert with me, if you will be so kind. We are to sing "The Messiah" and it is wonderfully grand you know.

Did you for a moment imagine I would write you another letter after what you said just to tell you about the Cleveland Reception! Hardly. It made me smile to think how astonished you must have been when you read the letter. I wish I might have seen your face. That was a little strange about the calendar, wasn't it. At least the way in which you put it seems so.[1]

> Yours sincerely,
> Ellen.

[1] Walsh visited in Chicago, as the letters indicated he would. While there "he was stricken with pneumonia" and stayed in the McClements' home, where Ellen, her sisters, and her mother took care of him. He could not return to Dakota for weeks. Statement of Mrs. Genevieve Walsh Gudger, along with her copy of the letters.

164

Chicago, February 2, 1888, 17° below.

Mon Ami,—

When I got home this evening I was surprised to find your letter.[1] I was frightened for the moment, fearing you might be ill. If I was surprised, I was also very glad to receive it, as I had already counted up the days and found the chances nil for receiving a letter before the middle of next week.

It seems a mere fancy that you were right here so short a while ago. Mamma said, too after you left, that the house felt as though there was no one in it. . . .

> Bye-bye.
> Len.

[1] Walsh, en route home, wrote a letter which is missing from the collection.

165

Dear Ellen,—

I have just arrived suffering in no way from my trip—not even the least bit tired. Indeed I am surprised that I feel so well after the long ride—particularly as I did an appalling amount of running around yesterday, fresh "obstacles" presenting themselves at every turn. . . . You see the trains running on the east side of the river had all left before I reached Lacrosse [Wisconsin]. I was under the necessity, therefore of going down on the west side and crossing by team.[1] The drive was very pretty, the most of the way along the base of towering cliffs and bluffs.

Henry is away behind with the office work, but I shall observe your caution and not attempt to do a thing until I have fully recovered. There's no escaping going to Bismarck though. I'll take care, however that I do not catch cold and the work will be very light.

I shall expect a letter by the time of my return from B.

Ever yours,
Tom.

[1] This indicates that the route lay south and then west again on the Chicago, Milwaukee, and St. Paul Railway.

166

Chicago, Feb. 7, 1888.

My dear Friend,—

I am very glad indeed that you felt so well after your journey, but you must not let your feelings of returning strength induce you to be less careful of yourself. You must take every precaution to avoid taking even a slight cold this winter—and don't you forget it.

Went down to rehearsal as usual. Sang Mendelssohn's "Hymn of Praise." It contains some admirable effects. One chorus certainly equals Berlioz' most thunderingly startling climaxes. Received an invitation to "assist at the Music Teachers' National Convention" next July. . . . They intend to devote a good deal of attention to American music, I believe, but I don't know as that's to be commended from any but a national standpoint. I shall not respond to that invitation as I should then have to attend rehearsals regularly. Mr. Tomlins is very anxious that at least one hundred and fifty of the Apollos join, and I shall go with that crowd as "the Apollos" will not have to attend all the rehearsals. I remember how provoked we were at the May Festival when, toward the last, the august Apollos joined us and sang no end of false notes into our ears. I shall know the feelings of the "ordinaries" when we enter the last rehearsals next summer.

Yours,

E.

167

Redfield, February 14, 1888.

My dear Ellen,—

I returned Wednesday, not from Bismarck but from Oakes. Did you know that oakes grew right on our open prairie. Fact. Must be a delightful place in which to tarry, you'll admit. Well, I tarried there. Owing to the delay of our train we failed to catch the N.P. regular and were obliged to resign ourselves to waiting twenty-four hours for the next train. The landlord expressed great regret that it was not the next succeeding evening we "got left" because they were to have a masquerade dance at the hotel. I didn't take kindly to the idea that evening but the next forenoon I began to think very seriously of staying for the dance and towards evening nothing could induce me to go on. Mr. Matthews of Brookings and Mr. Gamble of Yankton, fellow-travelers, kindly consented to look after my business in the supreme court. As the evening wore on I grew intensely interested in the dance.[1] The dulcet tones of the tuba and the "shrill piping of the wry-necked fife" or some other equally melodious instrument came stealing into my room at an early hour and I listened to them with the greatest eagerness until nearly sunrise. O music hath charms to soothe the savage soul. I grew very much attached to Oakes, so much so, that I sent out for a physician who advised me that the climate of Oakes was just what was needed for my enfeebled condition and advised me that I mustn't think of going home for another day at least.

You've guessed, of course, that this is all gammon. I've been desperately sick again, probably caught cold, though my lungs were entirely unaffected. They treated me well at Oakes but 32 degrees below zero didn't deter me from starting out Wednesday morning. . . . I've just been easing my mind to our landlord on the so-called meals they have been furnishing me. I'm going to board with a lady friend [Ellen McClements?] hereafter for a few months anyway. . . . It was foolhardy to attempt to go to Bismarck and I ought to have known it.

. . . Of course Irving's "Faust" is not Goethe's Faust, not anything like it, but he certainly hasn't improved on the original, either in the title character nor in Mephistopheles. The latter is the inferior character in the original, you know, and of course isn't equal to Milton's Satan. Still Goethe's creation is a consistent being. He possesses qualities you can define. I do not think Irving's meph. answers either test.

Three times as many words as this letter contains will be much sweetness long drawn out.

Sincerely yours,
Tom.

[1] John R. Gamble was a former member of the territorial council from Yankton. George A. Matthews had been elected to the same body in 1886.

168

Chicago, February 20, 1888.

Dear Tom,—

I think I need scarcely tell you how very, very sorry I was to have my fears confirmed by the letter received yesterday. Yet, I knew you were sick.

Why did you write in that way about yourself? It was just a little cruel I think. I read a letter as I read a book, and never look ahead to see what is coming, so, feeling as I did almost certain that you were sick, the first part of your letter puzzled me. I mistrusted a little, however, even your joke about the "oakes that grew up on your prairies." For a moment I was almost deceived about the dance, only mildly surprised at your suddenly devel-

159

oped admiration of the "light fantastic," and not mildly desirous of—well I'll say of asking you whether you thought dancing a good pastime to indulge in after being so sick.

Mon ami, why will you do those things which you know you ought not to do? What is "supreme court work," or any "reasons" under heaven, when compared with your welfare, with your health? Nothing!

I want to know what you meant by writing me such a long letter? Irving be hanged (excuse me but he must be sacrificed to my present feelings). I know what you wrote was good and all true too, but also know how tired you must have been after writing that letter. Please to remember that for the present I haven't time to read long letters though I'll write you two a week if you would like me to and if you can find nothing better to read. If you will write me just a little letter when you get this, and not wait till next Sunday it will please me. I'll tell you all the highly interesting news I can think of in answer to the little letter you will write me. . . .

Yours,
Ellen.

169

Redfield, February 19, 1888.

My dear Ellen,—

This is just to assure you that I'm getting on very nicely, go regularly to meals, about three blocks away, and eat heartily. Wish I might say that I'm quite strong again, but can't do so truthfully yet. However, I have every reason to be thankful for the progress I have made. Another week's rest will doubtless do much to bolster me up.

I can readily believe your house is haunted. I'm there in spirit most of the time. And they do "miss me when I'm gone," do they? Your mother was very, very kind to me. I almost believe she grew fond of me. Hasten the day when we shan't be rudely awakened from day-dreams of our late happy companionship by the reflection that there are nearly a thousand miles between us!

By the way Mr. Matthews succeeded with my motion quite beyond my expectations. He got an order sustaining it with $224 damages for the delay. This snug little sum with $300 more, our regular commission, makes this case net us a fee not wholly inconsiderable even for city practitioners. It is the largest we had yet realized out of any one case. Six cases for trial are awaiting my pleasure. . . . A term of court is about to be called, we are told, for Faulk county. We have several cases for trial and I shall probably try a number of cases for one of the leading firms out there. How would you like to be a lawyer and be under the necessity, actual or supposed, of being obliged to call in someone else to try the cases for you? It's a very satisfactory kind of practice for the senior counsel—all the glory of victory and no responsibility in case of defeat.

Mr. Dawes, one of our bankers, has been at Pierre the past week drilling a local opera company in "The Little Tycoon" in which Mr. D. appeared as General Knickerbocker. It was repeated "by request" and sung very nicely it is said. Dawes hasn't a very good voice but would rather sing than eat and he has some dramatic talent and a knack of organizing. He sang the same part when this opera was rendered here a year ago and strutted his brief hour with me the year before.[1]

Bye-bye.
Tom.

[1] Fred A. Dawes was manager of the Spink County Bank in Redfield and a cousin of Charles G. Dawes, later Vice President of the United States. Harlow, *Prairie Echoes*, pp. 24, 263.

170

Redfield, February 22, 1888.

My dear Ellen,—

Although my letter of Sunday will tell you all you wanted to know through that little one, I'll write today to tell you that I would like to have you write twice a week or every day if you can find time and that I can find nothing I should rather read. Also, that there wasn't the slightest occasion for my being scolded for writing about Faust and Irving. Far from tiring me it was a pleasant recreation and I didn't have to think at all, only to write, what I had thought before.

I shan't attempt to justify my mystical way of apprising you of my relapse . . . [*editor's omission*]. I was amused at a coincidence though. Like you I always read right on. I've mentioned to you how little prepared I was to hear the things that were said in a certain letter you wrote before the holidays—that one that didn't tell about the President's reception, and which, I pray, neither of us shall ever have occasion to regret even for a moment was written. Well, I read on and on, each moment growing more and more puzzled, seeking some well merited lashing of my many shortcomings, expecting anything but the hallowed words I found, until—well I didn't cry but I couldn't read any more and had only a vague general idea of what was on the last page. . . .

Masquerade here tonight. No, don't fear, I'm not going. One in a season is about all I can endure.

Your sick boy,
Tom.

171

Chicago, February 24, 1888.

Dear Friend,

I was very glad to learn from your letter of Sunday that you were feeling so well and from your letter received today that you are "picking up." If you had not had so much of that article which we can "best spare our friends"—good counsel—I should remark that because you are getting stronger is no reason why you should begin to be reckless.

No, Sir, I'm not going to own to you how really excellent I thought your remarks about "Faust" and the players, so you need not speak of "the weakness and incoherency" of what you wrote. Besides I'm not in an amiable mood tonight. I'm on the sick list myself—too much after-midnight repose and none before it, I guess. . . .

Sincerely,
E.

172

Redfield, Saturday, March 1, 1888.

Dear Ellen,—

We have not had any through mail for ten days. Your letters are probably held somewhere in the storm-swept region between the Dakota line and Chicago.

I am going to Huron this morning and may not return until Monday. I'll bribe our postmaster to send this letter south on the Milwaukee tomorrow morning. Have time now only to say that I'm getting on famously, doing a little work now and then only. . . .

Tom.

173

Redfield, March 7, 1888.

Dear Ellen,—

Our protracted blockade was raised Monday and your letter of the 25th came that day by way of St. Paul. The papers telling of the Apollo concert came this morning. . . .

Didn't you say that you had been entertained with Ramona? Well I was too, with the first part. I liked to learn of the life and customs of those people and the nature of that region lately come into such marked prominence. But the opening chapters led me to expect a better argument and conclusion. I have no patience with people who give up at trials such as overcame the chief characters in Ramona. Now, don't laugh while I ask in all seriousness why they didn't hire a lawyer. I'm sure the Mexican treaty contained a clause confirming all Mexican grants and titles and if it didn't, the blame should fall on the Mexicans, not on the Americans.[1]

I wrote you a short time ago of the approaching retirement of Judge Palmer of the Supreme Court. Well, his time has expired and Mr. Carland of Bismarck, the present U.S. Attorney, has [been] appointed to succeed him.[2] This creates a vacancy in the attorneyship. I was alone in the office yesterday morning when a gentleman came in and introduced himself. I recognized the name at once as that of a prominent federal official and a politician of territorial reputation at least. He proceeded at once to review the situation and said that taking central Dakota (which had peculiar claims) or the whole territory into consideration I ought to get the appointment. He begged me to allow him to present my name and said he had friends in Washington who could do a great deal. Now isn't that something of which one may feel rather proud without being exactly vain? All he knows about me is what he has heard and he travels around quite a little. Of course I expressed my appreciation of and gratitude for his interest in me but told him only that I'd think about it. I'm still thinking. I might possibly overcome my excessive antipathy to asking people to assist me and go in for it were it not almost if not quite essential to success to make obeisance to Church and I hardly think I'll do that.[3]

Did you hear they had discovered natural gas at Ashton? No hoax. Not the kind they ran the county seat campaign on, but real combustible, inflammable, natural gas. So what care we though blizzards be, we'll just turn on the gas.

Tom.

[1] *Ramona* was written by Helen Hunt Jackson in 1884. A friend of the Indians and a critic of U.S. land policy, she had also written *A Century of Dishonor* (1881).

[2] Judge C. S. Palmer of Sioux Falls and John E. Carland of Bismarck.

[3] Walsh had become allied with the Dakota Democrats led by M. H. Day and was increasingly opposed to Governor Church's administration. These factional differences were to intensify in the election year 1888.

174

Chicago, March 11, 1888.

Dear Friend:

Yours of the 7th received yesterday. . . .

I'll write of something that interests me more—the offer made you by the gentleman who called at your office. Yes, indeed, that was complimentary, but not at all surprising. You'll wait a long time before you'll s'prise dis chile.[1] I am about to say something that I do not wish you to look upon for a moment as advice. Even as an opinion I know it is wholly gratuitous, but are you not rash in allowing such an opportunity for advancement to pass by? I should suppose that such offers do not come frequently to men as young as you, and, from the title I should imagine the labors of the office would be directly in your line of business and therefore to your taste. In the course of a public career, I can readily imagine that a man must overlook many things—things against which his pride rises in revolt, yet I do think those very overlookings those subjugations of pride to policy (if you will) may lead to an outlook where he can bestow favor where once he asked it. Does not every man who is placed in such a position get somebody's help? I'd like to know any position worth taking that is not worked for nowadays. And you hesitate about allowing folks the pleasure of assisting one whom they evidently "delight to honor."

. . . Went to see Mrs. Potter that night in "Loyal Love."[2] She is very pretty, very graceful, and a fair actress, I thought. She smiles a little too often and her lips are colored too red. Like her better than Langtry.

Bye-bye
E.

[1] This dialect may be traced to the Uncle Remus stories, by Joel Chandler Harris, which were first published in book form in 1881. See *Uncle Remus: His Songs and His Sayings* (New York, 1881).

[2] Cora Urquhart Potter, born in New Orleans, made her professional debut in London in 1887 and immediately became internationally prominent as an actress. According to the *Chicago Tribune* of March 6, 1888, Mrs. Potter had paid her first visit to the "Chicago boards" the night before at McVicker's Theatre. The play was *Loyal Love*, "nothing less than an emasculated version of the touching story of Fair Rosamond that has been sung by a hundred poets and told in a hundred forms, and must be always tenderer in its native grace than in foreign guise."

175

Redfield, March 11, 1888.

Dear Ellen,—

. . . Why persist in assuring me that I may marry at will?[1] Have I not told you so? Long before I had said anything to you it was so. Marrying anyone but you has no place in my plan of life and has had none for years. It is altogether probable that I shall never marry unless you continue to think me worthy, as you once did. Some men think of it as a matter of course or from a business view. I don't. Would you marry a wealthy woman if you were a man? You never meant anything of the kind. If you did why throw yourself away on me, or doesn't the rule work both ways? It was one of my dreams that if I could get a comfortable home of which you should be mistress we might gain wealth by working together—each encouraging the other—and no other wealth ever spread its lures for me since I grew to be a man. . . .

I'm conscious of possessing a false pride which I often mistake for independence. Perhaps twas so in this case. At least I've done nothing although urged from a number of quarters.[2]

I noticed in today's paper that Louis James is playing "Gretchen —a new version of Faust and Marguerite"—in St. Paul. Wonder what it is. Do you know? [3]

Your

Tom.

[1] Either a letter from Ellen is missing or the relevant portion of one letter has been omitted.

[2] Referring apparently to the position of U.S. Attorney for Dakota Territory, in which he was interested.

[3] Louis James (1842-1910) had a long and prominent career in the theatre, beginning in 1864. He often played Shakespearean roles. *Gretchen* was a version of *Faust* written by Sir William Schwenck Gilbert of Gilbert and Sullivan fame. It was a melodrama in four acts, first presented on March 24, 1879.

176

Chicago, Mar. 19, 1888.

My dear Tom:

I came directly home this afternoon that I may answer your letter received at noon and mail it (my letter) when I go down to rehearsal tonight. Why such dispatch? Because you do get such nonsensical notions into that busy brain of yours, and they worry you no doubt, and I can't allow that. So I may have my "freedom" may I? Thanks awfully—I don't want it. You didn't know to what extent my last letter was serious. Strange coincidence, neither do I. Certainly I was serious in what I said to [you] about that office, in the way I said it. Not as advice, you remember but merely as an expression of my opinion of what you owed to yourself. . . .

I'll try to write a nice sensible letter next time but this one must do for now.

Your
E.

177

Dear Ellen,—

That letter drove away all those naughty nonsensical notions and I should have written before to tell you so only I haven't had a moment to do it, because, you must know, I have at last got to work again.

The territorial encampment of the G.A.R. occurs here during the ensuing week. This is becoming an event of the greatest significance because despite all assertions to the contrary and even, possibly of honest efforts to purge these gatherings of this element, they are made the most of by ambitious candidates for territorial offices.[1]

You must have misunderstood something in my last letter. I mean what I said about your comment on my allowing opportunities to go unimproved. No matter. I felt deeply gratified that you wrote so freely about it, and I know your views are right and that the reasons you urge should govern my action—only you credit me with greater talents, much greater, I fear, than one perfectly unbiased and equally capable of judging would. By the way, that attorneyship went to a gentleman entirely unknown at the bar, a Mr. [W. E.] Purcell of Wahpeton.

We have been house-cleaning the past week, got our rooms newly papered and renovated and carpet turned, put in a new bookcase and expect a set of Wisconsin Reports tomorrow. We are very nicely situated now, have the nicest office in town. A man's surroundings have no little influence on his habits.

I did penance for a number of things I said in my last letter and hope you have forgotten them all. I'll have to tell you some time soon how far from being "a man of wealth" your Brutus is and talk about that "someday" when you were to come to Dakota.

. . . Your letters are never lacking in sense. You have a way of getting a great deal of sense into your nonsense. Some people I know have a fatal habit of reversing this order.

Good-night.
Tom.

[1] He was doubtless referring to Republican politicians, many of whom shamelessly exploited the Grand Army of the Republic. Mary R. Dearing, *Veterans in Politics: The Story of the G.A.R.* (Baton Rouge, Louisiana, 1952), pp. 369-73 and *passim*.

178

Chicago, April 3, 1888.

Dear Brutus,—

. . . Don't care to go to the concert tonight for I feel tired to death—three Apollo rehearsals last week, and one Arion. Ran away from it at recess. Had an opportunity to see "The Ticket of Leave Man" last week. Wouldn't have gone for any money only I remembered you had played the Lancashire lad with great success. I didn't like the way it was given here. You and your troupe had better come on and show a Chicago audience what's what. Don't sacrifice your mustache again though . . . [*editor's omission*].[1]

The last Apollo concert of the season occurs Thursday night. We are to go right on rehearsing however as the club has been invited to sing one night before the National Music Teachers' Association next summer, July 5th. I shall not join the other chorus as I thought of doing. One rehearsal down town every week is enough for me with the incidentals that are sure to arise. Chicago never gives a person a rest.

I attended church last Sunday at the Cathedral of the Holy Name. I was speaking one day of my liking for oratorio music and a friend of mine invited me to go there Easter. The music was grand! The organ is a very fine one and there were any number of other instruments. The choir is a very large one. Dr. Barnes is one of the soloists. They sang the Hallelujah Chorus from the Messiah. The church is an elegant one and the congregation "the most fashionable one in town" of that denomination my friend assured me. To me it was all a grand, dignified pageant—the Arch-bishop and his assistants in their "cloth of gold," the flowers, the lights, the hush that at times fell upon that vast concourse of bowed heads, the solemn organ tones dying away among the arches, the incense rising at the altar. It was all a picture I can assure you and I enjoyed it greatly.

E.

[1] See other references to this play in Nos. 78 and 179.

179

Redfield, April 12, 1888.

My dear Ellen,—

Your letter didn't get here until yesterday and a pretty plight it was in. It bore no stamp and [had] evidently been fished up out of a river and dried at a blazing fire. It is probably one of the surviving victims of the New Hampton Ia. railroad wreck.

So you went to see me as the Ticket-of-Leave Man, did you? I don't remember having told you of the ridiculous feature of my brief career on the stage. Have I told it? Well, here's risking a tedious twice-told tale. You remember the grand finale in the play in which Bob forms the string of a bow of which the lesser lights are members, his head being supported in the lap of— what's her name—well, his wife, you know. We had drilled that scene with especial care on the theory, perhaps, that the audience deserved some recompense for sitting it out, and of all the details none had better his part than our stage carpenter who was ex-officio curtain boy. Now this stage carpenter deserves more than a passing mention. He was nearly six feet six, very slender and bothered with a game eye. He was a military man, ensign-sergeant, I believe. He was also a literary man, had organized a library. He was a druggist, an architect, and a Sunday-school teacher. He had a small hole in the side curtain through which he might occasionally get a glimpse of the audience. Well, when the great final act came his enthusiasm became so great, his expectancy of the wild

169

out-burst of applause so keen, that he got his only serviceable eye riveted on his port-hole in the curtain to observe its expression and became entirely oblivious of what was going on on the stage. On the stage everything went well. Each had said his part and in the most uncomfortable kind of a position I had closed. But the curtain never stirred. Now one doesn't mind very much lying down on the stage for just a minute with one's head in the lap of the beautiful heroine—paint an inch thick—provided it's in the play. But when it isn't, it grows tiresome as well as ridiculous, and then when it's kept right up the ridiculous feature wears off. Well, so it was. True had got entranced in some way but he finally came round all right and I don't think he heard what I said while I lay there but I've always been afraid the lady did.

. . . There was a time when we couldn't very well afford to be so awfully independent. That's a nice thing about the law business anyway—there's very little room for outside dictation, that is if the lawyer has any business. We have been enjoying a rather profitable season ever since I got back.

Don't you have vacation sometime soon? Don't you want to work your hand in? What will you do—write a speech or work up a brief?

Ever your
Tom.

180

Chicago, April 20, 1888.

My dear Friend:

You were right in your supposition. School closed today for two weeks. I'd feel lost without an "occupation" but I've ever so many things I want to do and several places I want to go. Let me see? Didn't you offer me a recreation? Which will I do—write a speech or work up a brief? You are too modest—why that "or"? Can I not combine your requests, and work up a "brief speech"? There's only one thing against the plan. You didn't specify the nature of the discourse. Was it to have been legal, aesthetic, political, agricultural, astronomical, or what. If only you had specified! Now, owing to the uncertainty of our city mails, the dangers "by flood and field," and the likelihood of a blockade in your land of zephyrs, this letter may not reach you till vacation is past.

I must tell you of how I may possibly spend my next summer vacation. I have been asked to join a party of "musical people" going to California. Their intention is to make the journey slowly, stopping off wherever inclined and giving musical entertainments now and then. The plan is to have a double quartette, two sopranos, two altos, two tenors, and two basses, a good pianist and perhaps an elocutionist. With the above voices, solos, duets, and trios can also be sung, or single quartettes for gentlemen's or ladies' voices only. I'd consent in a minute if I were sure it would be well managed. It might be lots of fun, I think.

About some of the music at the last Apollo concert. You were perfectly correct in your understanding of "unaccompanied" music. No instruments of any kind are used. The voices must necessarily be very accurate, or, all starting in together, there would be a discord if any part were even slightly "off pitch." In singing that way, a great deal depends upon the sopranos. . . .

I hope you are not working too hard. Care of your health is your paramount duty.

LN.

181

Redfield, April 29, 1888.

My dear Ellen,—

. . . But that is a very absurd excuse you offer to get out of writing a speech for me. What do you want a particular subject for? Why, it doesn't matter what you say, you know, only that you say something. In proof I'll try to send you the daily papers from Watertown next week.[1]

. . . That reminds me of a remark I noticed in one of the papers the other day. It was to the effect that Conkling could recite the whole of "Lallah Rookh" and knew Horace's odes as the ordinary reader does the "Psalm of Life." Do you believe it![2] I presume however that all or nearly all great speakers must possess an intimate acquaintance with the best things in literature and that they are great linguists because they have such acquaintance.

That California excursion will be a delightful affair I'm sure under the proper management. I didn't suppose though you were so much of a Bohemian.

Devotedly yours,
Tom.

[1] The Democratic territorial convention was about to meet in Watertown.

[2] Roscoe Conkling, a Republican senator from New York (1867-81), was the leader of the "Stalwart" faction of the Republican party. Longfellow's A Psalm of Life was published in 1839. Lallah Rookh, written in 1817 by the Irish poet Thomas Moore, was an Oriental romance, exceedingly popular though running over 250 pages.

182

Chicago, May 6, 1888.

My dear Friend,—

Are congratulations in order? If so—shake. Why didn't you tell me you were to be one of the delegates? [1] I beg pardon, of course your "wing" didn't have its "slate" made up. If I use your political slang incorrectly, don't mind please, I'll improve with time and tuition. I learn very quickly—some things; learned two new dances last Thursday night, the "York" and the "Gavotte." [2] Do you dance them?

Thank you very much for the papers you sent. I read every word that referred to your convention. What a formidable array of "crimes and misdemeanors" are laid against [Governor] Church. . . . I may be wrong, I doubtless am, but I can never believe in the policy that seeks to elevate one individual by encompassing the downfall of another. I mistrust the elevation. Could not some other course have been pursued that would have been quite, perhaps more, effectual? I suppose you knew all along that such charges might truthfully be made against the Governor, and I can now, since reading the arraignment, fully understand how you felt about accepting any favor at Gov. C's hands.

Will you tell me, please, the meaning of Alternates as used in connection with Delegates? Why do the Territories send delegates to the convention when the territorial vote is not taken for the President? By the way I wish I might have heard your "admirable" speech on the tariff question.

E.

¹ Walsh was nominated as one of two delegates to attend the Democratic national convention at St. Louis. He went, however, as a contesting delegate. The territorial convention at Watertown had resulted in a "split," as a result of which the forces of Governor Church nominated their delegates in one meeting while in another the opposing faction nominated Walsh of Spink County and Judge Bangs of Grand Forks County. See Kingsbury, *History of Dakota Territory*, II, 1520-21; *Dakota Pioneer* (Aberdeen), May 3, 1888.

² The gavotte was a French peasant dance, also adapted to ballet and opera. A description of the York has not been found.

183

Redfield, May 13, 1888.

Dear Ellen,—

You certainly deserve credit for patience at least in reading all the papers said about the Watertown convention. Perhaps congratulations had better be deferred until I get back from St. Louis when you may tender them in person, unless Grover [Cleveland] feels called upon to interfere in behalf of his pet. Did it occur to you that Chicago isn't very far away from the most usual route between here and St. Louis? Our delegation will doubtless go by way of Chicago. Of this I am not yet apprised, but if it doesn't either go or return that way I'll bolt—that is if my credentials will be honored at Robey St. Whatever the outcome may be we have fully demonstrated that Gov. Church is a failure. He will scarce ever again venture to dictate or control the choice or expression of the democrats of Dakota.

Recurring to myself—vanity thy name is—I was nominated by a Madison class-mate now practicing at Watertown. It was an exceedingly wintry day when we didn't get into some kind of a row there but we have harmonized in a way most beautiful to see since coming to the territory. We have been learning a few things. He was quite young then and I had recently been a school-master.

O, I beg your pardon. Alternates take the place of the regular delegates in case the latter are unable or fail for any other reason to attend the convention and then you know candidates for the higher places who fail may easily be placated with these honors. Besides there are always enough who want to go and they might as well have some official distinction. I presume the territories are as a matter of practical politics allowed a voice because a party which failed to recognize them would find itself on the list when they are admitted. Theoretically, as they are in a large measure governed by the President who appoints the governor, secretary, marshal and attorney, it is only right that they should have their "say." They ought to have a vote and would have one at least if a constitution were now framed in accordance with the political spirit of the age. But you will remember that "sovereign states" jealous of their power made our fundamental law. It's a lucky arrangement for us. The committee on credentials usually consists of one delegate from each state and territory. This gives Arizona as much to say as New York. The territories will all make common cause with us. Then the national committee of which Mr. Day is a member and which has a large influence is made up the same way. You may remember that at its recent meetings in Washington when the time and place of holding the convention was fixed Day held the territorial delegates firm and they dictated both the time and the place. . . .

Bye
Tom.

184

Chicago, May 16, 1888.

Dear Friend,—

Yes, I rather kalkerlated your delegation would go by way of this city—it's next to impossible to reach any place of importance except via Chicago, isn't it? I think Robey St. at large will honor your credentials, but whether any particular part of it will, is doubtful. Association has such an effect on a man and you, you know, have been associated with Dakota politicians. Need more be said?

Why didn't I say something about your chances of recognition at the convention? My silence certainly did not indicate any doubt of the justice of your cause; there can be no doubt of that, but justice is not always recognized. Notwithstanding that, however, had I said anything, I should have decided your chances good, for I have a great deal of faith in the triumph of a cause that is just, and in—you.

Who is "the owl"? Did you notice that, owl-like, he seems inclined to say to who instead of to whom?—to wit, "Who would you suggest as a typical young democrat?" . . .

If you'll tell me when you are likely to arrive at Robey St. I'll try to [be] there somewhere.

E.

185

Redfield, May 20, 1888.

Dear Ellen,—

I answer with more than ordinary promptness, if excuses are necessary because I want to ask you to render me some assistance in the matter of preparing our "case" to knock out their K.C. [King's Counsel?] at St. Louis. Some day when you are not particularly pressed with other duties I wish you would look up the works in the City Library and if it contains anything of value to us and you can place it at my service during the convention I shall deem it a great favor. The works on Parliamentary practice and the management of political conventions ought to discuss the issues. The technical points on which we rely are, 1, No particular place in the city was mentioned in the call as the place of holding the convention but the citizens of Watertown had prepared a hall for the use of the convention to which place the Church people repaired. Our friends went to another hall and were called to order by the Chairman of the territorial committee conceded to be the proper person to call the convention to order, 2, The Territorial committee passed a resolution just before the time of convening, calling upon all delegates to submit to that body their credentials, and authorizing the committee to prepare for use on the preliminary organization a roll of the delegates entitled to seats—that is, the resolution was an assumption on the part of the committee of the powers of a committee on credentials, so far as the preliminary organization was concerned. Now what I want is some authority on the limitation of the powers of such a committee and what right if any they have to say who shall or who shall not vote on the preliminary organization. Now, don't feel that you haven't done what might have been done if you fail to find anything going directly to these points. I should be wholly at a loss to know what to search myself. You understand this territorial committee was appointed last convention to attend to such matters as the conduct of the campaign, the calling of subsequent conventions, etc. There is no precedent in this county for assuming any such power as that undertaken by this body. . . . I shall feel much encouraged by the trust you express and hope for an impartial hearing. But we have heavy odds to contend against.

"The Owl" is a sphinx so far as my knowledge goes, but I suspect that his native fen is Aberdeen. He is rightly named, he sees so darkly in the broad day-light. He has a faculty for filling space, that's true and that's deemed a greater merit than choice grammar in a writer for a local paper. . . .

You didn't know, though, perhaps, that people, real sensible people come from Chicago to Redfield to study law. We have a young man in the office who has just come out to complete his studies under my direction, on the recommendation of an attorney there whom I met some time ago.

I've just been reading "Felix Holt." I never read a work of George Eliot's without being compelled to ponder over the depth of her wisdom which is never oppressive and her clear insight into human character and the springs of human action—the pettiness of some minds and the worldliness and selfishness of others often laid bare with a single stroke. I know of no passage in the book that might be considered eloquent, nor do I recall any in any of her works. There is a ruggedness in her sentences that prevents fine phrasing. The beauty is in the thought or in an epigram. It is one of the few novels of which you could listen to the reading of chapters wholly disconnected with the greatest interest.

Devotedly yours,
Tom.

186

Chicago, May 26, 1888.

Dear Friend,—

Your letter was duly received and I have tried to get you something in reference to the matter you mentioned. Went down Wednesday after school but didn't succeed very well. I think there is no work except those on Parliamentary Practices that treat of the subject. I got today, Cushings larger work, (a volume of over 1000 pages) and I think it must say about all that is to be said about such matters, excepting of course where assemblies make their own rules, etc. I have also Spofford's Manual. I have no doubt you know all about them, but you mentioned works on Parliamentary usages and I got them. I suppose them to be the best. Jefferson's is also in the library but I thought something more recent would be better. I see no reason why you shouldn't triumph, as I understand the case, if you have a fair field and equal favor.

Not knowing how long you may be able to stay in the city, and as you were not quite sure you would come this way, I have tried, in a very hurried manner, to state a few things that seem to me to have some relation to the matter in hand. If it has "nothing to do with the case" don't regret my having written it for I have enjoyed what I have read and have learned ever so many things I ought to have known.

Shall be glad to see you whenever you may come and wish I were able to render you some real assistance in this matter.[1]

Yours

E.

[1] Enclosed were four pages on the matter of parliamentary procedure. Statement of Mrs. Genevieve Walsh Gudger, along with her copy of the letter.

187

Redfield, May 30, 1888.

My dear Ellen,—

Your very valuable letter of Saturday is at hand. Your summary will be of such service that I need spend no time over

177

the matter in Chicago anyway. Your argument suggested to me an idea to [which Orestes] Brownson makes such frequent allusion in the American Republic. You'll remember it doubtless— namely that the creature can not be greater than the creator.[1] This committee was created by the convention, not of course by that particular body of men but by the party in convention assembled. How can it presume to lay down laws for the government of its sovereign, its creator? . . .

I shall go by way of Chicago, leaving here at 8 A.M. on Friday and arriving in your city about 3 P.M. on Saturday via the C.M. and St. P. Ry. I shall greet you Saturday evening—and it will seem an awful, awful long time till then.[2]

Tom.

[1] *The American Republic* was published in 1865, and according to Arthur M. Schlesinger, Jr., was the only "systematic" study that Brownson completed. Schlesinger, *Orestes A. Brownson: A Pilgrim's Progress* (Boston, 1939), pp. 260-61.

[2] Walsh's theories of parliamentary practice were not of much avail in St. Louis. The territorial faction led by Governor Church had prestige as well as numbers and was not to be stopped. According to the account in Kingsbury's history, the Church delegates attained a margin of two votes in the credentials committee. Thus Walsh was "unseated," as he put it. Kingsbury, *History of Dakota Territory*, II, 1522-23.

188

Chicago, June 11, 1888.

Dear Tom,—

I send you today, per American Express, a little birthday gift which I hope you will receive with my love and the earnest wish that this new year of your life may be a very happy one.

The books are not what I wanted. . . . You doubtless have at your command, mentally or otherwise the contents of these volumes but there may be some convenience in having the matter treated of in this shape.

Please don't work so hard. You were looking splendid better than I ever saw you before, when you were here, and you want to keep on looking so. The best way to accomplish it is 1st—

Don't work too much—2nd—Don't worry about anything—3rd
—Eat enough.

Yours,
Ellen.

189

Redfield, June 12, 1888.

My dear Ellen,—

I arrived in season last evening after a dull but not wholly
tiresome journey.

I have been subjected to no end of raillery all day but it is a
source of gratification to know that our being unseated at St.
Louis occasions universal regret here. . . .

I was the recipient today of two invitations to speak on the
4th, one from the citizens here—subject not named, presumably
spread-eagleism ad lib.—the other to address the farmers on the
tariff at a celebrated grove on an island about twenty miles up
the river where the yeomanry will celebrate. As my place here
can readily be supplied from our abundance of local oratorical
talent I regard with more favor the invitation to speak in the
primeval temple.

I shall try to go out to get a scent of the roses this week. Good-
night.

Devotedly yours,
Tom.

190

Chicago, June 12, 1888.

Dear Tom,—

Another note from me! The only way to balance matters
will be to write me a letter every day for a while. As I told you
the books which I sent were not what I was looking for. I want
you to return them if they are not something you really desire to
have—if they are not of real value to you. . . . I can return them

and get anything you may name in their place. Tell me something you would like to have. It would have given me such great pleasure to send in the first place something I was sure you would like, but I had no way of finding out.

Your
Ellen.

191

Redfield, June 12, 1888.

My dearest Ellen,—

Your letter and the elegant gift referred to in it were received today. Please accept my sincerest thanks for both. The books are superb. I'm sure you could have made no better selection even in Boston. I shall study the selections carefully. Contrary to your assumption I'm not familiar with many of them but, surprising as it may seem, hardly less with Frank Hurd's tariff speech than with the more historic efforts recorded in the collection.[1] It is indeed a choice selection and I shall prize it for its intrinsic worth as well as for the love and kind wishes you sent with it.

Say Ellen, we are not realizing all the possibilities of life, are we, now? If you could only smile on me once in a great while and say "Good-night," I wouldn't mind so much, but it's a long dreary prospect whenever I say Good-bye. Let me press you to consider whether we may not marry this fall. It will not be so pleasant to come here at this season, but then a year is a long, long time, isn't it? I think I could have things reasonably comfortable by that time—but of that you must be the judge. No man has any vested right to invite a woman into a state of starvation simply because she honors him with her love, or to ask her to share his home unless it approximates in comfort at least the one she abandons. Henry showed me just before he left a table of our receipts for the past year exhibiting a total of something over $3000. That will net us each about $1200 over and above office expenses, probably a little more than that. It occurs to me we ought to be able to get along on that income and the present year promises at least equally well. House rent will be limited to taxes and insurance. I believe I told you I had bought a house. It's a good investment though, even should we not use it right away. It's quite large but isn't very economically arranged, some slight changes will improve it in this respect however. . . . Now $1200 seems but a small pittance even to me and should we go to house-keeping on that there will be a continuous reminder in our desire of how wretchedly small it is, but it will suffice for me, if I am able to make anything like a safe estimate of the cost of running a house-hold. Your judgment is doubtless more reliable than mine in this matter. Now don't hesitate to say so if you think that isn't ample for your comfort. Next year will show better, I'm sure.

Those pictures I had taken are horrid things. I shouldn't think of sending you any. They published a cut in the Globe after one of them and all my ambition to be known as a handsome man is blighted in a day.

Your
Tom.

[1] Frank H. Hurd (a Democrat from Toledo, Ohio) served three terms in the U.S. House of Representatives between 1875 and 1885.

192

Redfield, June 14, 1888.

My dear Ellen,—

I shall do nothing of the kind. Return my books, indeed! When I prize them very highly aside from the fact that you sent them and I gave you a great deal of credit for making the selection. In all earnestness I'm proud of the books. Let me say right here that if you ever see those books again you will have to come to Dakota to perform that feat. . . .

If I only get another letter in the morning I'll be

Your enraptured,
Tom.

193

Chicago, June 20, 1888.

Dear Tom,—

. . . The reason that I did not write Sunday P.M. was that we had the pleasure of your brother's company at that time. I like your brother.

Good-night my esteemed friend,

E.

194

Chicago, July 3, 1888.

Dear Tom,—

I commenced a letter to you Sunday, another yesterday. Why didn't I complete the letters I had commenced? Because on Sunday I wrote that which I had reasons for thinking would be best unsaid when Monday arrived. What I wrote yesterday, I believe today to be unwise. I tell you honestly at the present time my future is a complete blank to me even as far as any plan is concerned. My folks know now that I have promised to marry you and they are most bitterly opposed to the arrangement. Do not let this hurt you any more than you can help. It is simply abominable I know, and makes me pretty sick at heart at times. Mamma is not included in anything I have said. She only thinks with regret of how far away Dakota is. I cannot ever tell you what I thought of what you said in your last letter in regard to my Mother. It would be impossible to thank you enough, and although that step will probably never be necessary, I am greatly pleased that you thought of mamma. . . .[1] Considering what I have stated you will doubtless think it would be wise for me to just leave all that is disagreeable here to take care of itself and seek forgetfulness in your home and you are right in thinking so. But, knowing that I shall surely not be the happier by staying here, I shall still remain for otherwise I could not approve of myself which is rather necessary to my existence.

Now I'll tell you what I want you to do. Tell me all about the place you have bought, how many rooms there are, how they are located, and be sure to tell me what direction the house faces. Are there any trees in the garden? Tell me all about everything. Will it bore you to hear about our closing exercises? . . .

Poor boy, aren't you tired of school? You were wrong about the Republican nominee weren't you? I was at the convention Saturday when McKinley made his little speech and I thought and so did nearly everyone, that the result would be as you anticipated. They had only four ballots that day and adjourned, I believe, through fear of McKinley. The present situation must be vastly more satisfactory to the democrats than to the republicans. There was not much enthusiasm shown at the convention, I thought.[2] I had a most excellent view being directly opposite the presiding officer, in the parquet circle. Judging by this convention, I know why you weren't seated at St. Louis. You hadn't a bald head—that is one of the first requisites, I'm sure.

Yours,
E.

[1] This is apparently a reference to one of Walsh's letters missing from the collection.

[2] Although Benjamin Harrison received the nomination, McKinley's star was in the ascendancy. Among those impressed with his "little speech" was Mark Hanna, and Hanna was looking for a new protégé. See Margaret Leech, *In the Days of McKinley* (New York, 1959), pp. 42-43.

195

Redfield, July 8, 1888.

Dear Ellen,—

The revelations of your last kind letter troubled me only by reason of the annoyance to which the facts necessarily subject you. I anticipated you would feel called upon to endure your surroundings until duty permitted you to leave them. But are you not a little fearful that your efforts will not only be unappreciated but ineffectual? As to your mother permit me to say that you will do me a favor to consider the arrangement I suggested as a personal and decided preference of my own and not a matter of necessity.

Don't trouble yourself about having spoiled my happiness. If

I have ever entertained any noble aims, your personality has been mingled with them. If I have led a life since my majority not wholly reproachful, to you the credit is largely due. In the anticipation of gratified ambition there was no pleasure like your smile of gratification. Whatever betide now, I have lived. But I have a most wholesome dread that you will find the criticisms of your sisters not wholly captious. I have an ever present sense that I have not within me those elements which wrest success from life, it will come, if at all, from the slow tedious development of only a modicum of talent. You deserve something better than a man of mild and unappreciated genius can ordinarily offer. . . .

I celebrated at Armadale as contemplated. It's the nicest place in Dakota. I had an attentive and appreciative audience.

The political campaign has opened. . . . There is a Republican Club in town. We are going to organize and challenge them to a series of discussions of the question (the tariff) from an economic or a political stand-point or both and a highly interesting time may be looked for. I can talk on that question and make my talk worth listening to.

Bye-bye
Tom.

196

Chicago, July 14, 1888.

Dear Tom,—

Thanks for the description of "the house." [1] I know now how to think of it. I should judge from your description and diagram that the house must be very nice indeed, though I do wish there were one more room down stairs and we would fit up the coziest little reading room, or study, or library, or whatever you've a mind to call it for you. I think the changes you mentioned will doubtless be an improvement. I am glad the grounds are so large, I just love a nice lawn. We can play tennis and croquet and ball. I really can catch a ball you know.

Do you know, I'm going to scold you now. The next time you want to say horrid things about yourself don't say them to me. What do you mean—if success comes to you? Are you not successful? Are you not honored among your fellowmen? Get rid of "that wholesome dread" of which you speak—you couldn't make me have a poor opinion of you even at your own request. . . . I really firmly believe that neither of us will ever regret the step we shall take next—June, if you wish it very much, and if nothing happens meantime to prevent it. By the way, mon cher, you will have to come east to get me of course. I would not like to be married in Chicago, but that is on account of the publicity that is necessary in this State. Not half the people here will submit to it and Wisconsin is often spoken of as the Gretna Green of Chicago people. . . . Do you think I want to look like a dowdy when I make my first appearance in the West? I must get something nice to wear and that requires time and meditation you know.

Your
E.

[1] Walsh's description was probably omitted from the preceding letter.

197

Redfield, July 17, 1888.

Dear Ellen,—

. . . That lake trip will be more than delightful. You mustn't fail to stop off at Sturgeon Bay. With your permission I shall write Mrs. MacEacham that you will stay with her a day or two.[1] She will hold me personally responsible if you do not and I'm sure you will be charmed with a brief stay in the place. There is no place along the lake at which you could while away a week more agreeably. Wish I could go with you. Guess I'll have to put it off until next June though. So be it.

That would be a charming idea to have a cozy little study but it would have to be yours too, or I shouldn't have any use for it. We may be able to fit up one of the rooms upstairs until we can build an addition or arrange some other way. We can have a good tennis court if the grass grows well, but you'll have to teach me how to play. I remember quite distinctly that you can catch a ball. Didn't I blister your hands with one once on a time?

There is still another chance we are told that the bill dividing our judicial district will pass. . . . He [O. S. Gifford, territorial delegate] is a positive injury to the territory at Washington. He doesn't get a thing done and members from adjoining states naturally feel that interference would be a discourtesy.[2] It will be a bountiful measure for us. [Judge] Spencer has almost quit trying to do the work, so much has accumulated beyond his capacity.

Your
Tom.

[1] When Walsh taught school at Sturgeon Bay, Wisconsin, his landlady was Mrs. Nettie MacEacham, a widow and former schoolteacher who became his personal friend. Editor's interview with William A. MacEacham (son of Archibald and Nettie MacEacham), Sturgeon Bay, Wisconsin, August 18, 1965. See also No. 202 and notes for No. 277.

[2] Gifford was the Republican who had beaten M. H. Day in 1886 in the race for territorial delegate to Congress. Walsh may have looked upon him with a jaundiced eye.

198

Chicago, July 22, 1888.

Dear Tom:

. . . I certainly would be delighted to meet your friend Mrs. MacEacham, and, as our boat stops at Sturgeon Bay it could only be a great pleasure for me to stop over a day as you suggest if it would not inconvenience Mrs. MacEacham. She may have other company you know or may be going away herself. It was most kind of her to have thought of sending the arbutus. It would have been joyfully received by me, it is so beautiful. I can never forget the cool, delicate perfume that always greeted me when I entered my room at Mrs. Tobey's the time you sent some.

Mrs. Boese has returned from a six weeks visit to Denver and vicinity and she is simply mad about the West. Such air. Such a sky! such stars! such moonlight! Chicago is nowhere.

Must be off.

Yours,
Ellen.

199

Redfield, July 28, 1888.

My dear Ellen,—

How are you progressing in Geography? If it has been as hot in Chicago as here you are excused for postponing your lesson. So I'll tell you that the Black Hills do not lie between here and Chicago, but that in going to the great metropolis from here you may and from Deadwood you must pass through Sioux City which is about 220 miles from here. The C. and N.W. road has a line about 300 miles long from Sioux City into the Hills region within Nine miles of Deadwood. This is the only line now penetrating the Hills. The mineral resources of the region beyond the Missouri is [*sic*] something fabulous the experts say, but they are so securely hidden away that they can be mined only at great expense at present. Our Hot Springs, in that region, are growing almost as famous as those of Arkansas.

Congress has finally passed the bill which gives our district another judge. It now needs only the President's signature and as it makes room for two more of the faithful and provides for an absolute necessity there is no reason to suppose that it will not speedily become a law. The new judge will probably appoint a term here shortly after his arrival and stay until the accumulated business is finished. At the last term not more than one-third of it was disposed of. As our fees depend to a large extent on the event of the suits you can readily perceive how important it is to us that they be finished up as speedily as possible. Besides one can hardly hope to become a lawyer with no more than eight or nine days court per year in which to acquire that tact and skill which are so essential and which practice alone can give.

. . . I really think you would readily admit that our people would suffer nothing in comparison with those in your neighborhood or with an equal number selected from any equal area of Chicago. Wouldn't the number of pianos in a village be a tolerably reliable indication of the culture and character of its people? Well, we have scarcely 1200 population and one could easily count twenty pianos in town. It would surprise you too, to meet some of the people who live on farms out in this country.

Your
Tom.

200

Chicago, August 6, 1888.

Dear Tom,—

We've been keeping house all alone. Mamma and Mary are visiting in Sheboygan. I did the tending to everything the first week, but this past week, everyone has attended to me for I've been very sick. They make no end of fun of me now because they say I'd better never think of "settling down in life" if a week's housekeeping comes so near killing me. Bad looking situation for you, isn't it, Tom? "Tell it not in Gath," but I do hate it awfully. Am all right again.

I went down town Friday night to one of the [Theodore] Thomas "summer night concerts." He plays here every night during July and August you know. The audience he draws nightly is really wonderful . . . . The "March" from Tannhaeuser was excellent of course, but the number which pleased me most was the "Funeral March" by Chopin, with the orchestration by Thomas himself. It was simply perfect. One wouldn't mind going to heaven accompanied by such strains.[1] Mrs. Boese and the children and I went one afternoon to the Eden Musée and heard the Hungarian band play. I had never been to that place. The first and second floors contain groups in wax that are really good. The balcony scene from Romeo and Juliet is there of course. Also Othello and Desdemona. In another group Queen Victoria is seated on a sofa talking to Lord Beaconsfield. Near them stands the Princess of Wales. Mrs. Cleveland is conversing with Pres. Carnot and Grover (as natural as life) is devoting himself to the little Emperor of China. Gladstone is entertained by, or is entertaining, the Prince of Wales, and the old Emperor of Brazil is bowing before the King of Sweden. The third floor is a hall and it is really very handsome. There are hundreds of Tropical plants arranged all around the walls and reflected in the mirrors with which the hall is lined.[2]

Good-night.

E.

[1] The entire program for August 3, 1888, is given in George P. Upton (ed.), *Theodore Thomas: A Musical Autobiography*, II (Chicago, 1905), 210. According to Upton, Thomas' summer night concerts in Chicago (1877-90) were "the most important and significant of all his popular concerts."

[2] An advertisement described the Eden Musée as "a large and commodious four-story and basement building, handsome in architecture, elegant in arrangement, and magnificent in decoration and embellishments." It was "completely filled with the most wonderful and natural-like wax people extant" and it also contained "one of the richest decorated and cosiest [?] Concert Halls in this country, wherein you may listen to Mr. Paul Olah's popular and well-rounded Hungarian Gypsy Orchestra, and wherein you may, while you so listen, partake of such refreshments as a strictly moral entertainment should furnish." Information derived from *Journal and Programme of the Letter Carriers' Association of Chicago* (Chicago, 1889), photo-copy provided by the Chicago Historical Society.

201

Redfield, August 8, 1888.

Dear Ellen,—

I was exceedingly sorry to learn that you had been ill and am still a little fearful that you could not have wholly recovered so quickly from malarial fever. Our neighbor, a young man across the hall, is down with the typhoid fever and it isn't very surprising either. It must be only by special grace that we have escaped so long. Our street is absolutely filthy and the city authorities take no steps to clean it up. They plead lack of funds consequent upon the cutting off of the revenue heretofore arising from liquor licenses.[1]

We are invited out to a card party tomorrow evening. It is to be in honor of a lady who is distinguished as the late president of the Iowa state woman's rights convention and one of the foremost expounders of those rights in that great state. Don't ask me if she plays cards? Nor if she does, whether she always asks which suit is trump, nor whether she ever trumps her partner's ace. I'll tell you all about these things when I write again. That reminds me I engaged to make some dates for your sister when the "crusade" should be inaugurated in Dakota. I must cultivate the lady and commend to her an able recruit.[2]

I have been riding considerably lately. I have the nicest little pony—a real broncho, but not at all vicious. She's full of life and enjoys a run as much as I do.

Good-night. Yours
Tom.

189

P. S. Got a letter from a member of the campaign committee this morning requesting me to be present at Sioux Falls on Saturday next to assist in firing the first guns, etc. But Achilles isn't quite mollified yet and won't go.[3]

[1] Local option was popular in many Dakota counties at this time, and apparently Spink County had gone dry. Kingsbury, *Dakota Territory*, II, 1532.

[2] Mary McClements was the sister Walsh probably had in mind.

[3] Having been "unseated" by Church Democrats in St. Louis, three months before, Walsh must have been referring to continuing soreness from that defeat.

202

Chicago, August 20, 1888.

Dear Tom,—

Your letter of the 8th inst. came into my possession about thirty seconds after I reached home this morning. I hope you are not sick, its a long time since you wrote that last letter and I believe typhoid fever is contagious.

. . . To you who know Mrs. MacEacham so well and who are so good a judge of character, any praise of her would be superfluous if not impertinent. Nothing could exceed her kindness to me. I was troubled for some days with tooth-ache or neuralgia or something and your kind friend just more than petted me. I liked it no end, I assure you. I'm not used to it you know; have always been trained to conceal anything like feeling of sentiment. (That's the Scotch of it you know). Just imagine me taking my breakfast every morning before rising and finally getting down stairs sometime near noontime. I enjoyed being there so much and was sorry to have to leave. . . . I want to thank you for the pleasure I had in visiting Mrs. Mc. She just worships you and I know she liked me a little bit on your account.

Good-night, Tom.
Ellen.

203

Dear Ellen,—

It's too bad you were not well but I can appreciate how tenderly you were cared for. Didn't you think Idlewild really romantic? Do you remember my writing about a certain occasion on which I sailed up the bay from there after laying becalmed for some time? I never experienced anything so exhilarating, captivating. I came nearer being a poet then than I ever expect to again. I felt the deep rapture of some of Byron's lines descriptive of similar scenes. It is impossible to experience it aboard a steamer as it is on land or in a skiff. You didn't sail, probably, or if you did, not on a clear moon-light-night with only breeze enough to make your vessel send.

We are to have the Andrews Opera Company through this section. They have their own orchestra and the company comprising thirty members travel in a special private car. I heard them play the Mikado at Huron long after it had got to be a chestnut and it was eminently funny and well sung.

. . . I said I wasn't very busy. That means I haven't busied myself. I ought to have been devoting my spare time to stringing together campaign yarns. Got a communication today from the Secretary of the territorial committee asking me to speak at Aberdeen Saturday night.

. . . My friend [Will] Sterling's laurels are more creditable. He has been district attorney down in his county for the past two years and they are trying to prevail upon him to run for the territorial council.

Bye-bye,
Tom.

204

Dear Tom,—

Guess I shall have to tell you about what prevented my writing to you, for it's rather amusing to think of what I have to undertake at times without knowing in the least how to do it.

The 24th annual reunion of the 105th Ill. Vol. is to occur at Bensonville next Tuesday, and Mr. B. was Captain of Co. I of that regiment. Congressman Mason is to be the "orator of the day" and Captain Bender is to deliver an address of welcome and introduce the speaker.[1] He asked me to write the address. Imagine it when I'd have to consult Webster to be perfectly sure of the correct application of the commonest military terms. He would not be convinced however that he could do it better himself, so I had to try. I had to send it up in the evening. Short notice for one who hadn't an idea on the subject. Think how I shall "be missed" by my neighbors should I leave here. You'll have a great deal to answer for.

Why didn't I write more about my trip? Ye gods! didn't I write eight pages. . . . I didn't see Idlewild so missed the opportunity to be, "if but for an hour," Tom, a poet.

Yours,
Ellen.

[1] Representative William E. Mason, Republican of Chicago, served in the House of Representatives from 1887 to 1891 and later had a term in the U.S. Senate, as well as five more years in the House (1917-21).

205

Huron, September 2, 1888.

Dear Ellen,—

You'll have to excuse the use of this paper. I might possibly get better but I had rather "take mine ease in mine inn" than prosecute a possibly fruitless search for an open stationery shop this hot evening. I'm going to Sioux Falls tomorrow. Our judge [Spencer] has just returned from a five weeks vacation out on the coast and through the Yellowstone Park. This jaunt doesn't seem to have satisfied him though. He leaves tomorrow for the east and we must go nearly two hundred miles farther to get our business done. You are undoubtedly right in saying that many of our abuses would be corrected if we were a state. Except a few days now and then Spencer hasn't held a term of court for six months. Our calendars are crowded, litigation is discouraged, cases in court delayed beyond all reason.

Went out to the farm to visit the friends of whom I wrote you some time ago. Made hay for half a day. O yes, the sun was shining the rest of the time, but I didn't work any more because it was shining too violently. There's no poetry in hay-making out here. Maud Muller's occupation is wholly gone.[1] They cut the grass with a mowing machine one day and the next drive over the sward with a loader which carries it right up to the wagon. . . . It does seem to me, though, that life would grow rather dreary to them. They talk though as if they had permanently settled down to farming.

I have the nicest little pony, full of life and vigor. A gentleman asked me to take it and break it for riding which I'm doing and at the same time acquiring such an appetite as I haven't enjoyed for a long time. Our evenings are usually quite cool and a ride after our hot days is exceedingly invigorating and conducive to sleep.

Did the Captain learn his piece quite well? And did you make him rehearse it "on a stool"? "A little more expression there, Captain." "Do not saw the air too much with your hand, thus." "No, not 'I have the bleasure,'—but p-p-pleasure." "Now, Captain, if you don't learn that better you will have to pull the paper out of your pocket like Gov. Church when he made his inaugural speech." Will coming generations learn of the Captain's triumph on the rostrum as well as of his deeds of valor in the field?

. . . He is now one of the leading lawyers of that city.[2] He was out here working up some evidence in a big divorce case. I'm afflicted myself occasionally with a feeling of unrest about going to a large city to practice. Wealth is so much dissipated here, that interests are small and litigation trifling. You must try so many cases in order to make anything and then you can't devote to any one the study it might receive. Occasionally though we get something worth fighting for. There's quite a handsome fee in the cases I'm interested in today if we win them, and the chances seem all that way now. I'll have to worry along a few more years anyway, acquire something more of the art of trying cases, and then if I keep at the top and your judgment coincides we may launch out.

Yours faithfully,
Tom.

[1] *Maud Muller*, by John Greenleaf Whittier, was published in 1867.
[2] The reference is to a Mr. Turner of Milwaukee (according to an interpolation by Mrs. Genevieve Walsh Gudger, in her copy of the letter). Further identification has not been established.

206

Chicago, September 6, 1888.

Dear Brutus,—

I came from school early this P.M. for the express purpose of writing to you, but I met the Captain in the yard and he had to tell me all about the Reunion. Do you know, he tells me (though he remarks that perhaps he ought not to speak of it) that he created quite a sensation out there. "Why," said he, "Col. Higgins came to me when I got through speaking and said, 'Capt., I always knew you could talk, but by —— I never knew you were an orator.'" He apologized for the dash, remarking that "all these military fellows use more or less strong language.". . .

E.

207

Redfield, September 9, 1888.

Gentle Portia,—

. . . Do you not remember some of Carruth's anecdotes illustrative of [the desire of] the true Dakotan to show a stranger the town?[1] It's deep rooted at Sioux Falls but there they have something to show. Did you know that the granite blocks used in paving your streets come from their quarries? It is an immense industry. I found time to go through the residence portion pretty thoroughly. It would surprise you to see the elegance and taste displayed and I may say the wealth lavished on the abodes of its citizens. They cost all the way from $10,000 to $40,000. All this was suggestive of wealth and affluence of which we in this section know nothing. And yet it occurred to me, although the city is the most promising in Dakota, that there was something unsubstantial or extravagant about this display, that it was quite ahead of the legitimate order, and out of keeping with the development of the country.

I didn't find the judge there, had to follow him to Elk Point. My mission was a success in every particular, winning for us practically two cases which we a short time ago appealed to the supreme court. As the same end we expected to reach in the supreme court has been accomplished we shall now probably withdraw our appeals. It's quite a victory, I assure you.

. . . My call was cut short by an appointment I made with Mr. Inman who used to be Chairman of the Territorial Democratic Committee. Our associations have been such that we have usually been opposed politically, although I have always entertained the warmest friendship for him and am now assured that it is fully reciprocated. He is very wealthy and entertained me right royally. The University of South Dakota is at Vermillion and Mr. I. is president of the board of regents.[2] I must confess that I had no idea of the high character of the institution. They had over 300 students last year coming from ten different states. This year they have a post-graduate course with six students. The faculty is said to be very superior. I met the president, Dr. Olson. He's a gentleman as well as a scholar and of the latter you may judge from the fact that he lectured on Greek at Chatauqua during the past vacation.[3]

There's one thing off my mind anyway. About ten days ago I wrote two pages of manuscript on a campaign speech. No further progress has since been made. I shall ship it down to you forthwith for completion — or perhaps you had better make a fresh start. Put the jokes in pretty frequently, never mind how chestnutty they are. I'll cull them for use in the rural districts. Be careful not to say anything about civil service reform but get in all your choice figures on the tariff. Give the lion's tail a gentle twist and tell about how the other fellows wouldn't let Dakota in. Here work up "broad and fertile acres," "boundless domain," etc., etc. Send it on as quickly as you can so I can practice a while before the looking glass after I learn it.

Bye-bye, Ellen.
Tom.

[1] A probable reference to Hayden Carruth, who edited the *Estelline Bell* from 1883 to 1886. Ellen must have met him on some occasion, perhaps in Chicago. Carruth went on from the *Estelline Bell* to be-

come an editorial writer for the *New York Tribune* and to fashion a literary career of some note.

[2] Darwin M. Inman was also president of the Bank of Vermillion. The college at Vermillion was known as the University of Dakota (having no "South" in its title) until 1889. It is unclear whether Walsh erred or whether an error was made in copying from the original.

[3] A better source than Walsh reveals that most of the students were in subordinate departments not granting collegiate degrees; that is, their work was approximately of a high school level. Lewis E. Akeley, *This Is What We Had in Mind: Early Memories of the University of South Dakota* (Vermillion, South Dakota, 1959), p. 35. Akeley joined the staff in 1887. His book describes the president, Dr. Olson, as an inspirational leader and a scholar. Olson received his undergraduate degree from the University of Chicago and had studied in two German universities. Unfortunately for his fledgling college, he died in a fire in Minneapolis in 1889. *Ibid.*, pp. 7, 33, 41-42.

208

Chicago, September 17, 1888.

Dear Friend,—

. . . You don't like this letter a bit do you? Well, you should not make fun of me then. I did think some of telling you of the picture at the exposition but I shall not this time.

Must close as we have our first Apollo rehearsal tonight.

Very respectfully,
E. C. M.

209

Redfield, September 23, 1888.

My dear Ellen,—

Of course I didn't like your letter a bit. You don't often do things just merely to inflict pain, do you? or was your letter intended as a sort of surgical operation? Your scalpel penetrates deep and rather mercilessly as it seems to me. I have been experiencing how "bitter is unjust reproof from the lips of those we love." Really I am unable to comprehend how you should imagine I was "making fun of" you. Imagine you writing anything which would be of service to me? I have imagined it. I've told you so. You ought not to have said that. Not exactly writing something for me to commit but assisting me to say the right thing or to say it in the right way — and you will, will you not?

A certain Mr. Crofoot of Huron has been appointed our judge of our new district. He wasn't my choice but the appointment is a creditable one. We have had a passing and pleasant acquaintance ever since I came to the territory. He is only thirty. . . .[1]

Yours
Tom.

[1] Louis W. Crofoot had come to Dakota from Pontiac, Michigan.

210

Chicago, Sept. 26, 1888.

My dear Tom,—

Did my last letter grieve you? Forgive me, mon cher, I am sorry. When I understand a subject, I can perhaps write something about it; but though I know a thing or two about the tariff my knowledge does not satisfy me. If it did, I would gladly do as you ask, just because you think I could. Shall I tell you the real truth, why I wouldn't write anything? I should be too awfully afraid you would think it silly.

. . . If you are not contented at Redfield, why stay there? You are young and can well afford to make a start elsewhere.

No. I'm not the least bit angry anymore, only with myself.

Yours
E.

211

Redfield, September 20, 1888.

Dear Ellen,—

. . . There's no room for a man here unless, in our own expressive vernacular he "rustles." You evidently mistook what

I said about desiring to go to the city to practice, or rather the reason of my discontent. I never thought more of Redfield or of its prospects than I do today. As for its people, they are certainly improving in character and in the matter of regard for myself I have lately received so flattering an expression of it that it constitutes no small inducement to me to make my home here. It is generally believed that our business nets as much as that of all the other firms in town combined. That probably isn't true, but we have a long lead and only yesterday received notice from the leading collection association that our names had been substituted as their correspondents in the place of our most formidable local rival. This firm's business constituted at least half of the work done by our friends during the past two years. So you see our business is fairly prosperous. But in that very fact lies the root of my dissatisfaction. I've got it into my head that my field isn't large enough, that I could manage larger interests and earn larger fees. I'm not troubled with my friend S's diffidence,[1] as you have probably discovered. But I have no notion of taking my chances equipped as I now am in a great city with no interest to bolster me up, one among the thousands with the chances on the start equal only to those of the lowliest. I went through the starvation period once and harbor no pleasing recollections of the process.

. . . He wanted some further counsel and Mr. Dawes, cashier of the bank, who from the first, for what reason I never learned, took a liking to me, sent him to us.

My hands are sorer than if I had been playing ball. I've been digging holes on our "homestead" in which to plant trees in the spring. You admire elms, do you not? I think of setting out a row around three sides — fourteen or fifteen in number. They may be gotten on the banks of the Jim, you know.

Politics are growing exceedingly interesting in these parts. I expect to "open the campaign" on our part at Doland next Friday. I'll let you off on that speech. I have collected considerable material and arranged some of it already into what seems to me pretty good shape. . . .

Your
Tom.

[1] Referring in all probability to Will Sterling of Huron.

212

Dear Tom,—

. . . Did I mistake what you said about Redfield? Well, all right. I can certainly understand your explanation of the situation. "Conceited" are you? Not a bit. You are only conscious of the power you possess, and why shouldn't you be? I have felt too that your present field of action is too small but I scarcely think the "walls" of your town will be impassable.

Good-night.

E.

213

Redfield, October 11, 1888.

Dear Ellen,—

You guessed it. I'm somewhat immersed in politics just now, and lest I shouldn't be able to write Sunday I'll take time by the forelock and send you something tonight.[1] Gen. Harrison Allen, the handsomest man in the territory, speaks here tonight. He wears his hair long — its slightly tinged with gray and always combed with perfect precision. His Prince Albert fits like a corset and is without a crease. He invariably salutes you militarily and is the picture of a holiday soldier. . . .[2] I spoke last Saturday night and beginning next Monday shall probably talk as often as every other night for the remainder of the campaign.

Haven't given up going to Chicago this fall by any means. I've fixed about December 1 now, but that is subject to change. It may be later. Do you have a vacation about Thanksgiving time? That would be a nice time to go down for recreation, wouldn't it?

You promised some time ago to tell me about the pictures at the Exposition. . . .

How much it would mean to democracy to have Dakota come into line — that's where she naturally belongs — and Harden's election would force from an unwilling senate, the boon of tariff reduction. It would serve notice on the republicans that if Dakota is to be held her interests, as well as those of New England, must be consulted.

Good-night, Ellen.

Tom.

[1] Walsh was campaigning for a seat on the territorial council. He was also drawn into the agrarian movement then sweeping the South and West. His nomination for the council occurred as the Democrats and agrarian leaders of Spink County effected a combination. The head of their ticket was John W. Harden, vice president of the Farmers Alliance and a Democrat, who received the territorial nomination for delegate to Congress. Kingsbury, *History of Dakota Territory*, II, 1531-32, 1540; *Redfield Observer*, October 4, 11, 18, 1888.

[2] General Allen of Fargo commanded the Grand Army of the Republic (Dakota branch) for the years 1887-88.

214

Chicago, October 16, 1888.

Dear Tom,—

Do you [know you] couldn't have decided on a better time to come to Chicago—that is a time that would suit me better. I was just thinking the other day that I wish you could be here to one of the Apollo concerts and if you come when you expect to you will be here just in time. The first concert occurs Friday, Nov. 30, the day after Thanksgiving. So it's decided, you'll take your Thanksgiving dinner with us, isn't it? I want you to come down before winter. You certainly must not come late in December, it might make you ill again. You've had enough pneumonia to quite satisfy you, I guess.

Do you know I am devoting my Saturdays to art now. Have been taking lessons for a month or so. I've always wished to paint but never seemed to get time. . . . My music teachers told me I might have made a good deal of my voice. I have been told so many pleasant-sounding things, and yet, if they are right who have said these things, what a monumental failure I am.

I wish you the most perfect success in your speech making. I judge from your letter that the "beautyman" [General Allen] was rather violent. Don't you ever be so, even when tempted to. The calm, logical, polished speaker is the successful one in the end, I think. He convinces the cultured, he rebukes his enemy's violence, and he keeps himself above the level of the mob who respect him for it.

Bye-bye.
Ellen.

215

Dear Ellen,—

I was out in the country last night endeavoring to edify the ruralities on the political situation and got back but an hour ago. I spoke three nights last week and have appointments for every night next week. . . . The papers are not likely to say anything that will please you to hear because, you know, I'm not talking very popular doctrine. Your idea of oratory meets exactly my idea of what constitutes excellence in that way. Our tastes do very frequently harmonize, don't they? Was not such a style as you suggest characteristic of Wendell Phillips? It seems to me I was told that he rarely changed his position or indulged in any gesticulation other than a slight swaying of the forearm. I can't understand it though when I read some of his fiery emphatic denunciatory speeches.[1] Thanks for your caution, too. How did you know I needed it? It is hard to resist. . . . Erskine's biographers say he used to jump up and strike his heels together twice in the air, while addressing a jury.[2] Choate began his address ordinarily with two overcoats on in cold weather, and as he became heated continued to divest himself of his clothing until he had quite passed the line of decorum.[3] Didn't Hamlet express it correctly in saying, "In the very torrent, tempest and as I may say whirlwind of passion you must beget a temperance that may give it smoothness." I wish you could hear me speak so you might criticise me mercilessly, nothing else would do.

Don't count on my being with you to a certainty on Thanksgiving. I'm going to try hard to go. I shall be greatly pleased, I assure you, to go to the Apollo concert if I am on hand.

Why shouldn't you tell me what was said about your painting? I should expect it anyway. I know you wouldn't touch it without doing well. The difficulty with many who essay the art is that they are unable to tell when a piece is well done or otherwise and lacking the conception, the execution is necessarily defective. I shall look forward with great interest to seeing your work. . . .

I'd like to read to you tonight, the Scotchman's talk about the cornfield, there was a life in the thing, it was full of suggestion, it reminded him of home and all that must be expressed in the picture [?]. Would you care to have me? I like to read to those who like to listen to me better than I like to talk.

Good-night.

Tom.

¹ Phillips, who died in 1884, was famous for his abolition crusades, his oratory, and his persistent concern with social ills.

² Thomas Erskine (1750-1823), British jurist celebrated for his ability as a trial lawyer.

³ Probably Rufus Choate (1799-1859), a lawyer and congressman from Massachusetts, noted as an orator.

216

Chicago, October 28, 1888.

Dear Friend,—

My suggestions on oratory? You "thank me for them." How did I know you needed caution? I had no idea, I assure you, that you could imagine I thought you in need of advice or that I could think it wise for anyone to drop his natural method of speaking at the suggestion of someone else. I did say that I hope you never indulge in that kind of oratory. I scarcely know why I said that for I did not and do not think you would be likely to. I was thinking more of the mode of delivery. Some speakers, you know, try to build up pedestals for themselves with the damaged remains of their opponents fame. . . . I did not mean to criticise the practice of making gestures. On the contrary I think hands can speak, and certainly the eyes, yes, every expression of the face adds to or detracts from what is said. It does occur to me, however, that I've known speakers who tried to make up in wildness of gesture and loudness of tone for what their discourse lacked in wisdom. . . . No, I didn't hear Blaine. I might have done so but I had seen and heard him before.

Who's going to be elected? Mr. Cleveland, of course. What under the sun would they elect Harrison for? In memory of his grandfather?

Now about the pictures I promised to tell you of. You showed your artistic judgment when you said the descriptions in the papers did not please you. They were absolutely meaningless to a great extent. "The Hunt Ball," an English picture by an American artist, Julius Stewart, is one of the brightest and happiest things on exhibition. It is really exquisite. I never saw anything more really perfect than the gossamer-like dresses and some of the ladies have such speaking faces that I found myself almost waiting to hear what they were saying. A most excellent picture and one of the largest, was "The Black Prince before the Body of the King of Bohemia after the Battle of Crecy."

. . . The Scotchman [?] was a born artist. When I was a little child we had quite a pretty place. The garden was very large and we had a lot of corn. I can hear now just how the corn used to rustle in the evening. I often listened to it though I was a little afraid too. Do you know that the leaves do not all rustle alike? I wonder if they have any consciousness of harmony.

Yours
Ellen.

217

Redfield, Nov. 6, 1888.

Dear Ellen,—

On Thursday, Friday and Saturday of last week I spoke twice, have missed one night during the last two weeks and four only in the last three. The day time intervening has been devoted to driving chiefly, and plying the persuasive arts of the politician — that is some of them — between times. My voice is as strong and clear as when I started out. I'm in good health and spirits. . . . The campaign has been in every way satisfactory to me and chiefly in the matter of the many friends I have gained in all parts of the two counties. I really grew eloquent last Saturday in a few passages, so that someone blurted out when I got through, "That's the talk of an honest man." Now isn't that something to be proud of without being vain. . . . Aren't you really afraid you guessed wrongly on the National ticket? This elegant weather augurs no good for the democracy in New York, yet if the local candidates do not trade there is no fear.

We have a great number of cases to prepare for trial. It is my purpose to devote myself to them at once and probably I shall be able to get so far along that I can take a week or ten days off about the last of the month.

Please consider neither the tardiness nor the brevity of this letter as worthy of imitation. It will seem an awful long time to me since hearing from you last however promptly you answer. I must get down on the street. Bye-bye.

Tom.

218

Chicago, Nov. 11, 1888.

Dear Friend,—

. . . Yes, I was somewhat afield in my speculations on the results of the election. My position was not a lonely one, however. I was surprised, infinitely surprised. Another quarter of a century of Republican victories will, perhaps, teach the Democrats a much needed lesson. It is most emphatically, a party divided against itself, to its own destruction. It is, doubtless, ridiculous in me to criticise so great an institution, but to me their conduct of a campaign seems bungling. In their management they are most lacking in what is exactly expressed by the French word finesse. They also take too much for granted and trust too much to "luck."

I didn't know you were running for office. I now understand that you have been speaking once and twice a day for three weeks (lacking four nights), endeavoring to get an office you don't want, an office that you believed, to begin with, that you couldn't get, that you didn't want if you could get it, that you spoke so much to get though you didn't want it, and that you feared, last Sunday, you would get, contrary to your first belief and your wishes, and in accordance with your efforts. Read me the riddle, I pray you.

Yours
Ellen.

219

Redfield, Nov. 16, 1888.

Dear Ellen,—

Your letter arrived but yesterday. A term of court is called for Clark county for December 4 at which I have several cases for trial. The preparation of these in addition to the work I had anticipated will make it quite out of the question to be with you on Thanksgiving. It would be such a pleasure to attend the concert with you too. I am resolved though to brave all the rigors of your climate and go down immediately after our term which will be about the close of next month, possibly in time to permit me to act as your escort to the next concert. As I understand it, the Club renders "The Messiah" annually during holiday week. May I go with you if I can get there. . . .

I'm not going to attempt to solve your riddle. The result of the election is perfectly satisfactory to me. Another defeated candidate was mildly bewailing our sad fortune. "But," said he, "it don't make any difference to you; defeat doesn't injure you." . . .[1]

Your,
Tom.

[1] Walsh could be pleased with many things about his campaign. His "eminent fitness" to sit on the council was attested to by such Republican sources as the *Redfield Observer* and the *Ashton Argus*. But he was a Democrat, calling especially for tariff reform, as did Cleveland in the national campaign and John W. Harden across Dakota Territory. The "error" of his ways left Walsh with little chance to win. He received some 1,110 votes to 1,870 for his Republican opponent. *Redfield Observer*, October 18, November 1, 15, 1888; *Ashton Argus* quoted in *Redfield Observer*, August 30, 1888.

220

Dear Friend,—

. . . Yes, you may go with me to hear the Messiah if you are very good meanwhile. I'd a great deal rather have you hear that than this first concert. I hope, however, it won't be terribly cold here. That seems a strange consideration to think of in connection with a person coming from Dakota.

. . . Tonight he [Tomlins] made us sing for three hours steadily. What does he care how he tires or ruins voices. Others will be found to replace them. Tomlins is a man I have really tried not to dislike but it's useless. To me, he seems a Napoleon of music. His constant appeal to his singers, "Make Me a name,"— all else is less than nothing.

Good-night.

E.

221

Redfield, December 1, 1888.

Dear Ellen,—

So you are a little averse to making a Parnassus of yourself that Tomlins may mount to glory, eh? Well that's right. Probably one owes it to an organization of that kind to inconvenience himself somewhat to contribute to the success of its public exhibitions, but it can hardly be demanded that one slave it like a ballet girl.

I do want to invoke your assistance again in a legal way. I have a very doubtful case coming up, and [am] much afraid I shall be obliged to go up on it. I have a reference to Harris vs. Frank 52 Miss. 155 and Jones vs. Webster 48 Ala. 109 quite favorable to the position I am compelled to take. . . . If these cases tend to support our position and you can spare time please send me a copy of them. But do not trouble yourself, please, if your other duties make it inconvenient, or if in your judgment the value of the decisions is disproportionate to the effort.

. . . Do you know what I always wish for when I think of visit-

ing Italy? A sail on the Bay of Naples—of course you would
never have guessed it—and I suppose it betrays no such admiration for the worthier, possibly matters of interest which that teem-
ing land affords.

Good-night.
Tom.

222

Chicago, Dec. 4, 1888.

Dear Friend,—

Those cases are hardly parallels of yours, both refer to
land leased for a number of years. I carefully read both cases,
however, for I knew I would not have time to copy them. . . .
You did not ask my opinion in the matter and I ask your pardon
for offering it. My excuse for so doing being the knowledge that
it can do no harm. You need pay no attention to it.

I'm really ashamed of this scrawl but I've been compelled to
write very fast.

E. C. M.

223

Redfield, December 10, 1888.

Dear Ellen,—

Thanks for your effort very much. I fear you went to too
much trouble. There are several suggestions in your remarks
about the case which deserve more attention than you seem to
think them worthy of. I shall appropriate some of them. There
is more force in your way of putting the argument on some
phases than as it had previously appealed to me.

. . . I fully agree with you too, [*in re Robert Elsmere*] in your
detestation of anyone so cowardly that he dare not think lest
perchance he should doubt.[1] A faith that will not bear the test
of reason, that can not endure the light of truth confesses itself
false. Did you get at the faith that Robert finally adopted with

anything like accuracy? If my faith were shattered I should have a sorry time reconstructing another.

Good-night.

Tom.

[1] *Robert Elsmere* (1888) was a novel by the English writer Mrs. Humphry Ward, relating to religion and the higher criticism.

224

Chicago, December 16, 1888.

Dear Friend,—

. . . If I can manage to get off and can otherwise arrange matters I'll sit beside you instead of in the chorus. Can't say just how it will be, but this I do say. I want you to attend the concert on the 27th also. At it we sing "The Tower of Babel" and the "Stabat Mater." The 28th we sing the Messiah. Can't you be here in time?

Hastily,

Ellen.

225

Redfield, December 20, 1888.

Dear Ellen,—

I snatch a few moments this noon to say that barring accidents I shall be in Chicago either Sunday or Monday afternoon. It is impossible for me to say now which day it will be for it will depend on whether court adjourns tomorrow evening as contemplated or whether some case pending may not necessitate a session on Saturday. I have been on one side of every case but one tried since the session began so such a contingency is most likely to detain me.

In greatest haste.

Tom.

226

My dear Tom,—

I am going down town in a few minutes so I thought it would be a good opportunity to mail a little note to you. Then I'm going to the public library to get a book, not on law, mon ami. I shall wait until you can be my stern teacher there. Then I'm going to the hair dresser's to get my "bangs" cut. Then I'm coming home to wait for your letter. . . .

Bye-bye.
E.

227

Redfield, Dakota, Jan. 1, 1889.

Dearest Ellen,—

You will observe that I got home as contemplated this evening still in time to return your New Year's greeting. You naughty, naughty girl, why didn't you let me thank you for the elegant handkerchiefs? If you had but seen the varying expressions of my countenance when I discovered them down in the car you might have felt the joke was worth playing though. They are very, very pretty indeed. With all fervor I wish you also a happy New Year!

. . . I shall go to work tomorrow with a sense of having been much refreshed by my vacation.

Present my regards to Mary and your mother, please, and write as soon as you can conveniently to

Your
Tom.

228

Redfield, Jan. 2, 1889.

Dear Ellen,—

That was indeed kind of Mary to feel an interest in my welfare. She asked me with such evident good-will if I should

like to live in Chicago that I yielded without reserve to tell
her of the perplexity I was even then in. And it gave me still
greater pleasure to have her ask at once, "What does Ellen
think about it?" Henry doesn't want me to go, primarily because
he says I can't stand the lake climate and secondarily because
he sees no pecuniary advantage in it. On the latter score the fact
that our cash receipts last month footed up $450 seems to him
unanswerable. . . . But the first year business doesn't seek you,
you must look for it, and then maybe you wouldn't mind keeping
office some of the time yourself. Yet there's such an immense
amount of satisfaction in being able to sit down quietly in your
office letting clients hunt you up instead of getting out to "rustle"
for business which process is always attendant with features
more or less disagreeable. The struggle for recognition in such
a city is a task even to a man of talents. I opine that a man may
become in no small degree distinguished at the bar there before
the business public even knows of his existence. Yet that wouldn't
deter me if I felt wholly at ease on the other matters. The Lake
climate doesn't seem to agree with me very well. . . . With
ordinary caution [however] and abundance of exercise there
ought to be no grounds for fear.

Court adjourns this week having disposed of perhaps half
of the business. No more court until next June. I had supposed
we had at least got rid of that feature of the practice in Dakota,
that better times were at hand in the matter of disposing of our
business, but it seems we aren't very much ahead yet.

Can't you really imagine that your note will interest me?
Imagine what I've done though—picked it up half a dozen times
to catch its perfume. Oh, I'm teachable.

Good-night.
Tom.

229

Chicago, Jan. 4, 1889.

Dear Tom,—

. . . So the young couple didn't afford you as much
amusement as they might. If I should ever go out to Dakota,

mon ami, I shall expect you to show your good sense by sitting in the smoker. Never mind if you don't like smoke, that isn't of the smallest consequence. Your duty will be to appear quite an old actor in the role of "Benedick, the married man," and a palpable neglect of your Beatrice is considered quite the correct thing in such a case I believe.[1] You may rely upon my seconding your efforts.

Were you really surprised? I didn't know as you would be. Perhaps you recall that I left the room just a little while before Mary came home from church. Well I felt quite guilty when I went back. I was almost sure you could read in my face that I had just taken my hand out of your overcoat pocket.

. . . Regardless of the fact that "calling" is out of date, we had quite a number, among them twenty-three of my boys, representing the three graduating classes.

Now don't write when you are tired, please. I'd rather wait for the letter and don't work so hard.

Your
Ellen.

[1] The reference is to Benedick and Beatrice in Shakespeare's *Much Ado About Nothing*. They finally agreed to marry, out of pity for each other.

230

Chicago, Jan. 6, 1889.

Dear Tom,—

I was amused about the perfume. Glad you are teachable. That's not my favorite kind, however. When I buy perfume, it is always Lubin's best, direct from Paris, and it's pretty sure to be either ext. of violets or heliotrope. I generally drop a few drops of anything that's handy into a new box of stationery.

I didn't finish this last night, partly because it got rather late, but chiefly because I am almost afraid to write upon the subject that I've thought most about lately—your coming or not coming to this city. You asked me though to think of the matter and tell you the result so I'll do so. In the first place it does not surprise me that your brother sees the matter as he appears to. Of course he doesn't want you to leave. To my mind you are better fitted for city than country life. (In what I say now I have no desire to disparage the latter, nor will I apologize for what I will necessarily have to say of you yourself.) Your tastes are naturally artistic, refined; and, though such tastes are not necessarily defaced by a residence in a small country town, certainly a city affords opportunities to enjoy and cultivate those tastes that a small town never can. Perhaps this phase of the situation is a strange one to mention first but to me life is worth living in so much as we progress, "rise from the lowly earth." As to your business prospects I should have no doubt of your doing well here. Your connection with the Osborne firm would be in itself a recommendation and possibly they would refer others to you. Besides if you had no other business for a time we could live on $100 a month. That's a queer statement for one who gets away with so much money as I do, but you see I've never tried to be particularly economical. But I could be economical. . . . Of raiment, my lord, I shall have a plenty. Perhaps a better plan would be, if you are willing, for you to come here and try it for a year, and if you don't like it, or the climate does not agree with you, what's to prevent your returning to Dakota? The school board will be rather willing to keep me another year I imagine and you would feel less responsibility if you were alone. The only thing that prevents me from unhesitatingly advising you to come is your fear that the climate may not be good for you, and that is the most important feature in the case. You know better the advantages of remaining in Dakota. Rest assured of this, whichever way you decide I shall feel that it is best so. I like the city but possibly might like Redfield a thousand times better. Besides you need not decide just at present, need you?

Bye-bye.
Ellen.

231

Redfield, Jan. 9, 1889.

Dear Ellen,—

. . . I have now to thank you for speaking so freely [about moving to Chicago]. That doesn't begin to express however my appreciation of what you said in the same connection to the effect that you could cheerfully endure the comparative poverty in which we might live the first year, or if it would lighten my burden continue teaching for another year. If you'll let me, I'll s'prise you for that. There—and—there. But, dearest Ellen, it will not be necessary to make either sacrifice. Conceding that I shall make nothing the first year but my salary I can get away from here in July with $800 cash. $400 to buy books and furniture will leave $400 surplus. That will fit a small house I imagine, and possibly leave something. Then if the house rent costs no more than $15—I'm getting that for mine here and that would be a small but steady income—so though we might not be able to live quite as well as we should like I don't feel that there is any danger of our coming to want. But you struck the key-note in saying you are anxious to live. So am I. The problem is where is life likely to yield the most. Here I am, to use the words of a generous rival who called this morning, "the leader of the bar." In Chicago I'm a non-entity. Here $3500 a year which I am likely to make is sufficient to maintain us in comparative affluence and leave enough for an annual trip to the city, in Chicago it's a mere pittance. Here I have a business established, there the uninviting task of building another confronts me. On the other hand success there means wealth and position worthy of being striven for, opportunities to do and be something, so that it might be said when my race is run by a few at least "well done." You'll write again about it, will you not? If I but felt assured that my health would not suffer I shouldn't be very long about making up my mind. The puerile obstacles I've alluded to would be only incentives and there would be so much to be proud of if you went through the struggle with me, a daily inspiration and a never failing support.

Good-night, Ellen.
Tom.

232

Dear Tom,—

Went to rehearsal last night and I wish you could have seen Mr. Tomlins. His mood was absolutely effervescent in its sparkling good humor. Compliments and smiles were scattered broadcast—all due to the fact that the singing of the chorus happened to just suit him in the beginning of the evening. After that his good humor made it impossible to sing wrongly. At our next concert, March 5th, we will sing "Manfred" and "The Golden Legend."

You want me to write again about the important question. Well I'll try to. I did not intend to say before that I should not give my opinion until you had decided what you were going to do. But my thoughts frequently run away from my pen with the result hinted at above. I meant to say that I would not express myself on the subject until you had done so. It would be foolish to do so only after you had decided. If I agreed with you then it couldn't make much difference and if I did not it couldn't be best to say much about it.

You make it difficult for me, mon ami, to have an unbiased opinion on either side. While reading your last letter, I quite agreed with you when you pleaded for Dakota, but [in] the next paragraph you so clearly defined the attractions of city life that my wavering opinions immediately turned from the home of the blizzard. So what's to be done about it, Tom? Don't you think you had better rely wholly upon your own judgment? If you did come here, we'd get along all right of course. What a goose you were to talk about sacrifices. I don't see where there would be any.

There was something in your next-to-last letter that I ought to have spoken of, but did not, though I fully intended to do so. This was it, "and then maybe you wouldn't mind keeping office some of the time yourself." Of course I shouldn't. I'd like it. Then I could learn something about the law if you would help me when you had time. And if you had some writing to do, I could do it for you. I really can write when I try.

I will paint you something with the greatest pleasure. You dear child, why didn't you ask me when you were down? Am I such an ogress? . . .

Good-night.

L. N.

233

Redfield, January 20, 1889.

Dear Ellen,—

I went to Aberdeen Friday evening. Since the division of the district, the pilgrimages I used to make to Huron are directed to the first named city. . . . That suggests another matter. Another gentleman occupying a similar position with the McCormick company, for whom I tried successfully a small though difficult case last week, said that their Minneapolis manager was out there a few days ago and expressed a desire to make arrangements with some young active attorney familiar with the Dakota practice to take charge of the legal business of the firm at Minneapolis. The matter was broached by myself and he offered to exert himself to induce his superior to look me up. If anything more comes of it I'll tell you. For a number of reasons I'm inclined to look more favorably on this than on what the other firm offers. In the first place their work is a "demnition grind,"[1] not much practice in court if I understood the thing aright, and as I intimated before, I believe that is an important circumstance to consider since actual experience is the only way of gaining that abundance of tact which the position demands. Another advantage lies in the fact that many of our clients do business there and in St. Paul and I could reasonably expect to get some of their business. It's an elegant city to live in too and, if I must confess it, I should feel much more like making an effort to become known and to cultivate the acquaintance of a small circle of friends. There is no occasion to be in a hurry. I apprehend my services will be just as valuable in a year from now as they are now. Indeed it seems likely that with the present prospect in the matter of trying cases, I shall gain not only in experience but, not unlikely, in reputation. . . . I am much inclined to think that the first year of our married life could be

215

spent here with greater happiness than amid the turmoil and bustle of the city. You'll have to learn to ride a bucking broncho and take a jaunt of three or four miles before breakfast to get the scent of our roses if they aren't all gone. Or a row on the river on a quiet Sunday afternoon would furnish some out-door diversion. What do you think of making this our temporary home instead of the city? . . . I'm not so terribly unsophisticated, you know. I've been around some. Handsome maidens are not wholly wanting even in Dakota and then I lived a year at Madison you remember, where one's social longings might be satiated if anywhere. But say, dear Ellen, if your suggestion of delaying our marriage was prompted in any sense by a suspicion that I might consider it an embarrassment in embarking in a new field, I pray you dismiss it, because I always think of you as a much needed help in such a crisis. You must tell me pretty soon where you want to be married.

Your devoted
Tom.

¹ A euphemistic form of "damnation grind."

234

Chicago, January 27, 1889.

My dear Tom,—

Have been taking a ten-mile ride—not on a broncho, nor merely for a breath of frost-laden air, but on cable and horse-car, and almost solely for the purpose of writing to you. The other end of the ten miles was ten miles from home, and there was no chance there [at home] for the absolute quiet that is necessary while penning the thoughtful kind of production I usually send you.

. . . When one thinks of the God and the religion of the old testament, when one hears some ministers tell what our life here ought to be in order to fit us for the next world, when one thinks of the ignorant multitudes, already bowed down with the miseries of earth, that blindly listen and believe and have added to their wretchedness here the fear or certainty of damnation hereafter, it makes one question whether what is termed goodness, or piety, or religion be not really absolute wickedness. . . .

Yes, I thought it might be less embarrassing for you to enter into business in a new place if you were alone. I fear you would find me poor help, a willing one however.

Yours,
E.

235

Redfield, January 30, 1889.

Dear Ellen,—

I leave tomorrow evening for Bismark. There's a promise of some sport at the capital. [Governor] Church and the legislators are fast reaching a point where open war is inevitable. They over-ride his vetoes just for the fun of the thing. Of course that isn't commendable but it has a tendency to make the debates of interest to a spectator. I have but one case on the calendar and shall probably have some leisure to devote to watching the progress of the fight.[1]

. . . I wish, Ellen, I deserved that abiding faith you have in me, but little as it is merited, I should have been less worthy of it had I not always believed that you entertained it in a small degree at least.

. . . I hope to read some of Burke to you some day. The wisdom of his utterances is no less noteworthy than the perfect rhetoric with which they are expressed.

Bye-bye.
Tom.

[1] Governor Church was faced not only by Republicans but by determined men who spoke for the farmers' interests. According to Howard Lamar, the Dakota Alliance had been campaigning for two years to gain control of the Assembly. In the organization of the new Assembly early in 1889 they controlled well over a majority in the lower house and selected the leaders of both houses. Lamar, *Dakota Territory*, pp. 274-78; Kingsbury, *History of Dakota Territory*, II, 1552-55 and *passim*.

236

Chicago, Feb. 4, 1889.

Dear Tom,—

I don't know if I shall have time to write a letter of the usual length before I go to rehearsal, but shall write something so that you may get it before you leave Bismark. You didn't say how long you would be there. . . .

Yours,

E.

237

Redfield, February 13, 1889.

Dear Ellen,—

. . . Mr. Hanson, assistant solicitor of the C.M. and St. Paul Co. was present and having the day before heard me argue my case before the supreme court he suggested that if I could only put off my trip to Chicago for a week until his return to Milwaukee he would recommend my appointment as local attorney for their road, which would entitle me to a pass over all their lines. So unless the G.M. [General Manager?] puts a veto on it I expect my commission in about ten days, as I concluded after some hesitation to accept his offer. I didn't express nor feel any particular gratitude at his offer but upon reflection I'm impressed with the belief that there may be something in it in time. The pass constitutes a retainer and then they pay me for any work just the same as other clients. I'll say to you because I know you will be glad to hear it that I received a number of very warm compliments on my argument, from attorneys whose commendation means something and points out the effort as singular at least. Mr. Hanson among others, although I was an almost unknown person to him, spoke to me and to others of the clearness and force with which my positions were stated.[1] A copy of my brief and abstract is sent you with the current mail.

I enjoyed the court quite well but the legislature was very

tiresome. Got in at the death of the woman suffrage bill. No, that isn't right. It never dies.[2]

Good-night.
Tom.

[1] The *Redfield Observer* of February 14, 1889, carried this account of Walsh's argument under "Local Miscellany": "T J Walsh argued his very important land case, Kalschener vs. Kellar [*sic*] et al., in the supreme court on Monday. He made a fine argument, and impression was general among attorneys that he will win his case. . . . Referring to Mr. Walsh, the Bismarck cor of the Aberdeen News says:

"Hon. T J Walsh, of Redfield, has been here several days conducting a case in the supreme court. His argument before the august body is very highly spoken of indeed by his brother attorneys and though opposed by Lawyer Winsor, of Sioux Falls, it is very confidentially expected he will get a verdict favorable to his client. Mr. Walsh has a bright future before him and deserves well, be it either in the practice of his profession or in political life."

[2] Governor Church's administration came to an end on March 22. He was exceedingly unpopular, and Dakota leaders prevailed upon the new President, Benjamin Harrison, to appoint a Republican. Arthur C. Mellette, formerly of Indiana, became the last territorial governor of Dakota. Kingsbury, *History of Dakota Territory*, II, 1564, 1568-69.

238

Chicago, Feb. 17, 1889.

Dear Tom,—

. . . I shall be very glad indeed if you can get down for the concert. Some excellent soloists are also engaged, Christine Nilsson among them.

That offer of Mr. Hanson's was very nice indeed, whether the position is a lucrative one or not.

If you get here in time you must go to the Art Institute.[1]

Bye-bye.
Ellen.

[1] The Art Institute was incorporated in 1879, but Ellen McClements was referring, in all probability, to the new quarters at the corner of Michigan Avenue and Van Buren Street which had opened to the public in the fall of 1887. Moses and Kirkland (eds.), *History of Chicago*, II, 126.

239

Redfield, February 24, 1889.

Dear Ellen,—

Of course you have read all about how we swagger around about our new statehood clothes that are being made. There's no particular demonstration being made but everybody entertains a feeling of great satisfaction. . . .[1] Delegates to a constitutional convention will be chosen May 14. In October state officers are elected and a vote is taken on the temporary capital.

Never mind what you said [about the name "Walsh"]. I dare say some who bore it were hanged for liberty and for crime. You'll not find that your worst burden. I'm selfish, sordidly so, and weak in many things in which I should be strong to be your Brutus. "I'm cabined, cribbed and coffined" even in speech and for this among other reasons I'm an unsocial fellow. Everybody likes Henry. . . .

I'm glad you challenged me to say what my first impression of you was. I like to think of it and the occasion of our first meeting. Do you? I was really startled to hear you sing and only then began to be interested, but I didn't feel on anything like even terms with you until you tried to throw burrs in my hair. I've always felt pleased at it myself and thought it honorable to both of us that my love for you found reasons for its existence and grew. Was that the time I made you catch croquet balls until your hands were all bruised up?

Bye-bye, Ellen.
Tom.

[1] President Cleveland had signed the enabling act on February 22, authorizing four "omnibus states" of South Dakota, North Dakota, Montana, and Washington to frame their constitutions.

240

Chicago, February 27, 1889.

Dear Tom,—

. . . What a lot of nonsense you can write when you try. I refer to what you said about selfishness, and being no talker,

etc., etc. You are a—but I wouldn't do myself so much injustice
if I were you.

Yours,
Ellen.

241

Aberdeen, Feb. 28, 1889.

Dear Ellen,—

I shall be in Chicago by Tuesday evening though I am
unable to say when you may expect me. I came up here to hear
this evening W. W. Erwin, conceded to be the greatest criminal
lawyer in the northwest, try a case. . . .

Good-night, Ellen.
Tom.

242

Redfield, March 8, 1889.

Dear Ellen,—

I expected a letter from you yesterday or today in re-
sponse to my telegram. I need not tell you how very grievously
I was disappointed in not being able to keep my appointment.
. . . I hope to be with you by Saturday of next week.

Bye-bye.
Tom.

243

Chicago, March 10, 1889.

Dear Tom,—

Why haven't you written? Are you sick or only busy.
If it's the latter, it is all right, but if you are sick I'd like to know
it. I received your telegram last Monday, but even then hoped

you would get here. During the concert I kept glancing at that vacant seat, hoping each time to see it vacant no longer. . . .[1]

I have seen Vereshchagin's great pictures and they are grand, sublime some of them. I don't wonder Russia has no use for them.[2] I wanted you to see them but the Exposition closes next Saturday. By the way, the picture I painted for you has been hanging up for a week awaiting a claimant. Am I to send it to you?

Your
Ellen.

[1] About this time in Redfield the "reading circle" was providing its own variety of entertainment. At a meeting on March 12, the program was to run the gamut from musical selections, to a review of *Silas Marner* by T. J. Walsh, to the battle of Saratoga and surrender of Burgoyne, to a biography of George Eliot, to a discussion of school management. *Redfield Observer*, March 7, 1889.

[2] Vasily Vereshchagin (1842-1904) portrayed in many of his paintings the brutal aspects of war, including the Russo-Turkish war of 1877-78. Doubtless it was this pacifistic "message" that stirred the criticism to which Ellen McClements referred.

244

Sioux Falls, Dakota, March 15, 1889.

Dear Ellen,—

I'll be close on the heels of this letter, not later than Sunday at 1 P.M. and possibly Saturday night rather late. But I may come up even if it is quite quite late, may I not? . . .[1]

Bye-bye for a short time which will still be long to

Your own
Tom.

[1] According to the *Redfield Observer* of March 21, 1889, Walsh went first to Sioux Falls, where he assisted in an attempt to make Redfield the capital of South Dakota. He then "hied himself to Chicago for business and pleasure."

245

Redfield, Blizzardom, March ——, 1889.

Dear Ellen,—

. . . I expect a judge ought not to have any ambition except for further judicial honors,[1] but then it's rather difficult to find perfection in these degenerate days.

It must have been exceedingly lonely riding home alone. I should have felt alarmed only I understood that you knew the driver.

Good-bye.

Tom.

[1] Walsh seems to have maintained this position consistently, although the judge alluded to in the passage above is not identified. More than twenty-five years later he argued that Charles Evans Hughes should not have left the Supreme Court to accept a presidential nomination. Walsh to Lyman J. Nash, August 19, 1916, Walsh Papers, Library of Congress.

246

Chicago, March 25, 1889.

My dear Tom,—

Do you know there is one point on which I cannot agree with you? Dakota is far away, and, stranger still, it is farther away at certain times than at others. It reaches its fartherest northwestern limit just about the time you arrive there after one of your eastern trips. Just about now it is at least 180 degrees from the mudless streets of Chicago.

. . . She [Kate] remarked that your mustache is too long, that it makes you look like a brigand. Such a remark does not seem wholly laudatory but it displays an interest never exhibited before. I predict that when she knows you a little better she will forgive even the long mustache which I admire. . . .

This letter is not likely to give you brainfever is it? But I remember how prone you are to read only such solid literature as the stuff which law books are made of, so, wholly for your own good, as a sort of mental playtime, I offer you something light for your perusal.

Good-night, dear Tom.

Yours,

L. N.

247

Redfield, March ——, 1889.

Dear Ellen,—

The letter that I looked for came this morning as promised. If there is ever one time more than another when your letters are a supreme delight to me it is immediately after returning from Chicago and living through that long dreary ride. I'm willing to admit it is a long distance. . . .

Yours,

Tom.

248

Chicago, April 1, 1889.

Dear Tom,—

Isn't this letter a surprise to you? I haven't the ghost of a thing to write about, but that's no matter, is it? Do you know what I shall miss most—well, after next July we'll say? Your letters. What are you going to do about it? Write me letters from the office? May I come down sometime to your sanctum and see how MacGregor looks on his native heath, with his proper surroundings? . . .

Bye-bye.

E.

249

Redfield, April 4, 1889.

Dear Ellen,—

. . . The storm tore up a number of the roofs about town, over-turned out-houses and did some minor damage. I never knew it to blow so hard and continuously before. Prairie fires were fanned into destructive activity by the wind and as a consequence there will be no little litigation against the railroad companies who are always charged with setting them. We took the initiatory steps in a case the other day against the Northwestern company for destroying a farmer's tree claim. There seems to be a sort of implied understanding that attorneys for one road shall not prosecute actions against another, but 'tis not so nominated in my bond and I have no sort of intention of honoring custom but by its breach.

After court I'll run down to Chicago, but, mind, only for a day or two. But I must hurry back to prepare for court here which is likely to last until it is time to go to Chicago again. Two days aren't very long but I wouldn't miss going down once more before—well before July, we'll say, to use your words, on any consideration. . . . You remember the injunction you laid on me, that I would have to ride in the smoker coming out. Well I serve notice right here that that will never do. You'll have to let me sit with you only to point out the places of note and interest along the line, as the more experienced traveler, you know.

We have been buying a driving horse. Henry went up to Mellette after it this evening. I think you will find it no small factor in making life in Dakota endurable.[1]

Good-night. Love.

Your Tom.

[1] The *Redfield Observer* reported on April 11, 1889: "The Walsh Bros. have recently purchased of True Childs, of Mellette, a six-year-old brown horse."

250

Redfield, April 6, 1889.

Dear Ellen,—

You said you like to get letters that come unexpectedly. I'm sure you were not looking for this. . . .

Have you ever observed how barren my speech is in this regard. My imagination isn't a very active faculty, although the efforts of other people in this field, being worthy, always command my appreciation. I don't remember ever having invented a figure of speech.

By the way, there is a sentiment existing and showing signs of development in favor of making me one of the Spink county delegates to the Sioux Falls constitutional convention which convenes July 4. If I should go it might make some difference as to the exact time when an event in which we ourselves are chiefly interested shall take place. If you could expedite your arrangements a little in view of that fact and permit our marriage before the assembling of the convention wouldn't it please you to attend? Or you may have something to suggest in view of this contingency. I had thought you might enjoy going around the lakes to Duluth and on from there to Minneapolis and St. Paul in coming out.

Here's a good-night kiss from

Tom.

251

Chicago, April ——, 1889.

Dear Tom,—

. . . Why, mon ami, I am the least imaginative person in the world, and as for any special style about my writings, I have none. I write as Mark A—— said he spoke, "right on" telling you for the most part that you very well "do know." [1] About your own letters you are singularly blind. I have never been disappointed in them; they satisfy me. I was much interested in all you said about your city's prospects, contrary to your expectations. My tastes are not wholly feminine, I fear. I suppose it would be more seemly for me to take a great interest in the way to make bread, the latest fads in fashion, etc., but somehow I can't.

I've just stopped to look up some date for your consideration. School will close June 28, your convention assembles July 4th. Wouldn't that be crowding matters somewhat? If nothing happens to render it impossible I shall not object if it pleases you. It would please me to attend the convention or to go [on] that lake trip you propose. I am always pretty well tired out though after the work attending the graduating exercises, so you'll have to take the risk of people thinking you've married a perfect fright. . . . Your house is not furnished is it? Can pretty things be gotten in Redfield?

Good-bye.
Yours,
E.

[1] In Shakespeare's *Julius Caesar*, Act iii, Scene 2, Mark Antony said:
> I come not, friends, to steal away your hearts: . . .
> For I have neither wit, nor words, nor worth,
> Action, nor utterance, nor the power of speech,
> To stir men's blood: I only speak right on;
> I tell you that which you yourselves do know: . . .

252

Redfield, April ——, 1889.

Dear Ellen,—

. . . I could get very neat furniture here or at Aberdeen but I always thought their prices outrageously high here. Besides to tell you the truth my experience in house-furnishing has been so very limited I'm not a little lacking in assurance about starting out. I did think some about buying in Chicago but freights, I apprehend, will consume most of the profit, only one might doubtless make a better selection there. I'll have to rely on you largely for suggestions. What shall the chamber set be, antique oak or cherry? You have doubtless seen the somewhat recent style of wall paper, heavy texture, neutral colors and plain—no figures. I haven't seen it on a wall but it is said to be quite attractive. Couldn't you get some samples?

Bye-bye, Sweetheart.
Tom.

253

Dear Tom:

. . . You spoke of my resigning my position before the close of school. You will have inferred from my last that such a course would be impossible but I should have explained why. In the first place I would not like to desert my class, really they would feel very badly about it. Even the decorations have to be all attended to by myself. Another thing the school board have been very kind to me and it would probably not be quite agreeable to them to have to look around for someone to take my place. . . . I shall take things as easy as possible. You know my school never causes me an anxious thought, and I was just thinking to-day that the pupils grow more considerate, more helpful, more thoughtful daily. In looking back over my school life, I can think of only two or three persons who ever annoyed me in school, and they did so for such a little time that I can scarcely recall that I was ever annoyed at all. I shall have all the final examinations over by the end of May and that will give me June for a leisurely preparation of closing exercises.

Ellen.

254

Redfield, April 12, 1889.

Dear Ellen,—

The receipt of your letter this afternoon was a very decided relief to me. Hadn't you better just observe yourself the admonition you give me and not try to do quite so much?

Our horse came down a week ago. He is not exactly the kind of horse for a pet. He's very large, but a nice driver and he carries himself well. But we have a baby pony. Our riding horse has a colt, a wee little thing, but he's agile and nicely developed.

. . . There is more to be gained in the way of reputation—notoriety perhaps—in winning one of those cases (criminal) than a half dozen civil actions demanding ever so much more study and ability.

I quite agree with you that we had better get, at the start, only such things as are necessary to fit us out comfortably and have those neat but not gaudy. As soon as I can get around to it I'll go up with a carpenter and have him figure on the changes proposed in the house. . . . I like your plan best because if we buy in Chicago you will have to do the selecting. It looks now as though there would be no occasion for hurrying our arrangements on account of the Sioux Falls constitution. It is going to be adopted beyond a question of a doubt and I have no particular desire to attend under those circumstances and even should I, there will be nothing that wouldn't be a bore to both of us then.

Did you get the flowers? Were they all withered and gone? They aren't very pretty but I thought you would be interested to know what they are like.

Bye-bye, Ellen.
Tom.

255

Chicago, April 15, 1889.

Dear Tom,—

. . . But, mon ami, you don't intend to depend on me for your meals do you? You'll starve, or die because you do eat if you place faith in my culinary skill. I can bake (everything except bread) but I can't cook. That is I don't succeed very well because I seldom try. You should have offered Mary your hand and heart. She's an excellent cook when she tries and she never will touch any other kind of work in the house, so it generally falls to me, when I'm home, to attend to the work outside the kitchen. Therefore it would be necessary to fit up one of the small rooms upstairs for a girl, but she need not be a "professional" as I think I have some faculty for managing (even in the kitchen) if I haven't to depend wholly upon myself. Aren't you finding out by degrees how rash your choice was?

I must ride, mustn't I when I come out there? Therefore a riding habit will be of the utmost importance. Do you folks put on a great deal of style when you go out riding? Shall I need a silk hat? By the way I wish you would wear one sometimes. It may be silly but I do think they are the only proper hat for a gentleman on dress parade. You would look very handsome in one I'm sure. You get a silk hat to please me, and I'll get and wear any kind of a hat or bonnet you describe.

I was much interested in what you said about your horse. But why isn't he black. We must have a span of blacks or creams when our ship comes in.

Yours,
E.

256

Redfield, April 15, 1889.

Dear Ellen,—

. . . I perceived that it would be almost out of the question for you to resign prior to the close of the term. There are obligations in such cases that one can hardly think of abandoning. So it will be July, unless the unexpected happens, as it proverbially does.

Bye-bye. Love.
Your Tom.

257

Sioux Falls, D.T., April 17, 1889.

Dear Ellen,—

. . . Its settled then that we stock up in Chicago. . . . Did you really think I was going to insist on your taking your points on the rudiments of the law by practice in the kitchen? It isn't so very pleasant down at the office but you may come down anytime, all the time, and have a desk too if you want it. Then when our ship comes in and I shan't be obliged to attend to the details and the mechanical part of the business and I can have a good working library at the house perhaps you can anticipate some pleasure in working together there, because then, you know, you'll be something of a lawyer yourself.

A riding habit isn't an entirely indispensable garment and really it would amuse you to observe the shifts sometimes resorted to in lieu of one. No, there isn't an excessive amount of style about any of them. They are usually made for service. Most of the ladies wear caps but a silk tile is always becoming, particularly to a lady of medium or above medium height. Do you really think I should grace a silk hat? How funny! I was actually contemplating purchasing one the other day. They may now be worn in these parts without danger, in fact they are getting quite common. But I always entertained an idea that my physical make-up wasn't particularly suited to that kind of head-gear.

Good-night.
Tom.

258

Chicago, April 22, 1889.

Dear Friend,—

I am glad that you feel as you do about my going to Europe. I have never thought seriously of it before when it has been proposed to me, but now that I have such an excellent opportunity, I had better accept it. They, however, will go directly to Christiania, I to Paris to study with Le Grange. . . .

My dear, dear, Tom—The other page is all nonsense, of course, at least that part which refers to my going. I wouldn't go, I wouldn't want to go, unless you could go along too.

Thanks awfully about information concerning a riding habit. I shall get a new one as I like to do things in proper attire. Don't worry you'll look quite charming in a silk hat though I like those large felt hats you wear quite as well, even better perhaps.

Good-night.
Ellen.

259

Redfield, April 23, 1889.

Dear Ellen,—

If you had just written another page of that heartless stuff I should certainly have felt that I am growing exceedingly and alarmingly nervous. If you really wanted to go I could hardly think of interposing an objection because that ship may be a long,

long time coming in. But wait, I have some news for you. You remember, doubtless, my telling you sometime ago of an offer I was not unlikely to receive to go to Minneapolis. Well, Mr. Daniels, the general agent for the company was at Aberdeen last week and came down here for the purpose as I afterwards learned of "sizing me up." I was absent at Sioux Falls but met him about an hour next day at Aberdeen. Daniels asked me what I would take to go down and take charge of their business. I found no difficulty in putting him off upon the promise at his invitation that I would call on him on my way back from Chicago. He has charge of the business of the company in a strip of country running from the Mississippi to the Missouri. I would be expected to try all their cases in that region which would necessarily involve frequent absences from home. And what will poor Ellen do then? I inferred also that he expected it would require and that I should devote all my time. Mr. Miller [?] undertook to find out for me if he could about what they expect to pay. Assuming that the work requires all my time what ought I to ask? Would $2500 be beyond my desert? I should be inclined to accept for $1000 less if they left me free to engage with other clients.

Bye-bye.
Tom.

260

Chicago, May 3, 1889.

Dear Tom,—

Our new principal came on Tuesday of last week. He expresses himself delighted with the school in general and the singing of my chorus in particular. He told them they are the best singers in the city schools and that Mr. Tomlins high school choruses do not produce as good tones as they. He has brought several people in to hear them, among them a new superintendent of singing who made them quite a little speech and said just about what the Principal did.

I read with a great deal of interest your article on the Sioux Falls constitution. Is it not strange that people should lend their support to such a faulty compilation? . . . Why didn't you do it sooner? Such a system of laws will be a "blot on the escutcheon" of the new state.[1] You have, I judge, an average percent of smart people out your way. Was it not their duty to find out all about the proposed constitution long ere this, or are some of them afraid to voice the faith that is in them? I like a proper amount of prudence, but I find it remarkably hard at times to draw the line where prudence ends and cowardice begins.

About the Minneapolis business. I shall not speak, since we are to "talk it over" when you come down. Only let me give you this caution. Do not go to Minneapolis because you imagine I might not like Redfield as well as a larger city. I think I should like to live in Dakota, if you thought it wisest, and I don't know but a progressive new State is better than an older one.

Yours,
Ellen.

[1] A constitution had been drawn up in 1885 at Sioux Falls, and the convention of 1889 was expected to approve that document. Therefore, Walsh could criticize in advance of the convention.

261

Redfield, May 8, 1889.

Dear Ellen,—

While absent on Monday I was nominated by the democrats as delegate to Sioux Falls. . . .[1] My article in the [Redfield] Journal seems to have gained me some notoriety.[2] Under the flaming heading "Another Heretic" the Brooking's Press, mildly opposed to the constitution, reprints the entire article. The Vermillion Republican also reproduces some of it. Should this opposition continue to develop and there are no prudential reasons to deter, and I should be a member of the convention, do you know what I shall do? Appeal to the respectable precedent of the national convention which though its members were elected to revise the Articles of Confederation as the members [of] this convention will be to revise the Sioux Falls constitution—for certain changes must be made you know—[went beyond its instructions,] and insist [likewise] on drafting a new document. Would that be too bold? I'll promise to make a speech if you come, provided I'm a delegate. . . .

Your Tom.

[1] The *Redfield Observer* of May 9, 1889, describes a fight in the Democratic county convention over the nominee to Sioux Falls, but "when the smoke of conflict cleared away" Walsh had been nominated. Winning the election was another matter. The enabling act in February had provided for minority representation in the election of delegates. Three were to be chosen from each county, and presumably the Republicans could get no more than two, but a prohibitionist became the third. Walsh was defeated despite tributes to his superior qualities, "eminent legal ability," etc. *Ibid.*, May 16, 1889.

[2] The *Redfield Observer* was formerly known as the *Journal Observer*. In all probability, Walsh's article appeared in this local paper.

262

Chicago, May 12, 1889.

Dear Tom,—

. . . It's nice enough to be popular with one's pupils but they come in at the most inopportune moments. Some of the larger boys were hurt greatly the other day because the new principal ordered them not to stand near the gate. He didn't know, of course, that they had been in the habit of awaiting my coming, and opening the door, getting my keys, etc., etc. I have often seen some of the teachers smiling, not quite pleasantly, at these little attentions of the pupils, but I never mind them, because I have faith to believe it doesn't hurt the boys. My pupils overestimate the little I can do for them always, and it seems to give them real pleasure to serve me in any way they can.

I'll look for you Friday night or Saturday A.M.

Yours,
Ellen.

263

Chicago, May 28, 1889.

My Dearest,—

I was wondering just now where my roving boy is, but somehow I cannot keep track of trains very well. . . .

Mrs. MacE sends her love [1] and so does

Your
E.

[1] Mrs. Nettie MacEacham was visiting in Chicago, and perhaps at
this time tentative arrangements were made for Walsh and Ellen to
spend their honeymoon at her home in Sturgeon Bay. In any event,
this was soon to happen.

264

Redfield, May 29, 1889.

Dearest Ellen,—

I arrived this morning. Didn't write you from Minneapolis because of lack of opportunity. I made no contract merely
because I am not quite ready yet to abandon the law business.
The work they desired me to undertake belongs rather to the field
of collections than law and on its being disclosed I said very positively that further negotiation was useless, that salary would be
no object to me.[1] I am sure you will approve my determination
not to let even a liberal salary lure me from the pursuit of a
strictly legitimate law business. Before calling on him, I dropped
in to see a friend who is practicing in the city. He is a cousin and
namesake of Senator Spooner of Wisconsin. He urged me to call
again after my interview which I did. He seems to be doing a
large business, but he labored hard and talked persuasively to
induce me to abandon my desire to go to the city to practice. His
argument pursued this line chiefly, that I had obtained an enviable reputation and position here, where a good lawyer is looked
up to by all classes and considered a leading and influential citizen. In the city I must for a long time at best occupy a subordinate position at the bar and that even should I rise to a position
on the level with the best, the men of wealth will still be far
above me upon the public tongue and in the public eye. He
ended by saying that I should think the matter over with great
care and if my determination remained unchanged to write him
and he would offer me terms on a partnership with him. . . .[2]

Your Tom.

[1] This and previous references (especially No. 233) suggest that the
job would have been with the McCormick Harvesting Co.

[2] This was Marshall A. Spooner, as revealed by his letter to Walsh of
October 25, 1890.

265

Chicago, June 5, 1889.

Dear Tom,—

Everything is on a fair road to success, I believe, in regard to our closing exercises. . . .

Now for that question you said should be settled at once. I will not be married here, but I don't see the use of going away off to Madison or Sioux Falls. Why not go to Kenosha, Racine, or any other place, it's immaterial to me. Mary will willingly go with us. We cannot, however be married as soon as you wish. It is simply impossible. Besides the house will not be ready and you know you hate hotels. You seem to have a partiality for the 15th. Shall we say then the 15th of August if nothing happens to prevent? That will give you time to get the house ready as you once expressed a wish to do and it will give me time to attend to a great many things I wish to see to. I shall be pleased to do the best I can here, if you desire it. I would prefer to go right into our own home.

Good-night, my Brutus.
Ellen.

266

Redfield, June 8, 1889.

Dearest Ellen,—

. . . Sunset Cox is to speak at Huron on the same day, the fourth of July.[1] I should have liked very much to have been able to hear him and to meet him. He will, I learn, spend the summer in the territories about to become states, taking an active part in their political campaigns, particularly in Montana and Washington where he will go on the stump in the hope of getting them to return democratic congressmen. He's ambitious and the people of these territories who owe so much to him, would delight in the opportunity to vote for him for president. Indeed it could not be asserted with positive certainty what even Dakota might do in such a case. He will be treated like a king at Huron. They are arranging for a magnificent ovation for him. $2500 will be spent on fireworks alone. He's unquestionably one of the brainiest men in Congress and what's more he's honest, not self-seeking.

Your Tom.

[1] Samuel "Sunset" Cox was a representative from New York, and formerly had served as a representative from Ohio, and a diplomat in Peru and Turkey. See the further references in No. 275 and accompanying note. David Lindsey's biography, *"Sunset" Cox: Irrepressible Democrat* (Detroit, 1959), reveals the strengths and weaknesses of a national Democratic leader of this period.

267

Chicago, June 10, 1889.

My dear Tom,—

Will you accept the accompanying book, with my love and best wishes on your birthday? . . .

I will send you "just one kiss" for your birthday.

Your
Ellen.

268

Chicago, June 12, 1889.

My Dearest,—

. . . Your letters—I don't remember a time when they were not looked for. . . . I received that big bunch of roses tonight. Most of the full blown ones had fallen off. I almost cried when I saw handfuls of those lovely pink petals. I put them in my rose jar however. The branches I put in a large jar of water and the buds are opening already. They are very fragrant. Thanks and a kiss for the roses.

Your Ellen.

269

Redfield, June 14, 1889.

My dear, dear Ellen,—

You are a dear good girl for remembering my birthday. When I begin talking law out of hours you will let me read to you from it, will you not?

We have been at work on Mr. Dawes' case since yesterday morning.[1] The jury retired at four this afternoon and are still out. . . . A messenger just came with the word that the jury had brought in a verdict for us.

Your Tom.

[1] A reference apparently to Dawes of the Spink County Bank.

270

Redfield, June 18, 1889.

Dear Ellen,—

. . . I was importuned this week to accept a retainer from the other railroad company, the C. and N.W., on the same terms as the St. Paul makes me but I haven't yet concluded to accept and hardly think I shall.

Your next will be expected promptly by

Your Tom.

271

Redfield, June 21, 1889.

Dearest Ellen,—

I write tonight only to relieve my disappointment at the continued failure of your letter to come. It seems a month since I got your last. After Friday you may be able to write often enough to make up for this long delay.

. . . I got a verdict this morning after the jury had been out all night. Thus far we have been very fortunate this term.

Do please drop me a post-card and I'll try to be satisfied.

With much love,
Your Tom.

272

Dearest Ellen,—

Your school closes next Friday, doesn't it? I'll warrant you are wearing yourself out too. Of course you want to make your exercises a success, but they will be that any way.

I read "William Shakespeare" this morning until I grew dazed. . . . Now do you know I could never read Don Quixote? It is just as dull, tiresome and sorrowful to me as the antics of the inmates of an asylum. If he didn't tell at the outset that the Don was demented I might endure it. I've tried three or four times to read it just because of the reputation the author has but can never get beyond a half a dozen chapters.

Bye-bye, Ellen,
Your Tom.

273

Redfield, June 29, 1889.

Dearest Ellen,—

I am greatly pleased to approve all the suggestions you make in the matter of our house-keeping. . . .[1] A term of the Supreme Court occurs early in September. It may be that the occasion will demand some work of me immediately before. In such a case couldn't you try hard to get ready, say a week before the 15th [of August]? Please leave the place of our "At Home" blank for a short period also. Are you surprised at that? You didn't think me such a vacillating, irresolute fellow, did you? The fact is that I am now negotiating with Mr. Spooner about going to Minneapolis and my dissatisfaction at the outlook here doesn't seem to dispel very rapidly. I ought to be thankful for and contented with much undeserved success. You may scold me about that if you like, but do please give me some advice and tell me what you would like—out frankly just as you did in the last letter.

How lucky you were to win that beautiful picture. Let me tell you something I've thought a number of times, that I shan't meet with so many disappointments when we are married, because you are always fortunate, except possibly when you met me. Things never go wrong with you. You get on anyway.

I shall approach the task of arranging things with a great deal of delicacy but then when they are once up and around it will not be a great task for you to re-adjust them. You didn't tell me what color to paint the house and you must give me some suggestions about the interior. Are you sure it will not be imposing too much work on you to ask you to select carpets and furniture and things of that kind. . . .

Tom.

[1] The letter referred to seems to have been lost.

274

Chicago, July 3, 1889.

Dear Tom,—

Will now try to answer your letters of last week. You ask me to tell you frankly what I would like, and I shall do so, but what I would prefer may not be best. Were I in your place I should not hesitate a moment about going to Minneapolis. That you will do well there is as certain as anything can be in this world. My creed is that any man, working earnestly in whatever his business may be, will be successful about 99 times out of 100. I mean a man of ordinary ability. Your danger is that you will work too earnestly, and your ability is not ordinary; so, with 100 people of your kind, I would put the chance of success, 100 times out of 100. . . . As you said, too, your remuneration is small in many cases—not in proportion to your labor by any means. In a city you might not have half as many cases, neither would you have to work as much, and the result would probably be quite as satisfactory. I should prefer to live in Minneapolis, but don't let that influence you.

Our graduating exercises were quite a success. Yes, we had a very pleasant time. You should have seen my flowers. I was just surrounded by bouquets and baskets chiefly roses.

Yours,
Ellen.

275

Dearest Ellen,—

I ask pardon for requesting your advice and then making up my mind before you had time to answer. I knew though that you would not misunderstand and that you would perceive there was no other course. It would be flying in the face of fate to go to Minneapolis now and try to "go it alone." About the ultimate results I never entertained any more doubt than you but I'm not you know, one of those who rush into the favor of people and meanwhile we must live. Opportunities are not likely to grow less numerous in the next few years and meanwhile I'm sure life will not be burdensome to either of us here where a comfortable existence at least is assured. . . .

Cox made a magnificent speech at Huron yesterday. It will probably be furnished in full by the dailies. If so I'll send you one.[1]

Here's a kiss from

Tom.

[1] On July 11 the *Dakota Huronite*, a weekly paper, published Congressman Cox's speech in full. It ran almost four complete pages and was, as Walsh said, a splendid effort. Cox avoided narrow patriotism and revealed a scholarly grasp of American history.

276

Chicago, July 4, 1889.

Dear Tom,—

Do you want me to write you another letter today?

. . . I'm not obedient so I hope the marriage ceremony of your church says nothing about "obey." The other two injunctions I fully agree with, but the other is a relic of an uncivilized past. By the way I was invited to attend a Catholic wedding last Monday, the first I have ever seen. I was charmed with it. Everything was quiet, and simple and short, nothing terrible or awe-inspiring about it. Let me warn you I shall call your pastor to time if he takes over five minutes to make you (shall I say "happy," just for form?) for life.

By this time you have made your speech. Did the admiring throng overwhelm you with applause? Do tell me about Eureka and the celebration.

Bye-bye. Yours
E.

277

Redfield, July 7, 1889.

Dearest Ellen,—

Of course I want you to write me another letter, and another, and another.

I have a young man in the office who has just graduated from the law school. He contemplates going to Salt Lake City this fall. I believe he is making an excellent choice of a location. The Dakota Editorial association went out to the Park last year, then down to Salt Lake and Denver, returning by way of Omaha. They were all greatly impressed with the achievements and prospects of the Mormon city. The people who built that town are scoffed at and vilified by those who aren't much better morally and infinitely inferior in point of energy and pluck. They have made a garden of a desert and if he who makes two blades of grass grow where but one was supported before, is a benefactor of the race, as is said, then may these people lay claim to that virtue.

It is becoming apparent to everyone and most painfully so to those who have invested in lands here that something must be done to alleviate or destroy the effect of the scorching winds that strike us at critical periods in the growth of the crop. The soil has wonderful fertility if there were enough moisture at the right time. Two weeks ago it was believed that the present crop was utterly ruined, but since then by reason of copious showers it has improved greatly in many places. Then yesterday another simoon broke upon us and the rain promised last night passed over. Unless we get a shower very speedily now, everything is gone for this year.[1]

My youngest brother graduated this year and the folks are anxious to send him to college. He's a bright boy and a good, cheerful, honest one. I wouldn't let them send him here.[2] Don't you think it makes a vast difference what kind of air there is about a college? Whether it's laden with a large sympathy with all humanity or impregnated with a sort of we-are-the-elect idea, tinctured with cant or the do-as-you-would-like-to-be-done-by doctrine; whether a great abundance of tolerance and liberality pervades it or if one must seek the fountain of knowledge in the icy air of Puritanic or Inquisitorial holiness? Don't you. . . .[3]

Bye-bye, love,
Tom.

[1] Average rainfall in Spink County is 19.21 inches. What the people of the county were discovering in the 1880's was that a cycle seemed to occur: first came good, favorable years, then the years of drought and of hot winds. See Robert S. Sampson in Harlow, *Prairie Echoes*, p. 41; Lamar, *Dakota Territory*, pp. 275, 279-80.

[2] John Walsh was seventeen at this time. Redfield College, for which Walsh had been hopeful in the beginning, apparently had not turned out well.

[3] So far as the editor is aware, there are no letters now extant for the remainder of 1889. Such letters as were written were few in number and rather personal, for Walsh went to Chicago in August, and on August 15 he and Ellen McClements were married. The *Sturgeon Bay* (Wis.) *Independent* reported in late August that the newlyweds were guests of Mrs. Nettie MacEacham, Walsh's long-time friend and former landlady. According to Mrs. MacEacham's son, William, who was fourteen years old at the time, this was quite a special occasion. He remembered details of the visit and particularly that he had taken a fishing trip with the Walshes, during which they caught string after string of northern perch and pike. Early in September the couple left the beautiful lake country and journeyed to Redfield. There their home was prepared for them; they entered hopefully upon a new life together. But the next year and a half was to prove a difficult time. The problems of this period in Redfield were later described by Genevieve Walsh Gudger (who was born in August, 1890, and had reason to investigate this first year of her life): "Weeks without rain had once more destroyed the crops and a particularly cruel winter broke the gallant spirits of many. Business was more than usually scant." Tom Walsh had to travel "unceasingly," trying his cases in Huron, Aberdeen, and other towns. His wife spent much of her time alone. Together or apart they now debated most seriously the possibilities of a move to another state. *Sturgeon Bay Independent*, August 25, 1889, quoted in the *Redfield Observer*, September 5, 1889; editor's interview with William A. MacEacham, August 18, 1965; Genevieve Walsh Gudger, "Farewell to Dakota," unpublished manuscript, a copy of which is in possession of the editor.

278

Thursday A.M. [Jan. 21, 1890,¹
Redfield, to T. J. W., Huron].

My dear, dear Tom,—²

You will think it strange that I should be writing this between 8 and 9 o'clock A.M. I thought of it however as soon as I awoke—a little before 8 o'clock. Just had my breakfast—in bed —and am writing this in the same place. Slept very soundly all night, since about 11 o'clock. It was a very cold night. Lena says there was nearly half an inch of ice on the water.³ I didn't feel cold however; there was a fire and besides I borrowed a coat of yours that you hung on a chair near the head of the bed. I don't feel so lonesome when I have something of yours near me.

Yesterday afternoon and evening seemed very long. I happened to glance at the clock at a little after three and I was so surprised—and disappointed. I thought it must be five at least. Wrong, isn't it? for one of my age to wish time to pass on swiftest wing. I don't always do so—only when Tom's away. I read a good deal more about the mighty-fighter [?]. I couldn't begin to tell you how many real and supposed foes he has vanquished. How different a French novel is from an English, American, or German one. It is one series of intrigues, from beginning to end. The novelist himself must necessarily be quite an expert, I should judge.

It is not at all windy this morning, and if it is not too chilly I am going to ask Mrs. Shelton to go for another drive. We will go over to the hills on the south.

If it remains pleasant I will have an early supper, 5 o'clock and go over to look Miss Eaton up. That is a nice time to ride on a pleasant day. This is Thursday, you know, so I want to be "at home" from 3 to 5 anyway. Tomorrow I shall try to return some of the many calls I owe, if I feel well. I felt quite well except a short time yesterday and hoping to continue so to do. You must not worry about me—it has enough to attend to without that. Don't go out when you are warm without your overcoat. Are you treating poor A. B. mercilessly?⁴ Shall wait all day for your letter. With an *awful* lot of love

Your Ellen.

P.S. No letter from home yet. I thought I would surely get one last night.

Sent to Chicago for some Henrietta cloth as I noticed in the Tribune they are having special sales of it at nearly all the stores. I will probably get there for 75¢ what I would pay $1.25 for here probably. Bye-bye, my Brutus—E.

[1] The date is derived from the envelope and may not be precisely correct.

[2] Only seven letters, or parts of letters, are included for the year 1890. First come three originals from Ellen, in Redfield, to her husband, who was off trying cases around the state. The new mode of life, and certain difficulties, are at least suggested. A fourth original letter is from Ellen in Chicago to her husband in Dakota. Three additional letters are copies, derived from the manuscript "Farewell to Dakota" by Genevieve Walsh Gudger. They relate almost entirely to dissatisfaction with Dakota and the eventual move to Helena, Montana.

[3] Lena was the maid.

[4] Probably the opposing attorney.

279

Thursday 7:40 P.M. [Jan. 24-25, 1890, Redfield, to T. J. W., Huron].

My Dearest,—

Your telegram has just been received. I have thought several times today that I would write tonight but had decided not to do so, as you might not get the letter. I thought you might get home tomorrow P.M. I am glad you are not going to try to do so since your business would probably suffer thereby. I hope to get a letter tomorrow though.

Didn't get up till two o'clock. What was there to get up for? You must not worry about me. I feel ever so much better tonight and ate two sardines and a whole biscuit for supper.

I thought I should hear from home today, but Lena didn't succeed in bringing me any letters. I sent her over to ask your brother if there was any mail for me.

Lena says there is another show in town tonight—Uncle Tom's Cabin—you may have heard of it. I have been telling Lena something about the story and she is going to get the book forthwith.

She bought herself a curling iron today, and her "bangs" are in full dress tonight. By the way, John Bell told her about the "show" and "didn't invite me to go" she says. He has just had la grippe. You must be very careful while you are away and not take cold. I have coughed scarcely any today. I expect to be all over it when you get home.

Have been reading "Adventures of a Phaeton"—The guitar and the abominable blue ribbon do figure pretty extensively. Katie made such sport of them that I can not appreciate them as I ought. The book will give me something to employ myself with till you come home.

You will not be surprised, will you, if my letter is short? I have not been out myself, have seen no one but Lena, have had no letters, and have seen no papers. My world is bounded by the snow drifts "round our dwelling," and it is now a world without light, for that is all in Huron. It will seem very long till you come home, but you must not come a moment sooner than 'tis' well. Me [?] needs an ever present ever-watchful eye upon him. I was going to write to you tomorrow morning instead of tonight but recollected how very doubtful it is that I shall be up very early. I am going to sleep very well and all night long so that I shall be much better tomorrow. Don't trouble yourself one bit about me please. There is not the least occasion. If I don't get a letter tomorrow, I shall write to Mr. H'—s next time.

Good night, dear Tom, Your Ellen.

280

Saturday 1:15 P.M. [Jan. ——, 1890,
Redfield, to T. J. W., Faulkton].

My dearest Tom,—

I thought I would not write till this P.M. as you might possibly come home on the noon train. I didn't really think you would come, but was waiting all the same. As no one was inconvenienced thereby, I kept dinner till 1 P.M. How are your or rather your opponents murderers, for of course they are guilty in this case . . . [*editor's omission*].

Last night was the windiest night I've known in Dakota. You can imagine how windy when I tell you that though all our windows and doors were shut tight the heavy curtains at the entrance to our room swung back and forth very noticeably. The wind was from the north east and prairie fires burned brightly all along the south western horizon. The sky was as red as it is at times at sunset, and at one time the flames shot up brightly for quite a while in one place. I thought it might be a hay stack or something of the kind. The wind was blowing the fire farther away, but when I looked last it still burned on. I didn't get to sleep very early I must confess—between twelve and one I guess. Had a return of my bad feelings, but that lotion seemed to help some in an hour or so. I had such a strange feeling in my head after I had been lying down before you left and I felt it all the evening. The top part of my head seemed so dull and stupid as though my brain had solidified. It does not feel so today however. Have been following the varied fortunes of Becky Sharp. I could almost admire her in the first part of the book but not after that.[1]

The flowers you got last Sunday are in full bloom. I'll try to send you one, though they are too thick to press nicely. It is not very pleasant today, rather dull and windy—think I shall put off those calls a while.

I hope you have not been worrying any about me. You must not—only take care of yourself and don't go out without your coat. I feel very well now and shall try very hard to continue to do so. Lena will take this down to the post office now and will bring me one from you I hope. Don't work too hard and take good care of my Tom. With much love Your Ellen.

Lena was in my room last night and said something about our revolvers. I told her I'd load mine and put it under my pillow. When it was loaded she begged so to have me not leave it so that I had to go to the door and shoot into the air. When she spoke I thoughtlessly pulled back the trigger and couldn't unload in any other way. The wind blew so you could scarcely hear the explosion. Lena breathed a sigh of relief when it was "all over." Isn't it ridiculous how much afraid the average woman is of firearms! Bye-bye Brutus.

Ellen.

[1] Referring to *Vanity Fair* by William Makepeace Thackeray.

281

My dear Tom,—

You are so good to write me so often, and I—I have now
missed three days since I left you. But I really couldn't write Sat.
or Sun., at least you were better off without such letters as I
might have written. You tell me to be "gay and hopeful." I actually smiled at the former. It seems such a mockery. I don't know
what is the reason, but I can't help feeling despondent nine-tenths
of the time, and I used to be full of hope always. When you come
next week I shall go home with you regardless of what the doctor says. I am now pretty well convinced that medicine will do
me no good. My head hasn't ached badly today but I cough almost constantly. I have no cold however, the cough is wholly due
to inflammation of the bronchi. You remember I had quite a severe cold last fall and the doctor thinks I never got over that
properly. I did tell him about how long I had the headache before I got la grippe. He doesn't say much though about what he
thinks. I shall see him again tomorrow and find out the extent of
that inflammation in the air tubes. I cough most usually when I
first lie down but today I've been annoyed with it more than
usual. Perhaps there's a limit though even to that, for I've
coughed very little since supper. I can't brag of my appetite yet.
I drink nothing but milk, lemonade, or water. Tea and coffee I
cannot look at.

Well this is quite sufficient on so unattractive a subject.

I can't see why my letters don't reach you sooner. I get yours
so promptly. Received two yesterday and one this P.M. Such a
long letter too, and I write such miserable things, but I have
nothing to write about. It was kind of your friends to inquire
for me. Tell them I'm all right. I don't care to have every one
know I'm somewhat ill.

Lena is careless. That was just like her forgetfulness. I am so
sorry you had to go out for your meals. Lena should have remained as long as you did. It is so far to the hotel. You need not
bring me anything when you come thanks. I took plenty of un-
derwear with me, and I have no possible use for more dresses.
You need not bring the parasol either that I mentioned in a re-

cent letter. I won't need it, and if I do I can send it to Katie at any time [?]. I shall like them to hear you sing, and in order that they may, I shall make a martyr of myself for a few songs. We have no music tonight, and as I sit here writing, and look at mamma across the table, reading, I cannot help thinking how lonesome she must be when Mary & Katie are both away and I am not here. Tonight as she reads she has on her face the pleasant smile that even years that contained much of sorrow and anxiety have been unable to obliterate.

Katie I have not seen today, at least not since two o'clock this morning, when my coughing awoke her and she offered to get me some "sugar or water or something." You not being present I preferred to get up myself and get a drink, but Kit was real nice about it. I was so sorry to have awakened her for she gets up quite early, but she said she was glad as it put an end to a disagreeable dream. I do not devote so much of my time to dreaming as formerly. Last night, however, a singing, drunken negro filled the chief role.

I have not heard from Annie since I came here, but Katie wrote [her] a few days ago. I shall give her your message when I write, or if Mary writes. You ask what I do during the day. Well, I am of use to mamma occasionally. Then I read some, and sew at times, and idle away the greater part of the time as has become habitual to me. I've just read "Lord Brakenbury" the last novel of Amelia B. Edwards.[1] I was interested in it. The book is well written and the story interesting. She frequently shows her deep research in regard to places and things, but it never seems forced. She does not at all remind me of "Pat Grant, Railroad Laborer." She is in town at present.[2]

There is no sign of snow here and Wicker Park and our front yard are getting green. Yes, I shall be very glad to see the flowers in Dakota, but about the walks and rides it tires me even to think. Don't make any plans, Tom, please. Just never expect anything —it's the only way to keep even with Fate.

Yes, I really do think you ought not to make any arrangements about coming here permanently. If you did, it would be on my account, and that I could not permit. I would rather *talk* to you about the other projects.

Messrs. Howard and Bromley are doubtless correct in their reports, though I can only guess at the meaning of "scooped."[3]

Mean, you term it? No, only generous. They are not women. I hope every thing will be as favorable as you desire.

I wish I could see Mrs. Sterling's article. She never impressed me as a genius quite.[4] Isn't this a long letter, and I'm tired too. Goodnight, dear Tom, Your Ellen.

I didn't know where to direct my last letter so sent it to Huron. I don't like to have my letters lying around in places where you are not so am inclined to direct this to Huron. Do you know so many of my boys [former students] asked me if I got their New Year's cards, but I didn't get one. They were all correctly directed too. It is passing strange if they were all lost, or were they not thought worth taking from the office? I know you would have brought them had you seen them. Mr. S. is better some say and expects to go to Europe in April. Some say he will never go. Your E.[5]

[1] Amelia B. Edwards, novelist and Egyptologist, died in 1892.

[2] *Pat Grant, Railroad Laborer*, sounds as if it were a dime novel but has not been identified as such.

[3] An unclear reference to C. T. Howard and N. P. Bromley, who were Redfield lawyers often in competition with the Walsh brothers.

[4] Whether this was Mrs. Thomas Sterling of Redfield or Mrs. William Sterling of Huron is not clear.

[5] As indicated by this and previous letters, Ellen McClements Walsh was suffering ill health. Her daughter has written that she never fully recovered; for the rest of her life she was to have recurrent headaches. After a stay in Chicago of more than a month during February-March, 1890, she returned to Redfield, and this was a happy time of a "particularly radiant" spring. "Rain was abundant," wild roses were beautiful along the banks of the Jim River, cacti blossoms were "gorgeously colored." However, with the coming of summer, the scorching winds returned and wheat and corn crops were withered away. Tom and Ellen Walsh resumed their deliberations: to what new place should they move? Genevieve Walsh Gudger, "Farewell to Dakota"; also letters by Ellen McClements Walsh, 1890, *passim*.

282

[T. J. Walsh, Redfield, to Mary McClements,
Aug. ——, 1890.]

. . . We have been thinking very much about getting away from here. On the whole business has been prosperous the last year and this summer in particular. I have been meeting with very uniform success and in some important cases. But the crop is almost a failure again and that means another year of business depression. Even if the harvest were bountiful litigation in this country will never involve large interests, so that one must try an immense number of cases to make any money. I don't see how we can get any nearer Chicago, though. Do you think of any intervening city that offers any inducements? Minneapolis and St. Paul are almost at a standstill just now and are crowded with lawyers. Ellen objects to my going back to the lake and I think wisely, so Duluth and Superior are out of the question. I would even dare Chicago if it were not for the same reason. Then there is Sioux City, Kansas City, Denver, Salt Lake and Helena. I don't like Sioux City. I have no sort of means to get any introduction to the business life of the next two named and who wants to live among the Mormons? In about a week I shall go to Helena to look over the ground. Have you noticed the advertisement of the place running in the Century? [1] The principal of the Winona schools [2] and his wife have been visiting friends there. He goes there to assume the principalship. Just think of it! There is an estate in litigation there now, you may have noticed mention of it in the papers, valued at $11,000,000. Nothing of that kind is likely to come up here in that many years. It is conceded to be the richest city of its size in the world and we think we may possibly be able to get a little of the wealth. It seems out of the world, but I am told that people there think no more of getting on the train and going to Chicago than we do. Then they run sleepers and diners clear through and its almost as comfortable as if one were at home. . . .

[1] *Century Magazine* of February, 1890, carried an article entitled "Washington and Montana, Have They Made a Mistake in Their Constitutions?" This was probably the item referred to, although not exactly in the nature of an "advertisement."

[2] In all likelihood Winona, Minnesota.

283

[Helena, Montana], September 17, 1890.

My dear Ellen,

. . . I have taken pains to reserve my judgment of the place. The main street is a little wider and a little crookeder than the principal street of Deadwood. Roughness and refinement jostle each other. The great peaks stand like sentries about the town—that is about half way round. To the northwest, north, east and southeast they stand farther off. I felt crowded down town but on taking a short walk, I found quite extensive plats suitable for residences, where the houses didn't seem engaged in a perpetual struggle to push their neighbors off their small piece of ground. The business houses are costly and some of them grand. The banks suggest ponderous wealth but there are no other startling indicia of its existence in super-abundance. I met a gentleman on the train who has charge of a lumber yard here. He graduated at Madison the year before I went there and we found we had a large number of acquaintances. I made no extensive incursions this afternoon. Called first on a gentleman, an attorney, who came from Sargent County, N.D. and whom I met in Bismark two years ago. He treated me very kindly and took me out to see some of the "Boys," who also acted very courteously. Among these latter is a nephew of E. A. Pew, who has been here only two weeks. "The boys," he said, had been very kind to him. He had been in court almost every day, asked by them to assist in the argument of some case so that he might make himself heard. "No money in it of course [he said] but I've made enough to pay office rent. Got a $500 retainer today." Mr. Newman agreed to call for me in the morning and take me up to the court-house.[1] They have a magnificent court-house, used temporarily as the State House too. If my courage, like Bob Acres' does not all ooze out,[2] I'll go in and pay my respects to the governor. Now you're ashamed of me, aren't you! But it isn't such a sweet kind of a job. Let me approach it ever so cutely, of course he will understand that I am soliciting. What if I am though? If I were he I should feel delighted to render any possible assistance to another in my situation, and I'm ready to render "quid pro quo." Haven't been able as yet to get any close figures but rent is high, both for office and dwelling.

W. W. Dixon of Butte was nominated Monday for Congress. The fight is bitter. . . .[3]

They tell me court is in session here always, and even then is away behind. Even in Sioux Falls they have long vacations. Then the U.S. Courts are here and also the Supreme Court of the State. The State Library comprising a good line of text books and nearly all the reports is here, so one need not put so much money in a library. . . .

Your
Tom.

[1] Probably Cephas P. Newman. Members of the Pew family, whom Walsh knew in Dakota, have not been completely identified.

[2] Bob Acres was a character in Richard B. Sheridan's comedy of manners, *The Rivals* (1775).

[3] William Wirt Dixon, who was born in Brooklyn, New York, had lived in many places in the West, including the Black Hills of Dakota, Helena, Montana, and Butte, Montana. He served in the territorial house of representatives in Montana, also in the constitutional conventions of 1884 and 1889. He was elected as a Democrat to the U.S. House of Representatives in 1890 and served one term.

284

[Helena, Montana], September 18, 1890.

My dearest Ellen,—

Your letter was such an encouragement. It drove away a most oppressive fit of the blues and I'm feeling almost jolly to-night. I begin to think Helena is quite a nice place after all and that it's just possible the undertaking of coming is not too great.

Well Mr. Newman called for me this morning. He introduced me to a number of attorneys at the court-house. I listened to the proceedings and quietly "sized up" the bar for an hour and then went down and paid my respects to the governor.[1] He arose when I entered and offered me his hand—treated me with frank and easy courtesy. We talked about general matters for awhile. I suggested that I had come to the state with a view to locating. He said this was a good town and mentioned several that were so. I said it impressed me as such, and the talk ended. He asked me to call again.

We shall manage some way. If we can stand the thing for three months I am confident I could make money here. . . .

This evening I went with Mr. Pew, a contractor formerly of Redfield, to see some houses. But I'll not speak of them. I should feel tomorrow night that everything that I could do has been done.[2]

Your

Tom.

[1] Joseph K. Toole (1851-1929) was a Democrat and the first governor of Montana, serving from 1889 until 1893; later he served in the same office from 1901 to 1908. In the years before Walsh's interview with him he had held for two terms the post of territorial delegate to Congress and other positions of importance in the territorial government.

[2] After Walsh returned to Redfield, the final plans were made. His daughter has provided a description. "The little house which they had occupied for only a year was sold, outstanding business disposed of. When all was in readiness, [train] tickets bought and household goods shipped, but $250 remained. With this small tangible capital, but with courage and hope in abundance, Tom and Ellen, with their four months old baby, set forth on the day before Christmas on their great adventure."

Thus T. J. Walsh—lawyer, politician, and student of government—moved his family and effects to Helena, Montana. After unpacking, he continued his former activities with hardly the loss of a stride. Almost immediately he became active in the Montana Democratic party, and when a contest occurred over the location of the state capital, he traveled across Montana campaigning vigorously in behalf of Helena. This early effort terminated successfully in 1894.

Thomas J. Walsh went on with his career, benefiting from a rich experience in Dakota state-making, and with notions about Washington, D.C., occasionally passing through his mind. He would reach his goals, professionally and politically, not by a change of methods but by a change of scenery.

Appendix I: The Wisconsin Years

Walsh's earliest letters date from 1881. Those included here are intended to be representative and to trace the Wisconsinite through his final two years of teaching and his year of law study at the University of Wisconsin, 1883-84. Annotation is lighter than for the Dakota collection. Only eight of these thirty-three (selected) letters are by Ellen McClements.

285

Sheboygan, Wis., July 28, 1881.

Mr. *Welsh,*—

Please accept my sincere congratulations upon two events—your success at Sturgeon Bay (poetic name), and your escape from Glenbeulah.[1]

Yours truly,
Ellen C. McClements.

P.S. I am also a subject for congratulations on account of the pleasure in store for me. I and my sixty-four private pupils start on a picnic in half an hour.

[1] Walsh was moving to Sturgeon Bay but had formerly been principal of the high school and a teacher at Glenbeulah, Wisconsin. His assistant there was Mary McClements. Walsh and Ellen McClements met for the first time when she came to visit her sister.

286

Two Rivers, Wis., July 29, 1881.

My dear Miss Ellen,—

The receipt of your very kind note gives me the greatest pleasure. Please accept thanks for your congratulations and kind wishes. The pleasure of attending a picnic at which you preside can be considered without fail as a foregone conclusion and so I present my compliments on the occasion without the least fear of being "too previous." You once went on an excursion down the peninsula! Might you be tempted to repeat it?

Yours with kindest wishes,
Thomas J. Walsh.

287

Sheboygan, Wis., September 29, 1881.

Dear Friend,—

Your letter was received Tuesday,[1] and notice, please, the readiness with which I comply with the request for an early reply. Notice also, my eagerness to have so truly meritorious an action recognized. Am glad to have this opportunity of writing you as I have something particular to say. When I wrote you that note upon your engagement at Sturgeon Bay, did you for a moment imagine I wished to impose upon you the burden of a continued correspondence? Your reply was quite correct and courteous. But it contained a question. I answered it, but in such a manner, I think, as to need no response.

As to the future correspondence which you suggest—the correspondence which "is to terminate at the desire of either party" —I have no objections provided you fully realize that the establishment of such a correspondence was not in my mind when I wrote. Let me warn you, however, that I am no letter writer, that is I cannot write a good letter. Don't you know, have you not discovered that I am stupid and tiresome to the last degree?

So you have taken to reading fiction. I suppose you do that on the principle that "a little nonsense now and then, etc." Have you finished "Jane Eyre"? Did you, with your taste for sensible reading, find it possible to struggle through all the sentiment of that truly delightful volume? I'm only joking; I did not admire it one bit either. Have you ever read "Felix Holt"? Felix was always a great favorite of mine, though I should have liked him better had he been a little tamer.

Please don't let your kindness in having read to us last winter prey upon you. I'm not a capable critic in that line, but I enjoyed it and thought it good. Besides, it is your Christian duty to give all the pleasure you can during your pilgrimage in this sinful world. That sounds good, doesn't it?

I'm awfully glad you got your Life Certificate. Of course I knew you would and that you expected one, but isn't it nice to really have it? I wish I had one. I hate to study. Mercy, how disgusted you look! It am a fact though, massa. . . .[2]

Yours truly,
Ellen C. McClements.

[1] As indicated by the date and context, Walsh's letter is missing from the collection.
[2] The certificate mentioned was the result of a state examination, requiring knowledge of college subjects.

288

Sturgeon Bay, Wis., November 3, 1881.

My dear Miss Ellen,

No, I should no more think of being displeased than you could harbor a desire to offend. I am no master of words and had that parodoxical old Frenchman [Voltaire] postponed the publication of his maxim until he had perused a specimen of my composition I could excuse him for saying that words were intended to conceal thoughts rather than express them.

We, too, had a teacher's meeting. . . . It takes all the spirit out of a teacher, after spending a gallon more or less of the midnight oil in concocting a theory on some dark point, to be then called upon to deliver it to desks, stoves and other sundry articles of furniture in lieu of the legitimate auditors.

I cannot sympathize with you in your choice of a hero, even though he be that man who "with one hand held successfully the rein of civil government and with the other hurled victoriously thunderbolts of war." I have no historic heroes, neither have I, on the other hand, any that I bear a marked dislike to, only so far as disliking their evil deeds. Yet it seems to me that in Cromwell the vices outweighted his talents, and I never heard it asserted that he had any virtues. Surely you would not worship success when it lacked the last mentioned qualities.

I think it well for Macaulay that he never essayed the drama. He would certainly have fallen into the same error of which he justly accuses Byron—that of making all his heroes prototypes of himself. Not exactly in the same sense however. Byron makes his heroes act as Byron would act. Macaulay makes them speak as Macaulay writes.

I have finished "Pompeii" the second time, an honor no other novel enjoyed. I do not think I ever heard it praised too highly and any encomiums from me would be superfluous when you have read it yourself. The manners and conversation of the classic peoples always had a charm for me, I know not why.

"Caesar" is my favorite in Shakespeare and "Sardanapalus" in Byron's dramas. The circumstances alone possess for me an intense interest without taking into consideration the grandeur and sublimity of language, the elevation and purity of sentiment, and the general ease and voluptuousness like unto life as we picture it in the climate and on the still, clear seas of the country in which the scene is laid. . . .

Most sincerely yours,
Thomas J. Walsh.

289

Sturgeon Bay, Wis., December 11, 1881.
My dear Miss Ellen,

I met the elite of Sturgeon Bay for the first time last Friday evening at a social gathering given by the members of a young men's club with the high-sounding title of the "Bon Ami." My first impression was very favorable indeed. They tried to make it pleasant for me although I was almost a total stranger. I had formed but few acquaintances, yet I spent a pleasant evening. It is the intention to meet every second Friday evening hereafter and to vary the principal amusement, dancing, with select reading, singing, etc. . . .

He (the clerk of the school-board) has quite a large library and has read extensively. His family and that of a Baptist minister meet weekly and discuss literature. I was invited some time ago to take part with them but have not thus far done so. I expect however to meet them next Tuesday evening when Moore will be overhauled.

Sincerely yours,
T. J. Walsh.

290

Two Rivers, Wis., December 29, 1881.

My dear Miss Ellen,

How have you been spending your vacation? I have devoured the greater part of "Ivanhoe" during such moments as I could spare from cracking nuts and the performance of sundry other Christmas rites of a like agreeable nature. We got possession of the parlor this afternoon and had littered it quite to our satisfaction when we were rather suddenly treated to a call by half a dozen ladies. The nuts were all gone, but the shells on the floor were not.

I was the recipient of a handsome Christmas present from my scholars on the day of closing—a handsome volume of Byron's poems elegantly bound in gilt and morocco. I was very much pleased at the kindness and attachment for me evidenced by it and prize it highly. . . .

Byron furnished the subject at the last meeting of the Club. Dr. [Henry T.] Scudder, our clerk, opened the exercises and after reading some harsh, but probably fair, criticism from Taine, recited the whole of the "Prisoner of Chillon." I have always admired it but never appreciated its merits to such an extent as I think I do now. I love to listen to the oral delivery of excellent compositions even though it be not done exactly to my own idea. For this reason I sometimes read myself when no one else will. The piece received a new interest, and I take it up again with increased pleasure.

I desire to commend your purpose of an early removal to wider scenes of action. I am certain that in such a field as Chicago your talents and ability, along with application, must secure for you the recognition that will probably never be awarded at home.

With the compliments of the season and the deepest regard,

I am, yours,
Thomas J. Walsh.

291

Sturgeon Bay, Wis., February 5, 1882.

My dear Miss Ellen,

. . . Our literary society is thriving and is a source of much enjoyment to me. We disposed of Southey without much praise from anyone. Some of his descriptions, in which he seems to excel, are, however, very entrancing. The society is something of a bonanza to me. Wouldn't you belong to one if the members were invited before tea-time and served to oysters? That's me.

I begin to long for spring, feel that I should like to ramble around the woods, sail on the bay, or do some other unconscionable thing rather than listen all day to the "terrible tumble and rumble and roar" of the school-room.

Write soon.

Very sincerely yours,
Thomas J. Walsh.

292

Sturgeon Bay, Wis., March 9, 1882.

My dear Miss McClements,

Agreeably to my promise, I send you herewith a copy of what the photographer tells me is a picture of myself, though I should have doubted it on less conclusive evidence. And I embrace the opportunity of your permission to reply to your last letter.

I may have once told you that since I was quite a boy an ambition possessed me to enter the Military Academy, but circumstances have always been such as to prevent its fulfillment. A vacancy has occurred from this district which will be filled on the result of a competitive examination to be held at Oshkosh next month and I have thought seriously of attending although I fear my age would now be an obstacle to my admission. Did you ever think of me as a military man? How would I grace a uniform? However, I would hope by outside study to prepare myself for the practice of the law which must at some time be my profession. I must still pursue a college course before practicing or consent to waste the better portion of my life grubbing away in the inferior courts. I feel that I should be working at a disadvantage without the assistance of that discipline which the college only affords. Besides I am very deficient in language and believe the study of the classics can alone give me such fluency as is at least essential. I haven't the conversational talent of a ten-year old and my letters must be further evidence of the same fact. I don't want to go to Madison, though, and enter with the chits of girls that have graduated from the high schools and who after four years' work will be graciously given the certificates such as I now hold, and unless my salary be raised or my expenditures considerably curtailed neither this nor any other college will ever enroll me as a member.

Why did you never tell me when you visited at Glen that you had a preference for Byron. I would have read at any length for you. My brother gets dreadfully bored with it when I am at home.

I have been extending my library somewhat. Some late additions are Thomson's "Poems," Taine's "English Literature," Lecky's "England in the 18th Century," "Corinne" by Madame DeStael and "Vanity Fair" rather miscellaneous, isn't it?

We have varied the work of our literary society and propose devoting some time now to historical discussion. I am pretty well acquainted with history and shall feel much more at home here than in the domain of poetry.

In concluding a correspondence which has been a source of the greatest pleasure to me both in the receiving and in the writing and which I trust may be renewed at some future time, allow me to express my regret at not being able to write something that would furnish you more entertaining reading matter. My meagerness of language has been before alluded to. I have often thought that it was owing to a meagerness of ideas in most folks and might be so in my case. However I trust you feel no sense of relief at your freedom and believe me it is with the sincerest regret that I sign

Yours no more,
T. J. Walsh.

293

Sheboygan, Wis., March 25, 1882.

My dear Friend,—

I was greatly pleased to receive your letter and picture last Friday. Thanks, very much, for both.What made you speak in such a manner of your picture? It is good. I like it ever so much. It must be owned that there is an expression on the face, in the eyes I guess it is, which suggests contempt for the rest of mankind in particular and all things in the world in general. Forgive me that remark, won't you? You may take carte blanche to criticise mine in return. I love a dimpled chin, when the depression is not too marked. Yours is just right.

No, you never mentioned to me your wish to enter the Military Academy. I never felt at liberty to speak of it, but I am so glad that you do not intend to waste your life in the school-room. It is presumptuous for me to dare to advise you, but do go to Oshkosh. I feel certain you will succeed if your age is not an objection as you suggested. Now I will answer those two questions of yours. No, I had never thought of you as a "military man" but have no objection to a little mental exertion in that line should you carry out your present plans. Secondly, you will in my estimation, grace a uniform so well that I now enter a petition for another picture when you shall have donned your shoulder straps.

Now I wish to inform you that I am very much displeased with you. Don't you know it is the worst possible policy to run yourself down to anyone? Of course, to me it does not matter because I know how much to credit of what you say, but what do you mean by stating that you have not the conversational talent of a ten-year old? Were I a Methodist, or anything to speak of, I would say that it seems like tempting Providence to make such a statement. Now let me tell you something, frankly, just as if I were a gentleman friend of yours. Instead of having a lack of talent in the talking line, you possess the gift of talking fluently, gracefully, strongly, convincingly, and that is just what you will need as a lawyer. Where did I find out all this? Granted that I have had few opportunities of hearing you speak, but I usually judge quickly, and generally correctly. That night at Glen, though you confessed you had made not the slightest effort your part of the debate was by far the best. Mr. B. spoke very well and you kindly took up his points one by one, and, by your rendering, illustrated very plainly how much better you could express the same thoughts and then relentlessly showed the opposition's want of argument in the case. You are able too, I think to enter heartily into a subject, to the utter exclusion of surroundings. That power is necessary to the successful actor or speaker.

. . .

I've changed my mind about the matter and you may write whenever you choose. Whose business is it anyway whether I write or not? Besides I'm anxious to know about the Oshkosh business.

Yours truly,
E. C. M.

294

Sturgeon Bay, Wis., April 5, 1882.

My dear Miss McClements,

. . . I didn't go to Oshkosh. I was never wholly decided in the matter and the probability of failure, together with considerations of expediency, which probably should have been disregarded, conspired to keep me away.

A meeting was held here March 17, for the purpose of organizing a branch land-league,[1] on which occasion I was orator-in-chief, and I did a little more, I believe, than was expected of me. My address was requested for publication but I persisted in refusing, not being at all desirous that the good effects of its oral rendition should be totally destroyed by a careful perusal. Indeed I was really astonished at the compliments I received. The President met me a few days subsequently and said that my talent lay in the direction of the law, in which opinion I silently agreed, and promised to secure me a position in the office of his brother, a prominent lawyer in New York City, if I desired to read.

Yours very sincerely,
Thomas J. Walsh.

¹ Walsh was possibly referring to an organization based upon the ideas of Henry George. Such land leagues were common in the period, and Walsh had read *Progress and Poverty* in 1880, one year after publication. Walsh to F. C. Leubuscher, July 7, 1930, Walsh Papers, Library of Congress. But the specific subject of his speech was the land problem in Ireland, revealed by his manuscript in the Gudger Collection.

295

Sturgeon Bay, Wis., May 3, 1882.

My dear Miss Ellen,

. . . The fishing season has come round and no end of perch are being caught. I have enjoyed myself at it a few times, that is to say I had something more than the "fly on the end." The flowers are also blooming and I do some work in botany. I have a class of three studying it who are quite proficient. My own work is done merely for the pleasure and recreation I derive from it.

You expressed your satisfaction some time ago when I said that I contemplated retiring from teaching sometime soon. Would it surprise you if that should arrive with the termination of the present year? It is probable that the school here will be again offered me, which proposal may be accompanied by an increase of salary and though the school is nearly to my satisfaction, the people generally quite agreeable to me, particularly so some literary acquaintances and the place healthy, I consider retiring at once. In any event another year must see me out of the school-room permanently.

Will you kindly let me know if you have anything on George Eliot which you think would be of service to one of our girls who is writing an essay on that head and if so generously forward it?

Sincerely,
T. J. Walsh.

296

Sturgeon Bay, Wis., May 14, 1882.

My dear Miss Ellen,

. . . *[editor's omission].* My brother [Henry] has been thinking of completing the examinations for the unlimited certificate in August. If he concludes to attend I shall go directly home after the close of school and assist him in working up; if not I purpose remaining here a short while at least. He has always borne the heavy end of the load for me, uncomplainingly submitted to much inconvenience to render surer my chances of success and been a model older brother generally. I make no boast of generosity but were our home a baronial estate I could see him possess it entire without an envious thought, so much more does he deserve it than I.

Really you ought to read "Corinne." You need pay no attention to the plot. It is quite senseless and improbable, but there are many parts which I know would be of interest to you. One would expect nothing less of a lady so talented, who held such a prominent place in the affairs of all Europe, who could rally all the wits of England and rival Fox, Sheridan and Moore in conversation in their native tongue.[1]

I believe I told you some time since of my having been elected assistant editor of the educational column in our local paper. Since that time the principal editor has not contributed above three or four ten-line articles. His self-denial in thus granting me such an opportunity for increasing my skill in journalism is certainly highly appreciated, but were the duties even lightened by an occasional official notice (he being our county superintendent) his sacrifices would be still more gratefully felt. I purpose acting hereafter as if I were in name as in fact the sole editor.

Yours,
Thomas J. Walsh.

[1] The novel *Corinne* (1807) was written by Madame de Staël, whom Walsh accurately described as a talented woman of wide influence.

297

Sturgeon Bay, Wis., May 28, 1882.

My dear Miss Ellen,

I know of no authoritative declaration in polemic literature on the justifiableness of a platonic correspondence between two young people of opposite sexes, the execution of which usually takes place on the Sabbath. My own conviction in regard to the matter, however, is that nothing in the Mosaic law or the first of the Church forbids it. Yet as the pious mind looks rather to the spirit of the law, and as you made mention once of your religious sentiments, the import of which I do not now recall and am a trifle too indolent at the present moment to undo the parcel of letters done up in the pink ribbon from which I might possibly learn, I am reminded that your conscience may not be quite as serviceable as mine in the matter. If so, please let me know and I'll—I'll date my letters one day back hereafter.

The method of introducing your last letter is unique and would have been complimentary did it not savour of burlesque.[1] With my accustomed presumption, I considered it the former. If I mistook I am sorry you were so unfortunate in selecting a subject for your facetiousness, for Brutus was a man after my own mind. Really, now, would it not be a noble ambition to desire to "so live that when the summons" came, "the whole world might stand up and say 'This was a man!' "?

With kindest regards,
T. J. Walsh.

[1] "Most noble Brutus!"

298

Sheboygan, Wis., June 12, 1882.

Dear Friend,—

Writing on the Sabbath again you see, but honestly I do be so busy during the week that I seldom write a letter. Which is worse, writing letters on Sunday or going boating? Let me try to remember. Did not I see some such sentence as this in a recent letter from you written on the Sabbath: "I would be out sailing but I could not get a boat." I do not know if you have ever fished on Sunday, but, somehow, a verse I saw the other day seems appropriate here.

This morn the gentle maiden will hie away to mass;
This morn her wayward brother will angle for the bass;
And while the gentle maiden sits quietly in church,
This wayward brother, with a fly, will try to catch a perch.
And while the gentle maiden before the altar kneels,
This very wayward brother will sit and bob for eels.

I don't think I'll finish this letter—or rather I believe I will for you would not know otherwise, would you, why I hesitate to do so. Well it is because of that—"pink ribbon." How could you be so unkind! Some people never destroy a letter, but I did not imagine you to be one of them. . . . Be good, won't you, and burn those letters. I wouldn't mind your having them in the least, for you would lay them aside and forget them, but in all probability there will be a Mrs. W. some day and she'll be sure to stumble upon your old letters. Knowing you "won't mind" she will read them and will probably ask you what has become of the girls who wrote "those silly letters." No, thank you, I would rather not have mine among them.

E. C. M.

299

Manitowoc, Wis., July 7, 1882.

My dear Miss Ellen,

I took advantage of the statement you made in your last that you would be absent from home for some days during the first part of your vacation, to put off for a few days beyond the usual time, my answer. And now I break in upon my work to fulfill that pleasant duty, for you must know that I am really at work.

Began last Wednesday in the above mentioned city the study of law. I had contemplated, as I informed you, to spend the greater part of my vacation at home prosecuting some work in the sciences but the resolution of my brother to postpone attending the examinations for another year caused me to change my original intentions. My tutor is an old teacher of mine, I say old because, although he is still quite a young man, it is some time ago since I went to school to him.[1] He taught me, I distinctly remember, to add columns of figures, or rather under him I learned to do so, for I may say that no one ever taught me mathematics. I learned it.

I get on very well. Am reading Blackstone and, contrary to almost universal experience, find it interesting and entertaining. At the present rate I can easily finish Blackstone during vacation and perhaps a volume of Kent. That will be a start at any rate. The gentleman I study with has always taken a great deal of interest in me, has requested me a number of times to come and read with him. He doesn't have a great deal to do, and has therefore both the time and the inclination to assist me in case I should need help. I went up to tea with him the other evening. His wife is a very fine lady reputed to be the best Latin scholar in the city. Both are graduates of Lawrence University. . . .[2]

Yours,
Thomas J. Walsh.

[1] Judge J. S. Anderson of Manitowoc. Walsh later wrote to his old teacher: "It may be pleasing to you to know, in what you speak of as your 'old age,' that I attribute in no small measure to your friendly aid and intelligent direction of my studies, whatever success I have met with in my professional and political career." Walsh to J. S. Anderson, September 13, 1923, Walsh Papers, Library of Congress.

[2] Lawrence University of Appleton, Wisconsin, became Lawrence College in 1908. In 1964, after taking in Milwaukee-Downer College, it became a university again.

300

Sheboygan, Wis., July 16, 1882.

Dear Friend,—

Your letter and I reached home at almost the same moment. I went to Chicago to attend the teacher's examination. Do you think it strange, knowing that you expect to go there soon, that I did not tell you that I was going? Let me explain. Had I failed to secure a certificate neither you nor anyone else that I could prevent would ever have known that I had gone down. That's a vile sort of pride, isn't it? Yet I might as well try to change the ever-lasting hills as to try to change that part of my nature. In the chances of passing, the odds were so much against me that I hardly dared hope to succeed. There were five hundred applicants, at least, and in the paper you can see the number who obtained certificates—forty-six, I believe. I did not consider the questions asked very difficult. I answered every one except two. One I did not know, and the other I had not time to write.

So you are deep in the intricacies of Blackstone. How I envy you! Do you know, it seems strange to me how works a century old can be indispensable to the law, yet I believe every lawyer begins with Blackstone. Of course it must be well to be acquainted with his writings, if only as a matter of history, but are they of real service, can they be practically applied at the present time and in this country? . . .

Don't study too hard.

Yours,
E.

301

Manitowoc, Wis., July 27, 1882.

My dear Miss Ellen,

You must, by this time, have heard definitely in regard to your hopes of securing a situation in the sinful city and as there is no reasonable ground to doubt your success, having gained the hills that overlook Rome already, congratulations are in order, without question. Accept mine, extended heartily and earnestly. As I stated to you before, last winter, so I have no hesitancy in asserting now that I believe your talents and industry will have a wider field and be likely to receive a juster recognition away from home. "Prophet, seek not for fame in thine own land" is one of those maxims which, though not universally true, challenge our respectful consideration. . . .

I feel like never more confiding a single purpose of mine in you. Had I known beforehand of your doubts and fears, your dangers and hopes, I should have felt a much greater degree of pleasure, I think, on learning of your complete success [in the teacher's examination].

I still continue to find Blackstone interesting reading. Expect to finish in eight or ten days more. You are in error in supposing that all lawyers read either Blackstone or Kent and so far as orthography, or grammar, or penmanship is concerned it is a peculiar privilege of the fraternity that no rule but their own wills is binding, of which privilege unlimited advantage is taken. I took the liberty to point out a number of grammatical errors in the great authority which now engages my attention, to my tutor who curtly told me that if I wanted to be a lawyer I should be obliged to quit being a school-master.

Yes, some parts of Blackstone are now obsolete, yet the great fundamental principles of law with which the work chiefly concerns itself are as true now and ever will be as true as in the days of its renowned author. The science of law has made great advance within the last century and a half, as well as politics and the material sciences. But law had at that time in England reached a degree of perfection far in advance of the others as compared with their condition in our day, and for that reason, although a text-book on chemistry or physics of that date would be hardly the thing to put into the hands of an embryo scientist, this by no means holds good with a work on the principles of law. . . .

I find it very pleasant down here, though I keep quite close to the office. Read at least ten hours a day.

Yours,
Thomas J. Walsh.

302

Sunday P.M., August 13, 1882.

My dear Friend,—

Yes, it has been fully decided that I am to have a school in the "sinful city." After the last meeting of the Board, the Chicago Times contained the names of those that had been "elected to be assigned places by the Superintendent." Thirteen were selected, and I was one of them. The day after the meeting of the Board, the Superintendent wrote me of the fact, and told me also that he would assign me a place at once. . . .

Have you read Mark Twain's latest, "The White Elephant"?

I have not, but I saw a very severe criticism on it some time ago. It spoke of Mark as the erratic crank who imagines he possesses the combined wit and humor of the nineteenth century. In referring to the book, it said that in searching the whole field of literature a bigger fraud could not be found outside of Tice's weather prognostications;[1] and that a money-loving publisher, seconded by his own desire to accumulate shekels, had led him to write the book when he had nothing to write. Such reviewers make one look with satisfaction on lovely obscurity, far removed from printer's ink and all wise critics.

E. C. M.

[1] John H. Tice wrote *Elements of Meteorology* (1875). His weather predictions in the newspaper were partly made, he said, to excite an interest in science. *Ibid.*, p. 4.

303

Sturgeon Bay, Wis., August 28, 1882.

My dear Miss Ellen,

I arrived here a week ago and began work at the Institute next morning.[1]

Two friends and myself enjoyed a sail down to Idlewilde yesterday afternoon. We didn't go down very fast though—four miles in as many hours—very little wind and that against us; but our return was something too grand for my feeble, languid pen. The wind, which had been blowing fitfully, all went down with the sun and the surface of the bay acquired the smoothness and glassiness of ice, broken only by an occasional swell from the parent bay whose waters were not so speedily quieted. The sails flapped lazily with the swell and then hung motionless. The fish sported in the water quite to the surface, occasionally throwing their bodies entirely out of the water after flies or moths. The precipitous, rocky shores frowned over the darkness that shrouded the waters at their base. The sun set in a blaze of red that covered nearly half the sky and varied with the retiring orb through all the intervening shades until the atmosphere at the horizon assumed the brightest azure. Then all became perfectly clear without a cloud to mar the harmony or break the monotony. To crown all the full moon shone down in all her loveliness "leaving that beautiful which still was so and making that which was not." A gentle breeze sprang up which increased gradually until we were wafted, rather than sailed, along at a rate which, though extremely pleasant, tended from that very reason to lessen our enjoyment by bringing us more rapidly to our destination. . . . Miss McClements, unless you intend going to Naples, come to Sturgeon Bay sometime.

Yours,

T. J. W.

[1] Walsh had returned to Sturgeon Bay for another school year following a brief visit in Sheboygan with Ellen McClements.

304

Chicago, Ill., September 6, 1882.

My dear Friend,

I can now look forward to your letters as oases in my desert. Remember I am "a stranger in a strange land" and have pity on my loneliness. . . .

I suppose you would like to know all about Chicago. My school, the Wicker Park, is one of the best in the city. When school closed tonight one thousand and fifty-eight pupils had been registered. The teachers are all very amiable.

I'll just take enough time to give you a piece of my mind. "Perhaps I owe you an apology for my abrupt visit, etc." An apology indeed! What made you think so? Was it because you found me in a calico dress and curl papers, or were you made to feel yourself unwelcome? If it was the former, believe me it was the first time I had not dressed for dinner during the vacation and I was mad enough, but not at you. If it was the latter, I am sorry indeed. For myself I can say there was no one I would rather have seen. . . .

E. C. M.

305

Sturgeon Bay, Wis., October 29, 1882.

My dear Ellen,

You mistake in classing me with those of the "sterner sex" who look with something of mingled pity and contempt on a woman who essays to discuss topics which, according to the narrow vision of those social tyrants, are "out of her sphere." Nor do I believe that the number of these is nearly as great as some of the "sisters" seem to think. I am a "women's rights" man and do not think it either politic or just in the state to deny to woman the right of suffrage if she chooses to exercise it. . . .

The prohibition movement is likely to play an important part in the coming election. Several speakers hold forth on the subject here tonight. As the matter has now been degraded to a mere political issue it seems almost in violation of good taste, if not the rules of piety, to dedicate the Sabbath to such a purpose. The movement seems to be engineered by the Temple of Honor and Good Templars principally, and doesn't yet number among its ranks any of the advanced intelligence of the community. Yet I am of the opinion that the organization, unless through the folly of its own members, will continue to grow in strength until it will obtain in a few years the balance of power. At any rate it seems certain that the decline and disintegration of the two old parties will not be much longer delayed and some others must rise to take their places. There does not seem to be any reason for a young man to pin his faith to either if he expects advancement. The lease of the Republican party is well nigh run and it is hardly possible that the Democratic party will ever again be rejuvenated without changing or at least adopting principles.

Bye-bye.
T. J. W.

306

My dear Ellen,

For your proposition to make the treasures of the magnificent public library of Chicago accessible to me I know not how to express my gratitude nor how I can impose upon you a task which might prove burdensome. But as you appear to have made the offer in all seriousness I shall promise to avail myself of the opportunity the first time I find it impossible to secure the desired information here.

When you say "tell me some more books," I am let out of the difficulty. Why not keep right on with the Holmes breakfast-table series? I haven't read the Professor, but the Poet is in my opinion nothing inferior to the most widely known of the series. If you don't smile audibly now and then, and then go back and read that page again, and then think about it, it's your fault and not the Poet's.[1]

Your confession that you once entertained a liking for law is also of some assistance to me. Did you expect me to throw up my hands aghast at the paragraph? Well you were terribly fooled if you did. It pleased me to discover another circumstance in which there is a similitude of tastes between us. If you have no antipathy to questions of politics and government I should recommend for your purpose a work I have lately read, by a French author, De Tocqueville, entitled "Democracy in America." It has established a world-wide reputation. I shall not risk an opinion of my own but give you that of O. W. Holmes, Jr., lately elevated to the Supreme Bench of Massachusetts. "The work" he says, "is interesting, startling, profound, liberal and instructive. The author is remarkably fearless, candid, and unprejudiced in his discussions and reflections." I am now reading Brownson's "American Republic," a work highly recommended. Smith's "Wealth of Nations" gave me about all the wisdom I possess on the subject of political economy. It holds about the same reputation in the subject of which it treats as Blackstone's "Commentaries" in the department of the law. Macaulay's Essays you have read of course.

If anything I ever wrote gave you an idea that I thought you displeased with teaching it made me say what I did not desire to nor believe. It was sufficient for me, Miss McClements, to have seen your school to convince me that you are one of the ideal teachers among whom are not numbered any who hate teaching. That's flat and sounds like flattery, but as I believe you consider me above any such vulgarity I make the assertion without hesitancy and you needn't mind contradicting it.

Yours with sincerest regards,
T. J. Walsh.

[1] Oliver Wendell Holmes's breakfast table articles appeared first in the *Atlantic Monthly* and were collected as *The Autocrat of the Breakfast-Table* (1858), *The Professor at the Breakfast-Table* (1860), and *The Poet at the Breakfast-Table* (1872).

307

Sturgeon Bay, Wis., June 12, 1883.

My dear Ellen,

In accordance with the wishes you so kindly expressed, school terminated in a highly pleasant manner.

I intend to "loaf" for a few days more and then go into the office here of a friend. Mr. Scudder desired very much to have me read with him, but the other gentleman is an older acquaintance and I knew expected that I would stay with him. I hope to be able to do enough this summer to enable me to enter the senior year class at Madison next fall. My brother and a common friend of ours will also attend the law school next year so that there is little danger of any of us being afflicted with lonesomeness. . . .

Very sincerely
Your friend,
T. J. Walsh.

308

Mon cher Ami,

So you've really said adieu to the pedagogue's desk! I'm glad of it, having always maintained that no man who amounts to a very great deal will stick to the profession. . . .

Did you really "loaf" for a few days? How could you spare the time? Why didn't you go right to work, and keep on working until the day you start for Madison? Do you know what you need? A good shaking; and I'd like to do it—or I guess I wouldn't either. I don't like to hurt anyone too awfully much. But I tell you someone ought to shut your books as fast as you open them. Do be sensible and give yourself a good rest.

Yours very sincerely,
E. C. M.

309

Sturgeon Bay, Wis., July 17, 1883.

My dear Ellen,

Court sits tomorrow and matters around town are lively as a consequence. The lawyer assumes a more rapid gait, smiles more benignantly than usual, and endeavers to impress the un-initiated with an idea of the vastly precious nature of every moment of his time. Jurymen collect in knots and discourse learnedly on the abstruse questions of title and evidence. The sheriff whips his chargers into a more rapid trot and is not approached, much less molested in any way. In fact it's court week and bustle is the order of the day. Some few important cases are coming up for trial but this evening there seems to be a general disposition to settle and I learned that several, in the arguing of which I should have been interested, have been arranged between the parties. I have been asked if it were not the truth that I should apply for admission. My friend Scudder says that I could pass a better examination than Sherman [?] did, which I cannot conscientiously deny. The point is, I am studying law to know it and not to pass the examination. And so I shall keep on a while longer. Don't you think that is wise?

After court adjourns a party of about twenty-five will go to Strawberry Island near the mouth of Green Bay on a ten days' camping and fishing excursion. The grounds are represented as being the finest in this region and I anticipate having a first rate time. Don't you wish you were going along? Don't I too? It would be a remarkably fine antidote to any faults your city life may have engendered. Think of it! Ten days! Twenty-five miles from telegraphic communication even! Out on an island! Can you realize the joys?

No steps have yet been taken towards engaging anyone as my successor. . . . One of the applicants before alluded to is an old friend of mine who, however has neglected his studies of late. I quoted some for him and he surprised me with "Tom, you have a wonderful memory." Scudder's folks have often told me the same thing but I considered it only pardonable flattery of undeveloped friendship. Old friends never flatter though, do they? Now if I could only be taught to reason I might become smart "with the process of the suns," mightn't I?

Lovingly yours,
T. J. W.

310

Madison, Wis., September 9, 1883.

My dear Ellen,

We haven't done much in the way of law yet. Professor Carpenter examined us in his branch for admission to the senior class on Thursday. Sloan lectured on Friday but didn't question us.[1] So I am still in doubt whether they'll admit me to graduate this year or not. I think the lecture, judging from the first effort, will be both enjoyable and profitable.

I've been reading "Sartor Resartus" this morning.[2] I got it from the University library yesterday. Their reading room is one of the pleasantest I have ever been in. The roof is formed of ground glass and that in the windows is stained. The result is a mellow light that is extremely agreeable and which gives the room a very cheerful aspect. Much care must have been exercised in the selection of the books, they are all choice. I sat down to look them over but saw so many that I desired to read, that I became bewildered and left.

My friend Barnes was on the train, from Milwaukee, with me. He had taken Horace Greely's advice seriously and was on his way to Dakota or farther west, according to his humor when he gets there.[3]

Chancery Lane.

[1] Jarius H. Carpenter and Ithamar C. Sloan.

[2] This work, published in book form in 1838, was Thomas Carlyle's spiritual autobiography.

[3] John Barnes, of Manitowoc County, Wisconsin, did not stay long in the West and later became a justice of the Wisconsin Supreme Court.

311

Madison, Wis., Sept. 23, 1883.

Elaine the fair, Elaine the——

. . . Each recitation at the university takes up an hour. The same time is allotted to the lectures to the law class. We have organized a moot court before which forum I appeared and won my case on Thursday evening last. Also a debating society which meets every Monday evening. This body I attempted to convince at its last session that woman and suffrage, however great the affinities between them, were two forces which it would seem wise to keep separate. My cogent arguments didn't influence the jury though. I am a little apprehensive that if I should ever get into practice I shall meet with experience similar to that which awaited my debut before the law class—the court will sometimes be with me but the other fellow will catch the jury.

Yours sincerely,
T. J. W.

312

My dear Sister Nell,—

Lack of time prevents answering you today in rhyme, my Lucille, so you must extract what pleasure you can from a prosy prose letter until my pen grows as ready as yours or tariffs, taxes, wages and "sich" cease troubling me. I worked all day yesterday collecting material and am now ready to arrange it. If I can only succeed in giving the jury as clear an idea of the subject as exists in my own mind, they will be obliged to conclude with me that the protective tariff does not increase wages, however useful it may be in other respects.

Of course you were delighted with Patti. The papers have exhausted the vocabulary of praise on her and I have not seen a criticism that does not sound like a twice told tale. Is this not her last trip to America? Did Irving's playing surpass your expectation?[1] Those who have heard him say that words are inadequate to express its perfection. Matthew Arnold's lecture was a solemn farce if my opinion is of any value, and it ought to be because I have read considerably on the subject of which he spoke. His talk was a defence of the study of the classics but his arguments were old, his thoughts commonplace, and his manner awkward in the extreme. His gestures were constrained and spasmodic. The very best that could be said of him is that his language is exceedingly terse and has the rare merit of being plain. Edward Everett Hale's lecture was both more amusing and instructive. I was introduced to him next evening at the club. He is a very cheerful old gentleman with a touch of drollery about him. It is very easy work listening to him speak, and like Holmes, he not infrequently, right in the midst of a very solemn discussion, lets drop a humorous remark that would draw a grin from Nestor.

. . . Now if you (or I) should ever become known to fame, with what sentiments would we regard some prowler, gloating miserly over our letters, provided we retain consciousness of things transpiring in this nether world after we take our flight hence! These historical mousers seem to have left no drawer of Carlyle's unlocked, much to that worthy's displeasure, I dare say, if he knows of it.

You have probably ere this heard Irving and Terry.[2]

Yours,

T. J. W.

[1] Sir Henry Irving (1838-1905) was the first English actor to be knighted. He managed the Lyceum Theatre in London and was highly successful in a number of roles. In 1883-84 he embarked upon his first American tour; seven others were to follow.

[2] For more than twenty years Ellen Terry was Irving's leading lady.

313

Madison, Wis., April 27, 1884.

My dear Ellen,—

Many thanks for the [May] festival programs. How very German the music will be! One ought to be well coached on the Niebelungen in order fully to appreciate the verbal part of the singing. That, I suppose, is considered a matter of but little importance and yet when I listen to vocal music it loses half its charm for me if I do not understand what is being said.

O, Dean is to be here on the 28th of May.[1] I shall look to his coming with longing. It has not yet been advertised what he will play nor how long he will remain.

The Republican state convention is to be held here next week for the purpose of electing delegates to the Chicago Convention. They will probably be instructed for Fairchild as first choice[2] but as he hasn't the ghost of a chance of being nominated it is likely that some of the more prominent candidates will have "friends" at work to capture the delegates for their "men." A list of the preferences of the students for president was taken a week ago with a result which developed the fact that we are not apt to go without a president from dearth of candidates. Blaine led off, but the vote was very scattering.

. . . One of the young men of the law class with whom I am slightly intimate desires me very much to go with him to Dakota after graduation. His home is there and he is full of praises of the country.[3] Perhaps he may yet prevail but my intentions have not thus far settled into anything like resolution. They probably will not either until the time approaches when it becomes necessary to act and then I'll make up my mind, as I usually do, in about five minutes. It is very like the casting of a die though.

Yours sincerely,
Thomas J. Walsh.

[1] Dean has not been identified.

[2] Lucius Fairchild had served as governor of Wisconsin for three terms (1866-72) and as minister to Spain (1880-82). By 1884 his political influence in Wisconsin had waned. *Dictionary of Wisconsin Biography* (Madison, 1960), pp. 124-25.

[3] This must have been William B. Sterling of Huron, Dakota Territory. A roster of the law class may be found in *Catalogue of the University of Wisconsin for the Academic Year 1883-84* (Madison, October, 1883).

314

Madison, June 8, 1884.

My dear Ellen,—

According to program I left your city on Thursday morning. I was very desirous of staying to attend another and more momentous session of the convention but, impressed with the necessity of getting rid of some of the work so rapidly accumulating upon me, I denied myself the pleasure. Do your boys hurrah for Blaine? [1] I did not hear you express any preference for or against "the plumed knight" during my stay, or did I? The enthusiasm at this place over the nomination seems to be confined almost exclusively to the democrats. . . .

I like to listen to ladies "talk politics," always provided they do it intelligently which, I am compelled reluctantly to admit, they do not always do. Having formed no party ties or affiliations they usually discuss issues and candidates with a candor that is seldom heard in the discussions of men. I think this lady, from her almost absolute lack of bias, was able to grasp the situation more completely and to discuss it more intelligently.

I am going out into the country some day next week to try a case for one of the lawyers in town. This isn't exactly my "first case" but is the first I shall have tried, or tried to try since I began to devote my special attention to law.

. . . I hate Carlyle because he was selfish that he might be

281

miserable. The natural vivacity of his wife might occasionally interrupt the gloom in which his life must be continually enwrapped so that he could write bitter things of a world of which he knew nothing. To take her away out on a barren moor and set her to work like a pack-horse seems the work of a demon if the purpose is kept in view and we give him credit for being rational.[2]

Yours,
T. J. Walsh.

[1] Walsh had been having a busy time both as a participant in political affairs and as an observer. About the end of May he served as a delegate from Door County in the Wisconsin state Democratic convention. It met conveniently in Madison. The national convention that he attended in Chicago went on to nominate James G. Blaine for the presidency.

[2] This interpretation of Carlyle seems to have been quite inaccurate, and was possibly derived from the writings of James Anthony Froude. See Elizabeth Drew, *Jane Welsh and Jane Carlyle* (New York, 1928), pp. 7, 183.

315

Madison, June 10, 1884.

My dear Ellen,—

I have just completed my thesis. I toasted "The Democratic Party" last night, poured forth from the abundance of my mystical lore for the edification and entertainment of my brother Ryanites on Saturday evening,[1] and shan't have another thing to disturb the serenity of the remainder of my stay in Madison. Now you allow that nothwithstanding my natural tendency to be petulant, I haven't, in my letters, indulged in scolding to any degree. But I'm going to begin now. It was altogether wrong in you to impose upon yourself the task of reading over such a lot of matter as was necessary to make the resume you so kindly sent—matter that must be entirely indifferent or even tiresome to you. I should never think of asking you to so victimize yourself, even though I didn't happen to know about the examination papers and all the other work. Accept my kindest thanks and the assurance that a number of the extracts and suggestions were of assistance to me. You must promise to allow me to repay you with similar favors when you get into a like predicament. . . .

Au revoir,
T. J. Walsh.

[1] Walsh was a leader of the Ryan Debating Society in the law school and a principal author of the society's constitution. *The Badger* (University of Wisconsin), November 8, 1883, p. 5.

316

Two Rivers, June 23.

My dear Ellen,—

As you surmised, your last letter reached me just shortly before taking my departure from Madison. We were awarded our diplomas on Wednesday morning and were admitted to the Supreme and Federal Courts on the afternoon of the same day. I tarried in the city only until the departure of the next train and reached home the following evening. Many thanks for your kind wishes. It would be very comforting indeed could I entertain the same assurance of my success as you. But knowing my own shortcomings and the obstacles to be encountered it is impossible for me to consider the future without more or less anxiety. However there is nothing in it, so far as I can now see, which should excite alarm, but much for congratulation. Within the week I shall have determined definitely what course to pursue and then shall proceed in it with what vigor is at my command.

The Commencement exercises at the University proved of much interest to me. Some of them were highly entertaining. The Choral Club treated us to a concert on Monday evening at which was rendered the first part of "The Creation." Why do you smile? Of course I should nere think of instituting a comparison between the Chicago performance and our modest attempt to please, but really the music seemed more musical to me than much of what I listened to in Chicago. Many parts of "The Redemption" were exquisite even to my uncultured ear but others seemed harsh and unharmonious. What do you think of Nilson's scheme of founding a national conservatory of which she is to be the directress? [1] Patti I notice, has signed articles with Mapleson agreeing to come to America for the last time once more.

Cleveland seems to have the lead with considerable to spare, among the Democratic candidates. I have no objection to him and shall be glad to see him nominated but should prefer Bayard as a man better schooled in national affairs. Ben Butler is working hard to carry off the prize but, in my estimation, with little chance of securing it. . . .[2]

Yours,
T. J. W.

[1] A probable reference to Christine Nilsson.

[2] Benjamin Franklin Butler, who had been a Union general in the Civil War and a Radical Republican in Congress, later received Democratic and Greenback support. In 1884 he ran for the presidency on both the Greenback ticket and the Antimonopoly ticket.

317

Two Rivers, July 5, 1884.

My dear Ellen,—

I was pleased to hear of the very satisfactory manner in which your school closed. . . . Now, my dear friend, do not allow yourself to suspect for a moment that I ever hear of your successes with any feelings but the sincerest pleasure and if I do not hear of them from you who shall tell me? Why, I know I have gone on telling you of my own little triumphs as if they actually were of some interest to you because I thought they were. I spoke at the celebration here yesterday—in fact was "orator of the day," and a great many nice things were said about my little piece. My little sister's criticism was that I "scweamed" too much, but I managed to "scweam" for half an hour without growing very hoarse and my lungs haven't received so much healthy exercise in many a day. That isn't boasting, is it? But it's blowing.

'Tis indeed a pity that flowers should fade. Now here's this magnificent dish of white pond lilies which my sisters and I gathered yesterday already beginning to show signs of wilting. So they grow in the neighborhood of Sheboygan. Our river is famous for the production of them and I don't know of anyone but our folks who ever disturb them. . . .

Who is your candidate? You must answer now before the convention or your guess won't count.

T. J. Walsh.

318

Two Rivers, July 16, 1884.

My dear Ellen,—

Does Cleveland meet your approval as a candidate? I know of no good reason why the nomination doesn't meet my unqualified endorsement, but it doesn't. Perhaps it is because his career has been too successful, his rise too rapid for me—something of the upstart about him. And then, does not it require a long training in the management of public affairs in order to reign well, just as [much] special preparation as is necessary in every other sphere of human action. Would not his great abilities too, if such he possessed, be found out and have forced him before the public long before three short years ago? I'm sulking on the platform too. It's senselessly long and although it does not seem to me that the tariff plank can, as is said, be read one way by the free-traders and another by the protectionists, yet no immediate action is promised and a little tinkering here and there will satisfy all that is pledged.

I shall leave for Dakota with the intention to reside there permanently, sometime during the latter part of next week. . . . I refer to what you said about my seeming an old friend when you write but that when we talk you seem hardly to know me. Now the same thought has occurred to me very forcibly every time I called on you and I regret the few opportunities we have had to cultivate a personal acquaintance will be so materially lessened by my contemplated move. . . .

Yours,
T. J. W.

319

My dear Friend,—

. . . No, it would not surprise me in the least to learn that you are an out-and-out Republican. I am not going to labor now to make a proselyte. But if you really are a "tariff man" you had better surrender at once. I have a stack of pamphlets, tracts, manuscripts which I may inflict upon you. . . . If the farmer of Wisconsin may be taxed for the benefit of Maine manufacturers, why [can] not Wisconsin brewers be taxed to support the good prohibition people of Maine and Kansas? But what right has government to lay its strong hand on the earnings of one man and appropriate them to the use of another?

Do you return by way of Manitowoc? I shall be there frequently during the coming week and also next week in case I stay over. If you come that way drop me a line and I'll come around and say good-bye before I start trailing along after the star of empire.[1]

Yours,
T. J. Walsh.

[1] A farewell visit was arranged before Walsh went off to "that horrid wild region," as Ellen McClements described it. E. C. McClements to T. J. Walsh, July 23, 1884.

Appendix II: Acknowledgment

I have had a wealth of assistance in completing this book and take pleasure in acknowledging it. Mrs. Gudger, with whom I first talked about her father in 1950, has never failed to answer questions or cheerfully to attempt to do so. She has shown an appreciation for the historian's craft and has made this book possible, first, by lending her parents' letters; second, by leaving me at liberty to write as I wish. Donald Jackson of the University of Illinois Press made invaluable suggestions concerning format and editorial procedures, and Mrs. Elizabeth Dulany of the Press contributed her copyediting skills. The Research Board of the University of Illinois has provided in recent years three assistants who helped enormously in the research on these letters. They are Richard A. Swanson, Donald E. Shepardson, and Michael L. Warren. The Research Board and the Department of History also made funds available for typing and other purposes. During my investigation of South Dakota history, Professors Cedric C. Cummins and Herbert S. Schell of the University of South Dakota gave generous assistance. My friend Cedric Cummins acted as an unofficial adviser and also arranged for Donald Walker, then a graduate student in his department, to do research in South Dakota newspapers. Special thanks must go to Mr. T. E. Ratcliffe and his staff at the reference desk of the University of Illinois Library; other members of the library staff also helped. To my great benefit, three friends and colleagues in the Department of History read the manuscript at different stages; they are Robert W. Johannsen, Clark C. Spence, and Robert M. Sutton. The mistakes that remain are, of course, my own.

Others have helped in a variety of ways, responding to my questions and appeals. They include the following: Mrs. Raymond T. Birge, Berkeley, California, and Dana W. Walsh, Los Angeles, children of Henry C. Walsh; J. E. Boell, university archivist, and J. Frank Cook, assistant archivist, Division of Archives, University of Wisconsin; A. E. Crook, Frankfort, South Dakota; L. M. Eldredge, librarian, Yankton College, Yankton, South Dakota; Margaret Gleason, reference librarian, and Josephine L. Harper, manuscripts librarian, The State Historical Society of Wisconsin; Frances Goudy, special collections librarian, Vassar College Library, Poughkeepsie, New York; Mildred M. Jaynes, Redfield, South Dakota; James E. Morris, reference librarian, the Chicago Historical Society; Will G. Robinson, secretary, the South Dakota State Historical Society; and the staff of the Library, Historical Society of Montana, Helena.

Selective Bibliography

Literary works from the period, though frequently mentioned in the letters and notes, are not included here. Nor are general works of reference.

I. Primary

A. Personal Papers

Vilas, William Freeman. Papers, State Historical Society of Wisconsin, Madison.

Walsh, Thomas James. Papers, Library of Congress.

B. Editor's Interviews

Senator Henry F. Ashurst, September 9, 1949.

Genevieve Walsh Gudger, February 16, 21, 1950.

William A. MacEacham, August 18, 1965.

Senator James E. Murray, August 27, 1949.

C. Official

Department of Public Instruction, City of Chicago. *Thirty-second Annual Report of the Board of Education for the Year Ending June 30, 1886.* Chicago, 1887.

Fuller & Johnson Manufacturing Co. v. *Foster,* 4 Territory of Dakota, 329 (1886).

Kalscheuer vs. *Upton et al.,* 6 Territory of Dakota, 449 (1889).

Levisee, Aaron B. and L. (eds.). *Revised Codes of the Dakota Territory, 1883.* St. Paul, Minnesota, 1885.

Register of Deeds Office, Sheboygan, Wisconsin. "Registration of Deaths, County of Sheboygan."

U.S. Congress. *Congressional Record,* 48 Cong., 2 Sess. (March 2, 1885); 49 Cong., 1 Sess. (January 29, February 5, 1886).

University of Wisconsin. *Catalogue for the Academic Year 1883-84* (Madison, October, 1883).

D. Newspapers

The Badger (University of Wisconsin), November 8, 1883.

Chicago Inter-Ocean, February 6, 1886; June 26, 1886; May 8, 1887.

Chicago Tribune, November 21, 1884; December 5, 1884; July 25, 1887; March 6, 1888; December 4, 1960.
Dakota Huronite (Huron), July 11, 1889.
Dakota Pioneer (Aberdeen), May 3, 1888.
Manitowoc Co. Chronicle (Two Rivers), Special Edition, September 20, 1892.
Redfield Observer, August 9, 1888–July 3, 1890.
Sioux Falls Daily Argus, September 29, 1886.

II. Secondary

A. Books

Adams, Isaac E. *Political Oratory of Emery A. Storrs from Lincoln to Garfield*. Chicago and New York, 1888.

Akeley, Lewis E. *This Is What We Had in Mind: Early Memories of the University of South Dakota*. Vermillion, South Dakota, 1959.

Cady, Edwin H. *The Gentleman in America: A Literary Study in American Culture*. Syracuse, New York, 1949.

Curti, Merle, and Carstensen, Vernon. *The University of Wisconsin: A History, 1848-1925*. Vol. I. Madison, 1949.

David, Henry. *History of the Haymarket Affair*. New York, 1936.

Dearing, Mary R. *Veterans in Politics: The Story of the G.A.R.* Baton Rouge, Louisiana, 1952.

Drew, Elizabeth. *Jane Welsh and Jane Carlyle*. New York, 1928.

Earhart, Mary. *Frances Willard: From Prayers to Politics*. Chicago, 1944.

Harlow, Dana D. *Prairie Echoes: Spink County in the Making*. Aberdeen, South Dakota, 1961.

Humphrey, Seth K. *Following the Prairie Frontier*. Minneapolis, 1931.

Kingsbury, George W. *History of Dakota Territory*. Vol. II. Chicago, 1915.

La Follette, Belle C. and Fola. *Robert M. La Follette*. Vol. I. New York, 1953.

Lamar, Howard R. *Dakota Territory, 1861-1889: A Study of Frontier Politics*. New Haven, 1956.

Lawson, John D. (ed.). *American State Trials*. Vol. XII. St. Louis, 1919.

Leech, Margaret. *In the Days of McKinley*. New York, 1959.

Lindsey, David. *"Sunset" Cox: Irrepressible Democrat*. Detroit, 1959.

Merrill, Samuel Horace. *William Freeman Vilas: Doctrinaire Democrat*. Madison, Wisconsin, 1954.

Moses, John, and Kirkland, Joseph (eds.). *History of Chicago*. Vol. II. Chicago, 1895.

Peck, Harry Thurston. *Twenty Years of the Republic, 1885-1905*. New York, 1907.

Pierce, Bessie L. *A History of Chicago*. Vols. II, III. New York, 1940, 1957.

Pomeroy, Earl S. *The Territories and the United States, 1861-1890*. Philadelphia, 1947.

Robinson, Doane. *Encyclopedia of South Dakota*. Pierre, South Dakota, 1925.

Roosevelt, Theodore. *Hunting Trips of a Ranchman: Sketches of Sport on the Northern Cattle Plains*. New York, 1885.

Schell, Herbert S. *History of South Dakota*. Lincoln, Nebraska, 1961.

Schlesinger, Arthur M., Jr. *Orestes A. Brownson: A Pilgrim's Progress*. Boston, 1939.

Tolles, Winton. *Tom Taylor and the Victorian Drama*. Columbia University Studies in English and Comparative Literature, No. 148. New York, 1940.

Upton, George P. (ed.). *Theodore Thomas: A Musical Autobiography*. Vol. II. Chicago, 1905.

B. Miscellaneous

Adee, Alvey A. "Reminiscences of Castelar," *Century Magazine*, XXXI (March, 1886).

Armstrong, William J. "Castelar, the Orator," *Century Magazine*, XXXI (March, 1886).

Bates, J. Leonard. "Walsh of Montana in Dakota Territory: Political Beginnings, 1884-90," *Pacific Northwest Quarterly*, LVI (July, 1965).

Dictionary of Wisconsin Biography. Madison, 1960.

Gudger, Genevieve Walsh. "Farewell to Dakota" (one chapter of an incomplete biography of Thomas J. Walsh, written in the 1940's).

"Washington and Montana, Have They Made a Mistake in Their Constitutions?" *Century Magazine*, XXXIX (February, 1890).

Index

Abbott, Emma: in *The Mikado*, 54; sketch of, 55n. *See also* Music

Aberdeen (Dakota Territory): as legal center, 215

Agrarian movement: and politicians, 38; Walsh's role, 199-200, 205. *See also* Dakota Democrats

Agricultural Society (Spink County): Walsh as secretary, 46

Agriculture: prosperous conditions, 1; profits in real estate, 2; anxiety over crops, 38, 242; large wheat farm, 46; and "yeomanry," 179, 201; no poetry in, 193; Alliance movement, 217n. *See also* Weather

Aldrich, Thomas Bailey, 151n

Allen, Harrison (general): described, 199, 200; and Grand Army of the Republic, 200n

Ambitions: and encouragement, 128, 140-41, 149, 263-64; and disappointments, 129, 150, 239-40; dislike of fawning, 131, 166, 167; and wealth, 166; and self-doubt, 184, 217, 283; in law, 261; importance of leaving home, 269. *See also* Law practice; Success

Anderson, J. S. (judge): as Walsh's teacher, 268

Andersen School (Chicago): Ellen McClements has position in, 43, 44; school described,

50; class party for Ellen, 77; closing exercises, 78, 84-85, 128, 130, 228, 236, 239, 240; school engineer described, 121; has devoted pupils, 130, 211, 234; regrets at leaving, 228, 230; and praise of singing, 232; mentioned, 94, 183. *See also* Teaching

Andrews Opera Company: praised, 191

Apollo Club (Chicago): Ellen McClements is admitted, 137-38; concerts, 156, 163, 168, 171, 200, 205; and false notes, 158; and rehearsals, 168, 196. *See also* Music; Tomlins, William L.

Apollo Hall (Chicago), 27

Arion Club (Chicago): Ellen McClements is member, 54, 57; program mentioned, 80; rehearsal, 168. *See also* Music

Armadale (Dakota Territory): as nicest place in Dakota, 184

Arnold, Matthew: lecture criticized, 279

Art: interests in, 9, 10, 109, 110n; and imagination, 96-97, 98; Ellen McClements studies, 200; and Walsh's comments, 201-2; paintings described, 203; and Ellen's painting, 214-15, 222. *See also* Exposition building

Art Institute (Chicago): establishment, 219

Articles of Confederation, 233

293

Church, Louis Kossuth (governor): Walsh criticizes as Dakota judge, 73-74, 78-79, 119; as next governor, 108; visits Walsh brothers, 116; and patronage, 116; veto power, 118, 119; unpopularity, 119, 120, 131, 172, 173, 193, 217; Walsh's alienation from, 164; as leader of Democratic faction, 175-76, 178n; administration ends, 217, 219n. *See also* Dakota Democrats

Civil War: memories of, 63

Cleveland, Grover: race against Blaine in 1884, 9n, 284, 285; importance of victory for Dakota Territory, 14, 15n, 17; reception in Chicago, 151, 156; defeat in 1888, 203, 204; and "omnibus" bill, 220n; criticized, 285; mentioned, 155, 162, 188, 205n

Colleges: public ones preferable, xvii, 108, 243; and legal training, 261

Conkling, Roscoe: as orator, 171; as Republican leader, 172n

County offices: contested in 1886, 103

County seat fight (Spink County): background, 6, 7n, 10, 14-15; seizure of records, 13, 16-17, 22; the "war," 18-20, 21n; "grand larceny" in Dakota, 25; new elections proposed, 25; residue of ill will, 45, 46; Walsh and trial of Redfield men, 45, 67, 68n, 69; Redfield's campaign, 64, 67-68, 88, 92, 93, 95, 101-2, 103; benefits to Redfield, 103-4, 121-22; mentioned, 164. *See also* Redfield

Dakota Democrats: quality praised, 10, 40, 41, 88; territorial conventions, 10, 48, 53-54, 97, 99-100; influence in Cleveland years, 14, 18, 99-

100; factionalism among, 164, 173n, 190; Walsh's nomination as contesting delegate to St. Louis, 172, 173, 174; and parliamentary question, 175-76, 177-78; defeat in St. Louis, 178n, 179, 190n; and campaign for the territorial council, 195, 199-200, 201, 203-4; defeat, 204-5

Dakota Education Association, 242

Dakota Territory: sectional rivalries, 2n-3n, 42n; and politics, 9, 11n, 116, 118, 236, 237n, 241; its people praised, 23, 55, 135, 161, 187, 194-95; and statehood movement, 51, 66-67, 68, 71, 97, 192, 220; as land of blizzards, 114, 119-20, 214, 223; judicial system and abuses in, 116, 192, 210; and high prices, 227. *See also* Church, Louis Kossuth; Judicial systems

Dawes, Charles G., 161n

Dawes, Fred A.: described, 161; and friendship of, 198

Day, M. H.: leads anti-Church faction, 99, 100, 164n; defeat for delegate in 1886, 104, 186n; on Democratic national committee, 174. *See also* Dakota Democrats

Deadwood (Dakota Territory), 94, 187, 252

de Staël, Madame: described, 265; mentioned, 62, 63n

Disraeli, Benjamin: writing praised, 114

Dixon, William Wirt: career summarized, 253

Don Quixote: Walsh's reaction to, 239

Drama: interest in, 8, 16, 25, 26, 28, 30, 31, 32, 56, 66, 113; and Walsh's theatrical debut, 71, 73, 75, 168, 169-70

Holidays: in Two Rivers, 21, 259, 284; Fourth of July celebrations, 43, 85-86, 179, 184, 236, 241, 242. *See also* Social customs; Sports

Holmes, Oliver Wendell: writings discussed, 274, 275n, 279

Holmes, Oliver Wendell, Jr.: quoted, 274

Hotel life, 55, 56, 110, 236

Household routine: and Walsh's absence, 244-47, 248-49. *See also* Marriage

Howard, C. T., 249

Hughes, Charles Evans: and judicial responsibility, 223n

Humor, 8, 24, 47, 58, 59-60, 61, 62, 69, 73, 75, 89, 98, 100, 135, 158-59, 169-70, 181, 183, 189, 210, 211, 216, 241, 261, 266-67, 276, 277, 284

Hurd, Frank H., 180, 181n

Huron (Dakota Territory): holds territorial fair, 95; as seat of fifth judicial circuit, 108, 126

Ingersoll, Robert G., 10-11n

Ingham, George C., 93, 94n

Inman, Darwin M.: and University of Dakota, 195, 196n

Irving, Sir Henry: acting praised, 138, 279, 280n; mentioned, 159, 160, 161

Jackson, Helen Hunt, 164n. *See also Ramona*

James, Louis, 166

James River: and Dakotans, 7, 135, 198, 250n

Jones, Samuel Porter, 72, 73n

Judicial systems: dissatisfaction with Dakota courts, 6, 64, 116, 185-86, 187, 192, 210, 253; and newspapers acting as juries, 89-90, 91; court day described, 276. *See also* Church, Louis Kossuth; Spencer, J. S.

Kalscheuer v. *Upton et al.*, 112-13n; Walsh's argument praised, 218, 219n

Keene, Thomas W., 8

La Follette, Belle Case, xvii, 83, 84n

La Follette, Robert M., 83, 84n

Lamar, Howard R., 217n

Lamar, L. Q. C. (Secretary of the Interior), 30, 31n

Langtry, Lillie, 113, 117, 165

Law practice: and rewards, 6, 7, 22, 32, 41, 57, 65, 104, 105, 110, 114, 121, 126, 133-34, 163-64, 167, 176, 195, 198, 204, 210, 215, 218, 238, 242, 251, 252, 253; discouraging aspects, 6, 9, 56-57, 64, 86, 119, 120, 170, 185-86, 187, 193, 210; comments on juries and judges, 9, 79, 124, 278; and choice of residence, 10, 11, 38, 39, 128, 193, 197-98, 199, 209-10, 211-13, 214, 215-16, 217, 223, 233, 235, 239, 240, 241, 243n, 249, 250-54, 280, 285, 286; and personal code, 16-17, 20, 47, 132, 163, 170, 215, 225, 235; habits of preparation, 33, 46-47, 50, 51n, 70-71, 95, 127, 130-31, 132, 139, 150, 167, 206, 207, 213, 223; some notable cases, 46-47, 67, 70-71, 112-13n, 132, 160-61; and branches of law, 53, 70-71, 105, 178, 228; and travel required, 95, 243n, 244-47; Ellen McClements as source of books and advice, 120, 128, 130-31, 132, 175-78, 206, 207. *See also* Walsh, Henry Comer

Lawrence University, 268

Literary societies, 23, 26, 222n, 258-59, 260, 261. *See also* Drama; Social customs

Literature: discussed, 23, 64-65, 114-15, 124, 125, 207-8, 244, 256-57, 258, 261, 265, 274

189n; and formal calling, 109-10, 111, 211, 244; a game of forfeits, 110, 111, 112, 113, 128-29. *See also* Humor; Religion; Sports

Southey, Robert, 260

Spencer, J. S. (judge), 108n, 123, 186, 192. *See also* Judicial systems

Spenser, Willard, 113n

Spink County: in frontier stage, 2, 6-7, 84, 123-24; economic conditions, 193, 243n, 251. *See also* County seat fight; Redfield

Spink County "war." *See* County seat fight

Spooner, John C. (senator), 235

Spooner, Marshall, 235

Sports, 61, 65, 68, 247, 264, 271-72; baseball, 44, 86; horses, 82, 84, 134, 135, 189, 193, 216, 225, 228, 230

Statehood (South Dakota): and Walsh's hopes, 220, 222n, 226, 229, 232-33. *See also* Dakota Territory; Sioux Falls

Sterling, Thomas S., 37n

Sterling, William B. (lawyer and Walsh's friend), 36-37n, 79, 122-23, 191, 198, 280, 281n

Stevenson, Robert Louis, 125n

Stewart, Julius, 203

Storrs, Emery A., 10, 11n, 51

Success: ideas on, 140, 154-55, 230, 240; and advancement of position, 24-25, 32, 33, 34, 47, 50, 53, 61, 164-65, 232, 252, 260, 284. *See also* Ambitions

Tariff: as great national issue, 99, 114, 115, 199-200, 285, 286; and efforts to reform, 173, 179, 184, 197, 205n, 279. *See also* Dakota Democrats

Taylor, Tom (dramatist), 71n, 117

Teaching: as profession, 42, 44, 49-50, 122, 133, 257, 261, 262, 264, 268-69, 270, 276; Walsh's

experience, 55, 77-78, 105, 255, 259, 260, 264, 271n; Ellen McClements' enjoyment of, 228, 274-75. *See also* Andersen School

Terry, Ellen, 280

Thackeray, William Makepeace: and *Vanity Fair*, 247

Thomas, Theodore: and summer concerts, 35n, 188

Thurman, Allen G., 29, 30n

Tice, John H., 271

The Ticket of Leave Man, 71. *See also* Drama

Tocqueville, Alexis de: *Democracy in America* discussed, 274

Tomlins, William L. (musical director), 27, 28, 35, 137-38, 157-58, 206, 214, 232. *See also* Apollo Club

Toole, Joseph K. (governor): Walsh visits in Helena, 252, 253, 254n. *See also* Law practice

Tripp, Bartlett (Democratic leader): described, 53

Twain, Mark: and reviewers, 270-71

Two Rivers (Wis.): Walsh's home town, xvi, 80. *See also* Holidays

Vereshchagin, Vasily, 222

Vilas, William F.: Walsh's admiration for, xvii, 29, 30n, 31, 50-51, 142

Voltaire, François, 257

Von Humboldt School (Chicago), 31, 43

Walker, Francis W., 91, 92n

Wallace, Lew (general), 113. *See also Ben-Hur*

Walsh, Henry Comer: as law partner, xviii, 2, 3n, 15, 112-13n, 133, 157, 161, 180, 198, 210, 211-12; interests, 89, 126, 136, 225, 265, 267-68, 275; and popularity, 94, 182, 220, 265; men-

tioned, 19, 106, 110. *See also*
Law practice
Walsh, Thomas J.: personality
traits, xiii-xviii, 4-5, 17, 20, 23,
36, 87-88, 89, 108, 109, 110,
132, 147, 207-8, 241, 273, 277;
pronunciation and spelling of
"Walsh," xiv, 5, 6, 134-35, 136,
220; political interests and
achievements, xv, 11n, 17, 29-
30, 34, 46, 254n, 285; as student and intellectual, xvi, 39-
40, 78, 106, 107, 108, 131, 139,
257-58, 267-68, 269-70, 274,
275; self-evaluation, 4, 15, 96-
97, 129, 132-33, 139, 166, 216,
220-21, 225-26, 261-62, 280-
81; and love of nature, 40, 45,
62, 191, 198, 206-7, 271-72.
See also Ambitions; Dakota
Democrats; Law practice
Walsh family: described, xvi, 21,
23, 134, 284; Felix (father), 91,
92; John, 242-43
Ward, Mrs. Humphry, 208
Wealth: and hopes for, 166, 168,
251; criticism of display, 194-
95. *See also* Ambitions; Success
Weather: extremes, 42, 46, 87,
114, 115n, 163, 205-6, 225,
242, 243n, 244, 246-47, 250,
251

West: and pioneer qualities, 4,
5n, 38; in eastern opinion, 58,
95, 134, 135, 186
Western News Company (Chicago), 31
Wheeler, Burton K.: and Walsh,
xiv-xv
Whittier, John Greenleaf, 194n
Wicker Park School (Chicago), 18,
32n, 117, 272, 284
Willard, Frances, 29
Willard, Sadie A., 84, 85n
Wilson, John R. (Democratic
leader): praised, 93-94, 99
Wisconsin, University of: Walsh
as law student, xvii, 58, 275,
277-83. *See also* Vilas, William
F.
Wisconsin: and campaign of 1884,
9
Woman's sphere: discussed, 27,
28-29, 88-89, 95, 189, 273, 281;
and woman's suffrage, 35, 36,
37, 38-39, 219, 278

Yankton: loses capital, 2n; described, 125
Yellowstone Park, 192

Zeisler, Sigismund, 91, 92n